"When Christ calls a man, he bids him come and die."

— Dietrich Bonhoeffer, *The Cost of Discipleship*

Things We Couldn't Say

Diet Eman

with

James Schaap

WILLIAM B. EERDMANS PUBLISHING COMPANY

GRAND RAPIDS, MICHIGAN

Copyright © 1994 by Wm. B. Eerdmans Publishing Co.

255 Jefferson Ave. S.E., Grand Rapids, Michigan 49503

Printed in the United States of America

00 99 98 97 96 95 94   7 6 5 4 3 2 1

Library of Congress Cataloging-in-Publication Data

Eman, Diet, 1920-

Things we couldn't say / Diet Eman with James Schaap.

p.   cm.

ISBN 0-8028-3763-8

1. Eman, Diet, 1920-   . 2. World War, 1939-1945 — Personal narratives, Dutch.

3. Holocaust, Jewish (1939-1945) — Netherlands.

4. World War, 1939-1945 — Jews — Rescue — Netherlands.

5. Righteous Gentiles in the Holocaust — Netherlands — Biography.

I. Schaap, James C., 1948-   . II. Title.

D811.5.E44   1994

940.53'18'09492 — dc20   94-18828

CIP

Again, a conversation with the doctor. We always come back to the same point: "The church may not mix in politics," he says. And I tell him that when you are a Christian and profess that God is almighty, there is no single area of life from which you can eliminate God.

from the diary of Diet Eman

To Mark,
without whose insistence this book never
would have been written,

and to Joy
and to all the friends I worked with
during those difficult years

Contents

Contents

The Hague, 1938

Above: The Eman family. Diet (Berendina) on bottom left.

Right: Hein Sietsma, about 18 years old.

As far back as I can remember, my father ran a prosperous interior decorating business, with many people working for him making drapes and lace curtains, as well as hanging wallpaper and doing upholstery. He did a good deal of contract work for wealthy and important people in the Dutch city of The Hague.

But when I was nine years old, in 1929-30, a severe depression hit the Netherlands, just as it did the rest of Europe and America. At a time like that, no one can buy extras and accessories, nothing beyond the bare necessities. The depression left our family with little income — so little, in fact, that it looked like I was not going to be able to go on to the university. I wanted to, of course, and all my teachers wanted me to go on; but father said that I could not. After all, he said, I was just a girl.

That was the only time I remember my mother and father actually quarreling. Mother felt that I should go on, but Father said no — it was too expensive, and, after all, my brothers *had* to go to the university. I'd probably just get married anyway. Mother fought very hard, but she lost.

I was always a tomboy. When my sister was sixteen, she loved to wear high heels and have her hair just so. But when I was that age, wherever I went, my hair was always a mess. I loved climbing trees and having adventures out in the country. My brother Albert and I and our friends used to pedal our bikes outside The Hague to little villages and farms, out to where we found pastures with *sloten,* those little brooks and moats that are still there today.

Sometimes on the *tweede Paasdag,* the "second Easter day," or "second Pentecost," the Monday school holiday after the important religious holidays, we'd go out into the country and climb trees and jump ditches. Some of those *sloten* were quite wide, and of course eventually we'd fall into the water. That was part of the fun of it, and I loved it.

My sister would plead with my mother, "Don't let Diet do that," she would say. "She should be much more ladylike."

One day a man from our church, the *koster* we called him in Dutch, the church janitor and bookkeeper, spoke to my parents.

"I have an old friend whose name is Jilt Sietsma," said the *koster*, Mr. Reitsma. "One of his sons has found a job here in The Hague at Shell Oil. This son can't pay much, but he needs a place to live."

Father looked over at Mother, because he left those kinds of decisions up to her. And besides being the decision-maker, she had a big heart.

"I thought of the Emans," Mr. Reitsma went on, "because you are such a nice family. Could you maybe take this boy in — at least until he finds a place to live?"

My mother wasn't taken with the idea, at least at first.

"This boy is the oldest of a very large family," Mr. Reitsma said, "and it's a very sad story because the mother just recently died."

Immediately, my mother's heart melted. "I can't take a boarder right now — my life is too busy," she said. "But I can take another son."

I was seventeen at the time, the third child of four in the Eman family. My sister Stephana — we called her Fanny — was the oldest at 25; my brother Arjan — a very old Dutch name — was a year younger than Fanny. Then came the *kleintjes*, the little ones, me and my little brother Albert, seven and eight years younger. I personally didn't like the idea of another family member at all. We were a very happy family, and it seemed to me that having this strange guy in our house, a young man only a year older than I was at the time, was nothing to get too excited about.

4

Hein Sietsma, his name was, and he had been born in the town of Marum in Friesland. At the time he came to live with us, his father was the principal of a tiny Christian school in Holk, a place that was hardly a town at all — a little farming community just outside Nijkerk, Gelderland. When I was young, country places like Holk and Nijkerk seemed to me to be an entire age away from life in the city, in The Hague, where my family and I had always lived.

I even disliked the name *Hein.* To me, it was some kind of backward farmer's name — something like "Old McDonald." *Hein,* I thought, what kind of a bumpkin name is that? I was studying Spanish at the time, and I loved Spanish names like Ramon, for example. Wouldn't it be something, I thought, to fall in love with someone named Ramon? But Hein! Ach, a person named Hein in our home — and a male on top of it!

When my parents told me that he was coming to live with us, I threw a fit. "I hate it," I told them, "and his name is Hein, of all things!" I was sure he would have freckles and red hair, a regular Frisian bumpkin.

When this Frisian farmboy came to live with us, we gave him the bed in the study room. In the Netherlands we had a kind of bed that I've never seen in the States, something called an *opklapbed,* a wooden bed that appeared to be no more than a bookcase. It was very long and had curtains over it; and when you opened the curtains, you flipped out the bed from the wall and put it on the floor. So the *opklapbed* in the study at the front of the house was where we put this new member of our family.

Shortly after Hein came to live with us, I discovered that he was actually a pretty nice young man. But I had to stick to my guns. I had made it very clear to everyone that his coming to our house was an invasion. I tried really hard *not* to like him — I really did. And having him there among us did indeed alter our ways a bit. We didn't have any real bathrooms with tubs and showers — only sinks. Sometimes, in a rush, we had to wash right in the middle of things, in the kitchen sink. Washing in public like that simply had to be done at times, just so that everyone could make it to school or work on time. I'd run to the kitchen with little more on than my underwear, and I'd wash in the sink. With just our regular family there, my brother wouldn't even see me, if he happened to pass.

But when we had a strange fellow in the house, I couldn't do that anymore. Every morning I had to wait until I could wash up in my father and mother's bedroom, where there was a sink and I could wash in private. Every morning I had to wear a gown, once Hein came. So to me, Hein's becoming a member of our family — as my mother put it — meant making big changes. Nothing was ever the same again.

Hein worked at Shell Oil, and he was also studying at night because he wanted to learn French. He had meals with us, and he went to church with us, and to the *Jongelingsvereniging*, the young men's society, where he met a whole bunch of new friends. In fact, once he started living with us, our house was always full of people. I had my friends, of course, and my brother Albert had his friends, and now Hein brought in a lot of new friends. We had a piano and an organ, and my brother Albert, who was very musical, played the cello. (He always wanted to play music professionally; indeed, he was in an orchestra and played beautifully.) All of us — this whole group that was at our home — would sing together, and it was a wonderful time. That time before the war, our house was always full of young people, full of happiness.

It was 1937, I was only seventeen, and I was working at my first job at a bank in the middle of the oldest part of The Hague. I had two really good friends, Rie and Jet, and on

Saturdays we always went biking to the dunes along the coast or someplace out into the country. Rie and Jet, like me, were tomboys. We were still kids, and we did the craziest things.

The first time Hein asked me to go out biking with him on a Saturday, I said to my girlfriends. "Guess who asked me to go on a bicycle trip?" They just roared with laughter when I told them.

"What did you say?" they asked.

"Why of course I told him no," I said, almost as if offended by his having asked.

And the truth was that I didn't want to go with him. Why should I, when every Saturday I was having so much fun with my own friends? Besides, I certainly wouldn't have admitted that I rather liked him, not after the fit I'd thrown when my parents announced he was moving in. I couldn't admit that for a long time.

But one Saturday afternoon, when my girlfriends couldn't go, I decided to take this Hein Sietsma up on another one of his invitations to go biking. So we went, the two of us. And we talked. We talked and talked and talked — which is something everyone did when biking in Holland: ride along for miles and talk and talk.

"So how was it?" Rie and Jet asked when I saw them afterwards. "What happened?"

"Boring," I told them.

And it was. With the girls I did crazy things. But Hein was a year older than I was, and he was obviously much more mature. With my girlfriends I climbed trees, jumped ditches, and had tomboy adventures. This date with Hein had been really low on adventure: it *was* dull, really; all we'd done was talk. Okay, he was a nice guy. I found out he wasn't as bad as I thought when he first moved in. But at that time of my life, I told myself, if I had to choose how to spend my Saturday afternoons, I would much prefer spending them with my friends.

Much later, my mother told me that Hein had spoken to

her about me, had asked her what he could do to interest me. She had told him that I wasn't ready for the kind of thing he was ready for; I was just a girl who thought real excitement was running in the woods and jumping *sloten*. I was certainly not interested in boys, especially those who did nothing more than ask you boring questions. He told Mother he was crazy about me. "But it's like she doesn't even see me!" he said.

"Just slow down a bit," my mother told him. "Diet is not ready for this boyfriend business. Be patient," she said, or words to that effect.

Of course, she didn't tell me any of this at the time. I *was* still a tomboy.

Hein came to live with us at the end of 1937, and for a long time he just observed me, I suppose. I was eighteen when I went biking with him for the first time. And then, after a year or so, he moved out of our house and in with some friends. Suddenly I missed him, though I never admitted it to anyone. All the friends still came over to our house, but soon Hein was gone for good. He had been drafted into the Dutch military service. It was a time when the whole world we lived in, so innocently full of happiness and children's games, had become, suddenly, much more dangerous.

Everyone was being drafted. Hein was sent to Deventer, on the IJssel River just south of Kampen, not far from the German border. When he was there — when life was becoming more dangerous for all of us — I realized how much I cared about him. It must have been at that time that I realized I loved him. I figured it out when I knew that if something happened to him, I wouldn't know how to handle it. Maybe it was the danger of war that made me realize I loved him. He had tried to tell me he loved me in his own way, but I hadn't paid any attention before the threat of war.

The Hague, 1938

Hein would write my family from Deventer, and every family member wrote to him individually. But when I read his letters, I could feel the way he was reaching for something from me in particular, something to hold onto.

▲   ▲

December 13, 1939

This morning I traveled from The Hague to Nijkerk, on leave. I don't know what to think of Diet. I had intended to talk a moment very seriously with her, all alone, while I was going to look into her beautiful eyes. That moment did not come.

Partly, she is a riddle to me. Next time better!

A woman is sometimes a riddle.

Diet is a tomboy, and mischievous.

from the journal of Hein Sietsma

▼   ▼

All of the Netherlands was afraid in 1938, afraid because we could see what kind of power Hitler had already amassed. He had taken Austria when so many people thought he never would. We all believed that England and France would certainly act at that time, but they didn't. When Hitler took Poland, we all understood that danger was on its way. We didn't know for sure when it would come, of course, but we could not deny our fear that something bad was about to happen.

When there is danger on your doorstep, you want to act almost like an ostrich burying its head in the sand. We liked to think that what had happened in Austria and Poland could not happen in the Netherlands. Maybe that was the only way to go on with life — denying, avoiding the worst possible thoughts.

I began to realize then how stupid I had been in not paying more attention when Hein was hinting that he loved me. So when I got a letter from him saying that on his next three or four days off he would love to come to The Hague and see me — not just my family — I wrote back immediately and told him, very carefully of course, that his coming to see me seemed to me like a very nice idea indeed.

That weekend, when I went to the railway station to meet him, my heart was nearly out of control. That was when I knew I was in love with him. By then we had known each other for quite some time, but meeting him alone at the train station for the very first time, I felt as if I didn't want to lose this man, not ever. I knew then that I wanted him to be part of my life, and I understood, just from being with him, that he wanted the same for me.

We had more weekends like that first one, when Hein would come to The Hague on leave. We would talk and talk, and I found out what a really wonderful character he had. He had a great sense of humor: sometimes we didn't have to say anything at all to each other, just stare into each other's eyes, and we would burst out laughing. But we also talked deeply and could be very serious. Our love grew. That first time we had gone biking together, when I was still a tomboy and Hein still seemed to me to be an intruder into our household, I had thought all his talk was boring. Later on, something changed: I had fallen in love.

There were wonderful long bike rides together. We'd pack a lunch and have a picnic somewhere along the side of the road, at a spot with tall trees and beautiful scenery, somewhere along those *sloten.* We'd sit on the grass and eat our lunch — bread with cheese or peanut butter that we had made ourselves at home — and we'd drink our lemonade. There was no ice, of course, but that lemonade tasted wonderful right out of Hein's army canteen. Those were the best days, days when we could still have that kind of fun in 1938. Hein loved classical music, so we would go to concerts. For example, we heard Feike Asma, a very famous Frisian organist; and we always went to the St. Matthew's Passion.

We dated in a way that young people today might think very old-fashioned. Very few Dutch people could afford to be full-time students at that time — I was taking language classes — so we all had jobs, and in the evenings we would study on our own. Maybe on Saturday nights we would go to a concert or take a walk, if it was nice weather. Maybe we would simply visit friends. On Sundays we went to church and we would sit together; after church we had coffee together and dinner. Those were our dates. Hein loved to play chess and backgammon, and he taught me to play those games. That was our courtship, and that's how we fell in love — quietly but deeply.

My mother and father loved Hein like a son. Mother had a very hectic life — with both my friends and Hein's coming over all the time — but I know she loved all the activity. Whenever Hein got a weekend pass from the service, he would come to our house. This was often in preference to his own home, partly because Hein's father was a very, very strict man. Hein always respected his father, but sometimes he questioned his rather severe ways.

One day my father got a letter from Hein's father, who knew that his son was about to receive a three-day leave that began on a Sunday. Hein had planned to hop on the train before church on Sunday morning, which meant, of course, that he would be traveling on the Sabbath. His father asked my father to refuse to admit Hein into our home because he thought that Hein's taking the Sunday train was sinful. My father wrote Mr. Sietsma back after Hein had spent the weekend with us: "I'm glad that your son Hein came to The Hague and spent the day and went to church with us. I would have hated it if he had simply gone to a bar."

Hein was, in fact, often angry with his father. But both of us could also understand his father's ways. He was a man who was very sure of his ways, and he had a very large family, so large that his discipline had to be quite strict.

Hein tried to spread his leaves out so that he could get to his family in Holk, but he knew that he was never welcome at home if his leave began on the Sabbath. If he had only two days off, he would come to our house first. He knew that otherwise he would waste a whole day just having to avoid travel on Sunday.

We wrote each other very often. What I understand about myself now was that even though I was a tomboy when I was a girl, I was still something of an introvert. Even though I was often willing to be different, I found it very difficult to tell Hein exactly what I felt for him at that time. Maybe it took more courage than I had; maybe it was just something about us and about the time, but I found it very difficult to be open about my feelings. It strikes me now that I was so very young when all of this was happening.

Hein seemed to find it much easier to be open and honest in expressing his feelings toward me. I couldn't — I just couldn't. Maybe my reluctance was just a part of my own old-fashioned ways: "Don't ever show your feelings," was the kind of forced exterior that is quite typical of the Dutch. Sometimes, I know, I must have seemed to him to be quite cold. But that first time he came to see me in The Hague, when he came to see just *me,* I kissed him. At that moment I somehow knew that what I felt for him was something that was not going to simply pass away. He kissed me too — yes, he did. That was quite an experience for me. It was wonderful that first weekend, and it was just the beginning.

▲   ▲

November 17, 1939

Katrientje is a cute, fresh young girl with red cheeks. Nice to talk to and she knows her place among the "young people." A fun-type, a little tom-boyish.

But Diet has, apart from all these good qualities, also her childlike, simple faith and the inborn quality to see the good in everything. Conscious, or unconscious for her it is: "God is with me and therefore I am happy and try to look for the good in everybody, without pushing myself into the foreground."

Why does she not write? Does she not know that I am aching for a letter, for a word from her?

Diet, are you coming tomorrow?

I want to hold you to my heart and tell you that I love you completely. I have seen that you love me, my all.

from the journal of Hein Sietsma

▼   ▼

It was 1939, and a number of our close friends had also fallen in love by that time. Johan Van Gelder, a friend Hein had met at our church, was engaged. And the other Johan, whom we called "Bram" to distinguish them from each other, was engaged to Nel, another friend. We were all deeply in love — all three couples. The girls loved each other too, and the guys were very good buddies. We had a wonderful world. Nel, Bram's girl, also lived in The Hague. But Johan was from Amersfoort, and so was his fiancée, Fokje. She would come to The Hague some weekends to see him, and often she stayed with us. My parents' house was like a hotel: one weekend it would be this young man or woman, the next someone else.

▲   ▲

November 20, 1939

Birthday of Mr. Eman. Yesterday afternoon to The Hague. Made my own leave permit. Was at 4:30 p.m. in the Malakkastraat. Bram was also there. With Bram we went to pick Diet up from church. Diet and Rie don't see us. We pass them and turn around and follow them. Still they don't see us.

I hook my arm into hers.

from the journal of Hein Sietsma

November 1939

Sunday I had a big surprise. When I walked home from church, all of a sudden Hein was walking right next to me! I did not know what I saw!!

from the diary of Diet Eman

▼   ▼

In the Netherlands, the fifth of December is called Sinter-Klaas, and on that day we all make presents — sometimes silly, sometimes not — for our close friends and family. Once when we were swimming in the ocean, Hein had noticed that I was scared stiff of jellyfish. When the wind blew from a certain direction, hundreds of ugly blue jellyfish, it seemed, would come storming out of the sea. Some were huge, and they had horrible stinging tentacles. I was paralyzed with fear.

At the next Sinter Klaas, I was given a big wooden box; the note attached announced that it was a gift from Neptune, King of the Sea. In it was a big blob of jello. Hein had made a big blue jellyfish, and in the middle of that blob was a little bottle of my favorite perfume, *Maja*. He was a sweetheart, so often playing tricks like that. Sometimes when I went to bed at night — in those days you rolled your nightie under your pillow — I would grab my nightie and something would roll out, a box of perfume or an apple or something. He loved to play those little surprises, and they were always thoughtful.

We were all supposed to write poems to accompany our Sinter Klaas presents. Hein wrote a beautiful poem with that jellyfish present, a note that described how Neptune wept because I had been so afraid of one of the little creatures of his kingdom. I'll never forget it.

My sister was a young woman who liked high heels and hats and all such beautiful ladies' things. The guy she was dating was at our home one Sinter Klaas when everybody had a present for somebody. The rule was that the giver was supposed to wrap it up and write a poem, and the recipient had to read that poem aloud, whether he liked what it said or not. Sometimes, if one had a little habit that others found humorous or annoying, that little habit was likely to show up in the poem. But what was written was always playfully done, not something to make anyone furious. The gift might be just a little thing, but it was always wrapped deceptively in a big box, wrapped time and time again. Sometimes it had other people's names on each separate wrapping: on the outside the gift might say it was intended for Fanny; but once she opened the outside paper, she'd discover the next layer would say it was actually intended for Hein; then he would open it and say, "It's really for Father."

That year my mother had bought a beautiful lace brassiere for Fanny, who loved lace. Now a bra was a very private thing in those days. But Mother always got mixed up when she wrapped things, so that present ended up — where would you guess? — right in the hands of my sister's new boyfriend. This young man was what we call in Dutch a *droogkomiek:* he had a very dry sense of humor. He opened the package, held up this beautiful lace bra, and said in a flat tone, "Ja, what am I supposed to do with this?"

▲   ▲

December 5, 1939

Went on leave to The Hague last Sunday. The English church.

Yesterday we celebrated Sinterklaas.

Afterward in Diet's room. She was so beautiful: I don't think I ever saw her so beautiful.

When she says, "Why are you laughing, Hein?" and I look into her eyes which are always laughing when she looks up, I can only feel how wonderful it is that both of us have to laugh quietly when we look at each other. Sometimes we burst out laughing loudly, because we just can't say a thing.

When once there came a tear in her eye, I asked,
"What's the matter, Diet?"

And she said, "I had to think of . . ."

I didn't ask any further.

But it was so wonderful to have such a girl with you,
who trusts you, to know and to feel that she loves you and
that she is yours.

Such a girl you can never harm or hurt. You think
everything about her, her soul, herself — everything is
wonderful and you don't want to ruin anything. That can't
happen — it can never happen, fortunately. You only may
love and make her happy, like she makes you happy.

Diet, when I think of you, I am so happy.

Lord, give that I may love her.

from the journal of Hein Sietsma

▼   ▼

For young people like us, times were different from what
they are today. No young couples were married quickly in the
Netherlands — certainly not immediately after they fell in love,
or even right after they became engaged. They had to wait
because they had to save money for furniture, for linens, for
dishes, for all of their household needs. Usually, two or three
years would pass before a couple would finally get married. And
once they were, women usually did not work outside the home.
Becoming man and wife depended on the husband's having a
good job so that he could support an entire family. There was
not as much money or goods available in those post-Depression
times. And for us, Hitler and the threat of war made everything
even more unstable.

▲　　　▲

October 31, 1939

Today the thought continues to run through my mind that there is a good possibility the war will come to us also. I am always thinking that if it happened in *our* country it will be much worse than when it happens in other countries, but what makes us different from others?

If I think that Hein could be killed . . . now in Poland there will be girls who have lost their fiancés and women who will not see their husbands again here on earth.

O Father, console them and please spare our country from that terrible disaster, not because we are any better but only out of grace. And *if* it has to be different, then teach me to pray: "Your will be done."

O please protect him whom my soul loves!

from the journal of Diet Eman

▼　　　▼

The Invasion

113DE JAARGANG

Nieuwe Amsterdamsche Courant

AVONDBLAD

ABONNEMENTEN PER KWARTAAL,
PER MAAND EN PER WEEK.

ALGEMEEN HANDELSBLAD

No. 37104; Twaalf bladzijden

Directeur: Mr. B. M. Pinedo.

Vrijdag 10 Mei 1940

Uitgave van het „Algemeen Handelsblad" N.V.
N.Z. Voorburgwal 234-240, Amsterdam (C).

Hoofdredacteur: D. J. van Balkveld.

Nederland in oorlog met Duitschland

België, dat ook door Duitschland is aangevallen, en ons land hebben een beroep gedaan op de Geallieerden, die hebben toegezegd alle mogelijke hulp te zullen verleenen

Grenstroepen bieden verbitterd weerstand aan IJssel en Maas

Vannacht drie uur overschreden Duitsche troepen onze grenzen, ruim een uur later bombardeerde de Duitsche luchtmacht Nederlandsche vliegvelden en te zes uur bood de Duitsche gezant te 's-Gravenhage een verklaring aan, waarbij de inzet van de Duitsche troepenmacht werd aangekondigd en elke tegenstand doelloos verklaard.

De Nederlandsche Regeering heeft deze verklaring met verontwaardiging van de hand gewezen en geantwoord, zich in oorlog te beschouwen met het Duitsche Rijk.

De Nederlandsche grenstroepen bieden aan IJssel en Maas krachtig weerstand. Vier Duitsche pantsertreinen zijn buiten gevecht gesteld, waarvan er een tegelijk met de brug over de Maas te Venlo in de lucht vloog. Bij landingspogingen in het binnenland zijn ten minste 70 Duitsche vliegtuigen neergeschoten. Van verschillende plaatsen komen berichten, dat de Duitschers Nederlandsche krijgsgevangenen als dekking gebruiken.

Te vijf uur in den ochtend kon het Algemeen Hoofdkwartier reeds melden, dat onze weermacht en afweer paraat waren en de inundaties zich volgens plan voltrokken.

De Opperbevelhebber heeft een verordening uitgegeven, waarbij het allen

Duitschers of vreemdelingen van Duitsche afkomst verboden is zich in Nederland op straat of weg te bevinden.

Voorts heeft de Opperbevelhebber „Het Nationale Dagblad", „Volk en Vaderland" en „Het Volksdagblad" verboden, en een waarschuwing gericht tegen de burgerbevolking om zeer wantrouwend te staan tegenover radioberichten en strooibiljetten, die gewag maken van staken van het Nederlandsch verzet of van onderhandelingen met den vijand.

Volgens berichten van Reuter en Havas zijn in België het militaire hospitaal te Antwerpen verwoest, verscheidene huizen te Brussel door bommen vernield, het station Jemelles in vlammen gezet en het vliegveld Evere door Duitsche vliegtuigen met bommen bestookt.

Een Fransch leger rukt reeds op, ten einde België hulp te verleenen. Ook Britsche troepen zijn onderweg.

Koning Leopold van België heeft het opperbevel over de Belgische troepen overgenomen.

De ministers v. Kleffens en Welter

PROCLAMATIE VAN H. M. DE KONINGIN

Mijn Volk,

Nadat ons land met angstvallige nauwgezetheid al deze maanden een stipte neutraliteit had in acht genomen en terwijl het geen ander voornemen had dan deze houding streng en consequent vol te houden, is in den afgeloopen nacht door de Duitsche weermacht zonder de minste waarschuwing een plotselinge aanval op ons gebied gedaan. Dit niettegenstaande de plechtige toezegging, dat de neutraliteit van ons land zou worden ontzien zoolang wij haar zelf handhaafden. Ik richt hierbij een vlammend protest tegen deze voorbeeldelooze schending van de goede trouw en aantasting van wat tusschen beschaafde staten behoorlijk is.

Ik en Mijn Regeering zullen ook thans onzen plicht doen. Doet gij den uwe, overal en in alle omstandigheden, ieder op de plaats waarop hij is gesteld, met de uiterste waakzaamheid en met die innerlijke rust en overgave, waartoe een rein geweten in staat stelt.

Wilhelmina

zijn naar Londen vertrokken voor overleg met de Geallieerden.

In Amerika heeft het nieuws van den Duitschen inval een diepen indruk gemaakt.

"Netherlands at War with Germany," reads the headline. Queen Wilhemina issued a proclamation to her people that, despite efforts to remain neutral, Germany's aggression had forced Holland to declare war. The surprise attack on Holland had begun at 4:00 A.M., with strategic bombing and a combined military force of paratroopers and German soldiers who had infiltrated posing as civilians.

It was May 9, 1940, the Thursday night before Pentecost, some friends were visiting my family in our home. We the radio on and were listening to Hitler give one of his fine speeches. There were quite a few people in our house that night, and we all knew German. We heard Hitler say that the Netherlands did not have to fear because the Dutch had been neutral during the First World War, and he would respect our neutrality. We were not important to his campaign, so we didn't have to worry.

After our guests had left, we all went to bed. But only a few hours later, I awoke to what I recognized as a familiar sound. It was the staccato sound of someone beating a rug. In the Netherlands of that era, housewives kept a regular weekly schedule: Monday was laundry day; Tuesday was for ironing; Wednesday you cleaned the living room; Thursday, perhaps another room; and on Friday you cleaned the rugs with *mattenkloppers*, rugbeaters.

When I awoke very early that Friday morning, I immediately thought, "This is crazy! Some idiot is beating rugs right now, and it's pitch dark outside." What I heard was the "pop-pop-pop" as if someone were spanking rugs — only much faster. It was the first sound of the war.

Father and Mother were up too. They had gone into the street in front of the house, so I joined them. There in the dark sky above us we could see an air battle — planes and shooting. We could hear it too, of course, and we could see what was being shot at the planes from the ground, what they call flak. We all ran back into the house and turned the radio on. The broadcaster sounded very nervous; he told us that we were at war and that German paratroops had landed.

This happened only hours after Hitler had assured us that we in the Netherlands needn't worry! I don't think that I had ever been lied to by a government leader before that time, and I was furious that this liar had told us not to be worried at the very moment he was sending troops onto our soil.

And our Dutch army, what were they? Our government did not believe in having a real standing army, and they certainly hadn't planned on this war. Our soldiers were on bicycles — can you imagine? — with their aging rifles slung over their shoulders. Against the Germans they were powerless. On top of that, many Germans came into the Netherlands that night wearing Dutch army uniforms. It had been reported from time to time in our papers that many Dutch uniforms had been missing, but no one had put two and two together. Not, at least, until those first Germans came over our borders looking so much like our soldiers that our boys didn't even know whom to shoot at. Some Germans even invaded our country wearing priests' habits!

We didn't sleep at all that night. After going back inside and listening to the radio reports, we talked and made tea. We were very nervous. Finally, we went back to bed to try to get an hour or so of rest. But there was no rest. We were at war.

Yet, the next day, what was there to do but go back to work? I had been working for some time at the Twentsche Bank, a very good bank in the center of The Hague. So that morning I got on my bike as usual. I didn't worry about air bombardment or any kind of danger; I just went to work. My regular route was via Vondelstraat, a main artery into the city. At one point I was stopped on that street by the Dutch police, who commanded me to say the words *Scheveningen* and *Schapenscheerder*, to pronounce them slowly. It was a shibboleth. If you were a native speaker of Dutch, you could pronounce those words perfectly. Germans, however, could not. It was just hours after the initial attack, but there had already been so much infiltration into the country that those precautions had to be taken.

There had been fighting on the outskirts of The Hague that morning, and paratroopers were all around the airports. Adriaan, a young man who was then dating my sister Fanny, was in the service like Hein. He had taken a job that required a certain amount of time in the army. The deal he had signed up for was this: if he agreed to go into the military service, he would get a good government job once he got out. And his time in the service was almost over. Fanny and Adriaan were planning to get married in September, four months from the time of the invasion.

That night of May 9, Adriaan was standing guard with his buddy at Ypenburg, the little airfield just outside The Hague, where the Germans dropped hundreds of paratroopers. He and his buddy were killed guarding that little airfield; they were among the very first Dutch soldiers to die.

On the 15th of May, 1940, the Netherlands surrendered. Hitler had assumed that he could take this little country with their bicycle soldiers within a day, but it took him five. The Dutch surrendered only because Hitler's bombers had destroyed Rotterdam. They had bombed the middle of the city — where all the people were, of course — and had destroyed hospitals and churches as well. It must have been horrible.

I didn't know it then, but Hein had been transferred to Rotterdam before the bombing, and he saw the whole thing himself.

I had thought all along that Hein was stationed in the east, in that area from Deventer to Ede. I had been worried about him, of course, because his first assignment was close to the German border and to much of the fighting. One weekend Hein had asked me to come to Ede, and I had ridden up there on my bike. He had borrowed a motorbike from a friend, and we traveled on it for miles, even though I was scared stiff the whole time. But he was happy to be away from the military environment for a while.

Hein never liked the military; something in him just seemed to hate it. It struck him, he told me, that so much of what happened in military life was simply a waste of time. It was difficult for him to serve his time, even before the war, but it was not because he was unpatriotic. What he did during the rest of the Occupation showed his patriotism, without a doubt. But he felt strange about the kind of life that was expected of him if he wanted to be a good soldier.

▲ ▲

December 9, 1939

I long so much to be a civilian again. I have to force myself to do my duty. I don't have the authority that I should have, without making myself fierce so that the guys are scared of me. Maybe I allow them too much. I don't have enough knowledge of human nature. I am too easy-going. I always watch what the others, colleagues, do wrong and never want to do anything more than they are doing. I am an egotist. I always have to force myself to realize that it does not matter that I, again and again, struggle with empty service time, with exercises which are not worth a thing, with turns of duty which are worth nothing. I have to remember that it is much more important to be always on time, to create more action, and this way to stimulate the other guys to do well. I have to live more for "guys and service" as one concept. My looking at the faults of others has to disappear. In the first place I have to love. For Christ rules and He has conquered *all*.

December 25, 1939

A soldier at the cross. Christmas and the war. Swearing and Christmas leave. The song of the angels and street jokes. The little child in the manger is the Christ of the cross. The true Christmas spirit makes us see him as our King and Redeemer.

My will subordinate to his will. Away with slander. Away with egotism. Away with gossip. Away with thinking evil. Away with doing evil.

If we, Christians, get rid of all our faults and errors, we still have to look to help others, for true love for God reveals itself in love for your neighbor.

We should not seek ourselves, or boast of what we do, because we have no merit. He first took away our sins and then he fulfilled obedience for us. First he made us Adams in Paradise and then he fulfilled the covenant so that we, because of him, may go to heaven as redeemed.

Where is my gratitude? In comparison for his gift, what are these little things I am going through?

from the journal of Hein Sietsma

▼ ▼

In the first few days of the invasion, I was terribly worried because of the rumors and radio reports — while we still had them — of heavy fighting at the Grebbeberg. Our government had even blown up some dikes and dams to inundate the land. I thought constantly of Hein and tried to write him daily.

Because there were so many spies throughout the country, the government would not forward closed letters, only postcards, which could be read easily. So for a time I wrote Hein a postcard every day, not knowing where he was or whether or not he'd been harmed by the invasion and the fighting that followed.

▲   ▲

The Hague, May 12, 1940

Dearest,

You probably haven't received my letters, but you know that we're always praying for you and our boys. We're not afraid because you're in the Father's hands, where you're safe. We don't see him, but he is with us. He himself promised us that, and he will certainly do it in the hour of danger. He has found this necessary for us, and through it he brings us very close to him. There, it is good, isn't it?

How thankful I am that we were able to see each other last week, and that I was able to be with you.

I keep thinking back to our Easter holidays. Today it is Pentecost. The Lord remains the same. He is the Rock upon which we lean. He hears all our prayers and answers them in the way that he finds best for us. He never makes mistakes.

Till we meet again, dearest, here, or there where there is no more sorrow.

You are fighting, with God, for justice.

Don't ever worry about me, okay?

A kiss from your Diet

postcard from Diet Eman to Hein Sietsma

▼   ▼

Already in the early months of 1940, the government had moved the soldiers around because they were beginning to feel the Nazi threat acutely. So it wasn't until I heard from Hein after the invasion that I realized he had not been at Ede at all when the invasion took place. Instead, he'd been moved to Rotterdam, where he had witnessed the terrible bombing of that old, beautiful city.

▲   ▲

June 4, 1940

Pentecost I could not celebrate. *War of five days* and we were conquered. *Bitter* I have been. *Hate* I felt. *Courage*, for I did not shrink from death. *Only Diet* was there — because of her I still was careful.

I have been in the flames of the hell of Rotterdam. And the sun I saw through the black-gray column of smoke was changed into blood. And it spoke to me.

Much has happened, and I could not be silent.

Now we wait patiently, and sometimes impatiently, for we don't know the future. One day we will have peace again. One day we won't hear the engines of warplanes any longer. One day we will again live freely, lives of happiness and love and Dutch luxury. Maybe then people will acknowledge that neither the one, nor the other, but that *he* rules the world.

"Bong, bong, bong!" I want to shoot at them, those lousy planes, every time they do their pestilent buzzing over the city.

I wait for the hour, and that *will* come, when I can join and march against the enemy to fight for the liberty of Dieneke, my fatherland, and myself.

You filthy scum and bunch of bloody pus boils! Don't you think you are big heroes now that you have massacred a whole city of people who wanted only peace?

Rotterdam calls for revenge, you bunch of boils.

from the diary of Hein Sietsma

▼   ▼

Maybe it was better that I didn't know Hein was in Rotterdam to experience what he did, such a horrifying fiery bombardment. Some time later I received a card from him saying that he had been near Rotterdam, and he had survived. The card had a postmark on it, an advertising stamp that said, "Spend your vacation in your *peaceful* Fatherland." The corners of that card were actually smudged from the fires of Rotterdam.

The next terrible news we got was that our queen and all of the government officials had left the Netherlands and gone to England. I cannot express how horrible that made us feel. I heard it on the radio: "The queen has left for England." Our queen! It was an awful moment because it was as if our mother had left us behind for the Germans.

▲   ▲

June 4, 1940

And you, Wilhelmina, and our government — don't you think yourselves a bunch of wonderful people to save your skins elsewhere, and to let our men sacrifice their lives? Did you see them fight? Did you see them die? They loved him, and they loved their Fatherland and their queen, more

even than we who survived. They were so courageous —
those trusting, faithful soldiers. Thousands of them fell —
do you hear? And thousands also lost everything they had,
do you hear? Thousands?

And you left for safer regions, did you not? Heroes!!!
You only thought of yourselves, did you not?

But the best and the noblest gave their lives, you hear?

If you ever would come back, then you'll know that
the handful of guys who formed the core of our country,
the cream of the crop, is gone.

from the diary of Hein Sietsma

▼   ▼

We were so angry and bitter. We did not know enough
then to understand exactly what had happened. It would take
some time before we understood why the queen and the whole
government had abandoned us.

Those first few days — just before the Germans had actually marched in and taken control — the bank where I worked
was nearly overwhelmed with business. People wanted to take
their money out; they felt they had to buy food and other material
to stock up. Everything was in turmoil. During those five days
there were air raids as well: whenever there were sirens, we all
had to rush into the vaults, which was very scary. The Germans
weren't bombing precisely our area of the Netherlands at the
time, but we were still very afraid. When the planes came over,
we never knew where they would drop their bombs. Later, they
did attack The Hague, but I was not there at the time.

Then one day the tanks rolled into the heart of The Hague.
The German soldiers came marching in, doing their goose step,

their bright helmets shining. It was simply heart-breaking. Clearer even than the picture of those invading soldiers is my memory of the way tears streamed down my face, down all of our faces. There was such a sense of doom, the feeling that it was inevitable that the Germans would be ruling us until, somehow, it would be over.

That day, I became so angry about the Germans — all of this happening in *our* country, and we hadn't asked for any of it — that I made a vow: even though I could speak German fluently, I would not speak a word of their language as long as those German soldiers were in our country.

After they had taken over, the Germans often came into the bank where I was working, and I had to wait on them. I began my own resistance with a small bit of mischievousness in those first days. I knitted a sweater in our royal family's color, orange, and our national colors — red, white, and blue. The background of the sweater was bright orange wool, and I embroidered all over that with red, white and blue flowers. I wore that sweater to the bank, and there I stood, in full view of the Germans standing in line.

One day I was called in by the *procuratiehouder*, a holder of the power of attorney, the man who signed the checks.

"I think it's better if you go home and change into something else," he told me. But he also whispered to me that he loved the sweater.

▲   ▲

May 2, 1941

New order of the Reichskommissar! No longer any pictures of live members of the Royal family, van Oranje

Nassau, and no longer are we allowed to show the colors of the house! Ridiculous! The love for our Royal family remains in our hearts and you cannot pull that out!

from the diary of Diet Eman

▼   ▼

After those first few days of the invasion, Hein was brought to Gouda, along with many of our captured troops. I was so relieved when I finally received a card from him indicating that he was all right. But even that good news was hard for me to celebrate, because days before that, in the opening moments of the invasion, my sister had already lost her fiancé. In the face of her terrible loss — and the grief of my parents — I could not show my thrill at Hein's safety.

Fanny had heard the terrible news about Adriaan immediately, because when the Germans invaded, she was living in an apartment in Monster, very close to the place where Adriaan was shot. The invasion had begun in the early morning hours of Friday, and he was probably killed right away. That day, Fanny did not go to work but got on her bike and pedaled to The Hague, through the military lines. Somehow she had found out what had happened to Adriaan, and she came home to tell the family. She was just shattered.

It was very difficult to be in our home during those days because of the big shadow Adriaan's death cast over all of us. My sister and I shared a bedroom, and I listened to the sound of her sobbing every night. I didn't dare to say a thing to her because I thought I had no right to console her, not with Hein still alive.

Adriaan's buddy, who was also killed, had been an only

child of parents who were not Christians. After the death of their son they went to séances, and at one point they said to Fanny: "Whenever we go, we have regular contact with our son. And you know what, Fanny? Adriaan appears to us too, and he's been asking for you."

So my sister went along to those séances for some time. Her face began to take on a ghastly look — big, hollow black eyes. What's more, she lost a lot of weight. To me, the whole thing was sad, and very spooky too: she thought she was talking to Adriaan.

"Have you heard anything strange tonight?" she asked me one night. "Adriaan was here. He came in — his spirit was here in this very room with us."

We all watched her suffer as she continued to go to those séances. But we couldn't say anything. After all, she was an adult. I was twenty and she was twenty-eight; what can you say to someone that age? She would have been married in September if Adriaan had not died that first day of the war. We tried to tell her that séances were wrong according to the Bible. "Remember the witch of Endor," we'd tell her.

But she wouldn't hear of it. She said: "Adriaan always had one special name for me, a name he used only when we were alone. And he spoke that name to me there — in that seance."

When my grandmother came and saw Fanny, she became very frightened. "You have to get Fanny out of here," she told Mother, "or else she will die."

Mother told Fanny that she needed some kind of change, but Fanny wouldn't hear of moving.

"I'm not going to do anything," she said. "I'm not going to look for another job — nothing at all."

I believe it was her sewing that kept her imprisoned. Sewing was her job, and she was very good. When she did that work with her hands, she would sit there and think and think, because her fingers were busy by themselves. She would sit and twirl her fingers and stay in her despair: her fingers' solitary work became a refuge, a place to hide. We thought it would be better if she had other kinds of work to do.

Finally Mother said to her, "The best thing would be if you were in a household where there is no mother, because you are a terrific housewife." Fanny knew canning, cleaning, and, of course, sewing; and she loved housework. She and I were very much different in our desires. Her highest dream was to have a home of her own.

So Mother searched the want ads in the newspaper and found a notice: "Widower is looking for a lady to help him bring up his two children in the spirit of the *overleden* mother" — the mother who had passed away.

Mother answered that ad and told the man what had happened to Fanny: she didn't tell him about the séances, but she said that Fanny's fiancé had been killed in the invasion and that she needed a change, needed to get out of the house where she was surrounded by all her grief and where everything reminded her of Adriaan. So Fanny went to Apeldoorn, where this man lived, and became his housekeeper.

My brother Arjan had already joined the Indonesian service by that time (he later died in a Japanese prison camp), and now Fanny had also left the house where we had lived so happily before the war. Once the Germans marched into The Hague, that house, like so much else in the city, fell into fear and silence.

▲   ▲

January 1, 1941

What will this year bring us? Peace? Liberty? Reunion? Lord, you know it already! This time last year, when we were all together, we would never have thought that all this would happen! But you knew it. And we still have to give you thanks, for in some way this is necessary for the big plan you have for this world.

"Lord, you have taken every second of our life in your own Hand." ("Sacred Songs" by Rabindranath Tagore) And it has been good. You will take care of us in the future, and therefore a future with you is good. You also see Arjan, who has drawn closer to you because of all this. You see Hein, wherever he may be. You are with them.

You look down upon Fanny for whom this is so very difficult, and you guided her way to Apeldoorn. Please grant that for consolation she looks to you only and not to that contact during the seances, because that appearance would take the place of your Holy Spirit, and Adriaan himself would never have wanted this.

Lord, you who have guided our lives up till now and have been Love for us, we thank you for everything you gave us, and all we needed. We thank you for the happiness, peace, joy and now also for our sadness, Lord. Give us, for the coming year, the certainty that you will always be near us, always will hear us, and that your eye will look down upon us in love. Then we can enter this New Year with JOY.

from the diary of Diet Eman

▼   ▼

The Occupation Begins

She, in German: "Für meinen kranken M . . ."
["It's for my mother who is ill."]
He, in Dutch: "Geen praatjes, gevorderd!"
["Nonsense! Hand it over!"]
She, in Dutch: "O, is u Hollander **geweest**?!"
["Oh, so you **were** a Dutchman?!"]

P. de Zeeuw J. G.zn., *Vrij* (de Bilt: Uitg. Comp. De Branding, 1945).

▲　　　　▲

Easter 1941

A little bit different from last year's Easter! Then we were in the midst of war and now that horror is over. O God, still we were closer to you then. And did not this all happen to bring us closer to you? How can it be that all of us are getting so bitter, and that we feel guilty under your heavy hand.

Send Lord, your light and your *truth*. Never did we know what truth meant until now, when we are surrounded by lies. Bah, what an atmosphere around us — and are we the "lights" in the darkness, like you commanded us to be? There is no difference between me and the world. Am I of the world? Sometimes I am afraid that I am. Please loosen me from that, O Lord.

from the diary of Diet Eman

▼　　　　▼

Soon after the Occupation began, Hein was released, along with the rest of our captured soldiers. They were not taken prisoner because they were not the military brass. The Dutch army — or what was left of it — was simply dissolved. Hein returned to the office at Shell, where they passed him through various jobs in training to go abroad, which was something both of us had wanted to do before the war started.

It was no more than a few months after the Occupation began that we realized there were things that simply had to be done. When we saw injustice, we all felt it; we couldn't just sit there and do nothing. But what could we do? The atrocities toward the Jews all around were beginning, and we felt that it was our duty to act in some way. But it took time for us to know exactly what, when, and how we could do something.

Right from the beginning, the Occupation created ambiguities, arguments, and difficult struggles within Christian circles. When Jesus lived, his country was occupied by the Romans, and everyone remembered what he said: "Give Caesar what is Caesar's." Jesus Christ never preached rebellion against the Romans. Part of the struggle, the moral struggle, was the belief that what had happened in our little country was in fact ordained by God: some people claimed that we shouldn't interfere with what went on because the Occupation itself was God's will. Even my brother was originally inclined to think that one simply could not work against the Germans if one followed the teachings of Scripture.

The queen and the government had left for England in the early moments of the five-day invasion, and there was a whole group in Holland who said that the queen had no right to lead us anymore. Those of us who remained behind were required to obey the government that God had given us now — that is, the Germans. But Hein and I and many others felt our royal family had been crowned in a religious ceremony, with the words "by the grace of God." We felt the queen was our rightful government, and we felt that we were doing what the Lord wanted when we obeyed her. That's why, later in the occupation when the queen actually told the Dutch to go on strike against the Germans, we did it, although our actions cost many lives.

Many people in our church, the Christian Reformed Church, felt that the queen was still our head, not the Nazi puppets. But the church we called the "black-stocking church" leaned toward the other point of view: that our burden was to be in subjection to whatever higher powers God had placed over us. People who took that point of view were never very strong in the Resistance because they thought resistance against the established government was, quite simply, sin.

Those were the kinds of arguments we used to hear, and we would even have them among ourselves during those early days of the Occupation. We had especially good arguments at the home of one of my fellow bank employees, a man named Platteel. We talked about how we were to live now in this new arrangement with the Germans. He was older than I was, in his thirties, and was married with two little kids.

In those early days, members of the Platteel group would advise everyone what passages to read from the Bible, what scriptures we should consider when we were trying to reflect morally about our new national situation.

Some of the early Resistance people would sit down and take passages from the Bible that clearly showed the direction that we as Christians ought to take. Then they would write those passages on pieces of paper, and pass those notes around. A little note would say, "Read this passage, or that one." Mr. Platteel would give me such a note, passing it along after copying it many times. There were no copy machines in those days, so who knows how many times he wrote that out and gave it to someone? He would often distribute lists of readings on his own, and even that small gesture could be an encouragement, a direction for us to go in. Such little things were important because such little things gave our hearts strength.

We all felt terrible about what was happening around us. Hein and I would sit down and ask ourselves, "What can we do?" We always talked about it together, and then discussed how we felt with a few more people at my bank or at his office, people who thought the same way we did.

Once the Occupation began, the Germans began to make all kinds of rules: we were not allowed to listen to the BBC, for instance, though any number of people still did it secretly, of course. And then came the next order in the newspapers: "Everybody has to surrender their radios." Radios, in those days, were the size of televisions today; nobody had little pocket-sized appliances. So deciding whether or not to give them up to the Germans was a big decision. And the Germans made it very clear that if you didn't deliver your radios to them, you could be thrown in prison. People became very scared. In the Netherlands, people are accustomed to liberty; nobody had ever told us what to do before.

This is what we thought: "Do we simply obey those miserable Huns?" The question "Are we going to obey?" had to be asked and answered, asked and answered, over and over again. Some brave people made a hole in the wall of their homes, put in a shelf, and then placed the radio on that hiding place and hung a painting or a mirror over it.

Every evening at eight o'clock the BBC sent out information about the progress of the war and other matters. If you lived on a main street of the city, somebody from the family would walk the dog or just walk down the street to be sure there was no spy around. By that time there already were Dutch cowards — those who sided with the Germans — who had started to make money by turning in their own countrymen. If they betrayed you by pointing at your house, they made good money. Once those kinds of sides had formed, the real danger started: the Underground against the informers.

The Germans continued to say, "You are not allowed to do this, and you are not allowed to do that." They made prohibitory laws against just about everything, and they reported the news in such a crooked way that everyone assumed what we heard was just plain wrong. So we knew that the BBC on radio was our only source of reliable news. Those of us who met to discuss what could be done were a very few people then, very few. Because many people were intimidated by the Germans and did hand in their radios, we knew that few of those people were hearing the real news of the war, the news from England. Thus, our first act of disobedience was listening to the BBC, taking down the real news in shorthand, typing it out, and spreading it around. That was the beginning of most Resistance groups. If you were caught doing that, of course, you went to prison. But we did it anyway.

In The Hague we were surrounded by Germans immediately. They were everywhere, marching and just standing around on street corners. Even where you worked, you had to be careful about what you said because a lot of people in the office were pro-German, some of whom you would never have suspected it.

My heart nearly broke because my two dear girlfriends, Rie and Jet, the friends my age with whom I went jumping *sloten* and climbing trees and had so much in common — those best friends wouldn't think for a moment about resistance. As a matter of fact, my brother Albert had a kind of a crush on Jet, so those girls were always in our house. Albert and Jet were friends, and I was dating Hein; Rie's boyfriend, Paul, lived on our street, and his sister Jopie came along too. We were all the same age and we formed a kind of club, the Malakka Club, because we lived on Malakka Street, named for a part of Malaysia. We were always together on Saturdays, and it was quite a mixture: Jet, Rie, and Daniel were Christian Reformed, as were Albert and I and Gerald, another friend; but all the rest of the kids were of different faiths. There were even two brothers of a family that had no religion, Stan and Henk van Eekelen. Of the two, one became a fanatical communist, the other one a fanatical Nazi, of all things. Two brothers in the same house, two completely different world views!

Even before the war, my parents would often have Dutch soldiers over on Sunday. We lived beside an armory, and we would have several soldiers come to the house for dinner, and to play the organ and sing. My parents thought that was one way to support our boys.

Jet's family didn't invite boys from the armory into their home. Her family belonged to our church, but they had six kids, and they would say, "Yeah, yeah, our family is too busy. We can't do that." We accepted their decision. But they were really the same kind of people we were: they attended the same church and had the same basic beliefs. In fact, their father did the same work as my father did; they were sort of competitors. After church on Sundays, the girls would come to my house, and we would play Ping-Pong or *sjoelbak* (shuffleboard), or we would play four-handed piano.

But just a few weeks after the war broke out, one Sunday I entered their house, and there above the piano hung a portrait of Hitler! In addition, German soldiers were in their house that night. Jet's family was doing for German soldiers what we had done for the Dutch boys before the war. *Now*, after the Occupation had begun, they could do it for the enemy.

I had decorated my bicycle at that time by putting a little patriotic red-white-and-blue flag on it. Every night I rode home from the center of the city on my bike, the flag waving. One day Jet's brother Daniel ripped that red-white-and-blue flag off my bike. I was so deeply hurt that I wrote them a letter. "Until that picture is gone" — I meant that picture of Hitler — "I'll never set foot in your house again," I told them. I said I was angry, "because you had no place for the Dutch soldiers who gave their lives for our country, and now you treat the guys who have come into this country, totally uninvited, with hospitality."

▲   ▲

July 1941

Dear Rie and Jet:

Sometimes I would so very much like to know how you are doing. Sometimes I long so much for both of you. Especially when I look at our vacation photos. Then I can barely take it that things are now the way they are. You had such a large place in my heart and I loved you both, more than even Fanny. You probably are playing a lot of piano, eh, Jet? And what is Rie doing? I have the feeling that I barely know you anymore. Nel, Bram's girlfriend, sometimes laughs and makes movements and then I am thinking: "Who does she remind me of? — somebody does it just the same." And now I know it, Rie — it is you. When you were teasing someone, you laughed just like Nel does.

Did I do wrong in breaking with you? Would it have been my task to still try to keep you? Was it wrong that I did not want to come to your house any longer? Also not to be considered a traitor? I spoke to my father confessor [a man named Taverne, a man I helped], and he said, "The light may not be in communion with the dark forces."

I wish I was a light, but I am only a little flickering flame. I am so happy that Nel now came into my life. I still don't know her, but I feel that she will be able to replace something that I lost when I lost you.

from the diary of Diet Eman

▼   ▼

To this day, I don't understand their way of thinking. That family was so similar to ours in beliefs — same church, same profession, and same standard of living. Maybe I never knew what those people were really like. When we were younger, maybe we were just having too much fun. We never talked about important things, about politics; we never talked about serious things at all. We just had fun. I never knew them inside, I suppose. But maybe there was more to all of it. Those girls were my best friends, so I've often thought about what happened.

Hein and I and the group that met at Platteel's felt very strongly that what we were doing was right, both with our consciences and with God. What we were certain of was that there were things happening in our country that were wrong. But it was so difficult to know what to do. At first, we didn't know where to start. At that time the Germans had not yet started persecuting the Jews. What had aroused us was other things: laws against radios; rules about what we could listen to; laws forcing us to hand in copper, brass, and other metals; laws against everything. We the people of the Netherlands were accustomed to being free.

▲   ▲

July 7, 1941

Did not write in a long time and much has happened during that time. Two weeks ago, Russia joined. All metal has to be handed in. Political parties have to be dissolved. Their monies have to be handed in. Many arrests among the Roman Catholics, and we are *getting accustomed to this, that is the very worst of this all.*

And also, I forget to see that this all happens with

44

God's permission. I keep on staring at the injustice which our country and people are suffering, but I forget that you bring your trials on this earth because you deem this necessary, otherwise it would not have happened.

Teach me to see that this is you, who carries everything in your strong hands, then I can even be happy knowing that you are fulfilling your plans. Keep me from saying so many things which are not pleasing to you. Set a guard over my mouth, O Lord, and keep watch over the door of my lips.

from the diary of Diet Eman

▼   ▼

The Germans would print rules in the newspaper and broadcast them over the radio. They put up little signs on trains: "Be careful what you say." That's always what the Germans told each other: "Be careful with your conversations. The enemy is listening in." Of course, *we* were the enemy, and they were reminding their military that they should not talk about military things, because we would hear it. Then they began designating certain cars on the trains as belonging only to them. At that time in the Netherlands only the very rich had automobiles, and there was no gas. So the trains were a vital means of transportation. Everyone had bicycles, of course, but if you needed to go some distance you usually took the train. What they did was this: if it was a train of six cars, say, they would take two cars for themselves. They would put big signs on those cars: *Nur für Wehrmacht* ("Only for the German army").

When the Germans marked specific cars, those cars would almost always be empty, and the Dutch people had to stuff themselves into the one or two cars left for them. One time I fainted on the train, and I could not fall to the floor: there were too many people. I hung there, even though I had fainted dead away. Hein saw that I had fainted, but he was standing so far away from me that he could not get through the crowd. You were simply happy if you got on the train at all, never mind if you stayed together. We were already doing Underground work and on our way to Nijkerk that day, and I fainted shortly after we left The Hague.

The train stopped in Voorburg for two minutes, and the people around me saw me hanging there, green probably, and when the doors opened, they shoved me onto the platform. The doors closed, and the train simply left without me! Hein could not get to me. He had seen me lying there on the platform, but he was caught in his car because everyone was so cramped in. The train went all the way to Utrecht with him on it and me lying on the platform at Voorburg. Imagine, if you fainted, you couldn't even fall on the floor, you just hung there between people.

The way the Germans abused the railroad made me very angry, especially later, when I had to do so much traveling on those packed trains for the Resistance. So one time I walked right into one of those empty cars where the paper message — *Nur für Wehrmacht* — Gereserveerd voor Duitsche Weermacht — was stuck on the windows. I stood there with my back against the window, and behind my back I ripped the message off completely. Immediately, of course, the whole car filled up with Dutch people. That time, at least, the Dutch people had one extra car on their own train.

An officer at the bank by the name of Gitz used to give me occasional hints: "I have heard that some people are actually taking these Jews and hiding them," he said to me one day, as if it was an incredible shock that such a thing was being done. At that date, to be sure, it wasn't really done often. There were *onderduikers* already by that time, people who "dove under," went into hiding under a false name. But even hiding *onderduikers* was all very new then. Gitz was a man with whom I had a lot to do at the bank. "Have you heard of people who are in the Resistance, and who then have to go into hiding?" he asked me in a rather casual way.

"Ja, I've heard about that," I said, also very casually.

He often attempted to read my own feelings about the whole situation in that way, and I always was wary of him and his interest, even though, later on, he gave me more tips on people who were in the Underground and in other organizations. So Gitz helped me to get started, but always in a very guarded way. It wasn't easy to bring these things up with people you didn't know well: the price for being wrong about who could be trusted was very, very high.

Working together was absolutely required if our movement was going to grow. One of my uncles, my mother's brother, lived in The Hague and was doing important work for the Resistance when he showed interest in us. He worked for a printing outfit, which was ideal because he could secretly print the things we needed badly. He had his own contacts, so our circle grew because of our contact with him and his printing press.

When we started to do dangerous work — that is, when we began working to hide Jews — Herman, a Jewish man I worked with at the bank, told me about his Uncle Frits, who was doing all kinds of things for the Resistance. "Would you like to meet him?" he asked.

This Uncle Frits was not Jewish, but he had married Lena, Herman's mother's sister. Because his wife, his whole family, and all his relatives on his wife's side were in danger — being Jewish — he began to work hard for the Resistance. Uncle Frits had a strong sense of what was right and wrong.

He started doing all sorts of things with us. He came to the meetings at Platteel's, and, of course, he had even more contacts, including an accountant and his wife, Jenny, who was a housewife and very active and eager to work in the Underground. So at one point we had a big group of resisters in The Hague, and soon there were many things that we could do.

This is what happened: when all the problems for Jews burst out, when it became apparent that the Nazis were really starting to go after Jewish people, we saw our task. Up until that time we had been groping around with the constant question, "What can we do? What can we do?" But after the seizure of Jews became clear, that was simply not a question anymore. Our objective became very clear: to find places for Jews wherever we could.

When we formed ourselves into a Resistance group, we called ourselves "Group HEIN"; but the name had nothing to do with my fiancé's name. It was an acronym formed from the first letters of *Help Elkander in Nood*, which means "helping each other in need." Hein was one of the two leaders; the other was Ab van Meerveld, an old friend of his from The Veluwe, the part of the country where Hein had been raised and where his family still lived.

At first we didn't even think about a name; everything we did was so casual and limited. Our first activities consisted of spreading reliable news and trying to get people to England. Such small things, it seemed, and we were such ordinary people. But then our work started growing. And other small groups started to form in those early months. The Resistance was simply made up of people who were opposed to what was happening in the Occupation.

Distrust and suspicion surrounded us all the time. Young men could be stopped at any time on the streets and conscripted by the Germans. Germany was so short on manpower, their men spread over the whole of Europe as Occupation forces, that at home they had only young kids under fourteen and very old men. So they made it a rule that young able-bodied men of the countries they occupied had to go work in Germany. First it was an invitation; later it was forced labor. Those men were placed in factories, which became dangerous places when the Allies got involved, because they would often drop their bombs on those factories. Few Dutch men wanted to go to Germany to help the enemy; so our work began as an effort to hide not only Jews but also the *onderduikers,* Dutch men hiding for other reasons, such as to escape having to go work in Germany. The necessity of that effort had become very clear to us.

The *razzias,* the Gestapo raids, began to take place *after* the Germans were already coming after Jews; but our trying to help the *onderduikers* really started at about the same time that we started hiding Jews. When the Germans started taking other people too — not just Jewish men for forced labor camps — then the queen, in a radio broadcast, the queen made very clear to us that Dutch men should not go to Germany. Once again, just as with the confiscation of radios, Dutch people had to make a difficult choice. I realize now that more people than I once believed were simply very afraid; and many just obeyed all those crazy German rules.

Many men did go to Germany, but many others went into hiding. They worked on farms or did what they could in hiding; some worked in the Underground. No one had any inkling that the war would last for five years. At first, we really thought it would last only a year. We thought, these are modern times, after all, and this horrible barbarism will be defeated quickly.

We were sure America would join the war effort. We thought that Roosevelt would help free us. But we didn't have access to much world news, and thus we didn't know that in America there was terrific opposition to the war. We pictured America as the great land of justice and freedom and so on, and we thought that America and Roosevelt simply wouldn't stand for letting that little painter fellow out of Austria have his way with Europe.

At that time, the British were fighting for their lives against the bombardments. I still admire the British immensely because they had to send all their little kids out into the country in big trains, where they were taken in by farmers. Every night London was being bombed — the Blitzkrieg. Under those circumstances, when you are all in danger, you want to keep your kids by your side. And all the British housewives learned first aid and how to fight fires. After the bombardments, many English people would go out with their masks on to help. For them the war was simply horrible. I have the greatest respect for the courageous British.

If we hadn't believed in the Americans, I think we would have cracked up. We were so convinced they would join us because what we had already seen by 1941 was so evil. In our minds there was only one solution to all of this, and that was total war against Germany. But the Dutch had no weapons: we had only bicycle soldiers who were not really militarized and who carried guns that barely even shot straight. We had nothing.

It didn't take long, however, before our group of resisters had answers to the question we had constantly asked during those first days of the Occupation. Soon enough we knew what we could do. Soon enough we knew that the only way for us to act was to resist, even though the risk sometimes seemed very high.

▲   ▲

September 28, 1941

Rev. Bosch in the *Grote Kerk:* "Do not pray as in the Old Testament — 'Smash the heads of the children of those who persecute me against the rocks,' but pray instead, like Paul — 'I wished that you were like me, except for these chains.'"

Sometimes I cannot imagine that we as a people ever will be less hard again. Because of the things I say now, openly, without blushing. These thoughts of revenge I would earlier have wanted to dig a hole for saying — before this war. Only your Spirit can keep us from turning into animals. Send your Spirit into our hearts and lead us in your eternal way.

from the diary of Diet Eman

▼   ▼

A Place for Hein

When the queen left the country, we were angry and many Dutch people cried. What I thought was, "What mother leaves her kids behind when life gets tough?" I felt deserted, forgotten in her personal rush for safety. My first reaction was also Hein's first reaction, as well as the first reaction of many people in the Netherlands. Her leaving seemed understandable to us only from the standpoint of her desire to escape, which made her departure, in our eyes, even more deplorable. Later, we learned that King Leopold of Belgium had stayed with his people, had not run away as our queen had. His actions seemed those of a noble ruler, someone who truly cared about his people. But after the war we discovered that the Germans had put King Leopold in a big walled castle, where he was, in effect, imprisoned for the whole course of the war, never allowed to speak to his people, never allowed to lead them or even give them advice.

Our queen went to England with the whole Dutch government. And we all found out later that they had taken our national treasury, an enormous amount, along with them to England. Hitler had thought that he would march through the Netherlands within a day, seize the whole treasury, and use it to finance his huge war machine. Losing the Dutch wealth that the queen took along to England was a huge loss to his economy — and very disappointing to him.

We discovered that the queen, in fact, had done a very wise thing in leaving for England. We started to listen to the BBC immediately, and she gave many instructions to the Underground and other people of the Netherlands who remained loyal to the crown. Then, once it became clear that the queen had not abandoned her people but had done the wise thing, many Dutch people wanted badly to get to England themselves: we thought England would be the place from which we could best work against the Germans. General de Gaulle was in London, training the French; and we had our queen and all the government ministers there. "Get to England, get away from this" — that's what people thought. It was a very popular idea. Many of my friends became the *Engelandvaarders* — the sea travelers to England — and did just that.

That was Hein's great goal at first too, as well as his brother Henk's. During the summer of 1940, just after the Occupation began, many of us thought that we could be of greater use to our country in England. On his own, Henk started inquiring about ways to get to England. At the same time, Hein and I were in contact with a Jewish man named Mattijsen, who we thought was a communist and who was very active in the Underground movement. The Platteel group did a good deal of work with Mattijsen, and he helped guide us on many matters at the beginning.

Mattijsen lived in Scheveningen at that time, an area that soon became *Sperrgebiet*, forbidden territory, for ordinary people, but wasn't yet in those early days of the Occupation. He had a contact with a secret sender, he said, someone who maintained radio contact with England. Even though it was quite early in the Occupation, if we heard something we thought important, we would get the information to Mattijsen, who would then see that the information was sent to London. One day we heard that Hitler was coming to the Netherlands to talk to the top officials he had placed in power there, and that he would be staying at *Kasteel Oud Wassenaar*, a beautiful castle outside The Hague that had been remodeled into a hotel. We felt that if the English could drop just one bomb on that castle, it could wipe out Hitler and his top Occupation officers. I got the information from someone who worked in that hotel in a management position, but we kept it very secret until we got it to Mattijsen, and Mattijsen sent it to England.

That night we heard Allied planes and were eagerly waiting for news, but nothing happened. The plot didn't work out; but this was the kind of information we felt was so important to get to England.

Hein's brother Henk was then working in Amsterdam and living in a *pension* (a boarding house) with a wonderful family. Someone he had contacted told him that if he wanted to get to England he should see a man in a little cafe in Hilversum. The contact told Henk that when he entered the cafe he was to order a beer, and while he was drinking the beer he was to say a certain sentence; then the man would answer him with another sentence, and Henk would say something again, and after about four or five sentences that fit together like a puzzle, the man would know that he'd come to indicate he wanted to go to England and he could be trusted.

Henk never said anything to us about where he was going. He simply went to Hilversum, ordered his beer at the cafe, and said the password sentences. Immediately, the man he met was very nice.

"Oh yes," the man said, after taking him to the side, "I see you want to go to England. You are lucky: there is a submarine coming soon, and there is still a place. Actually there are several more places. Do you have any friends who want to go too?"

Henk gave him Hein's name, and the man took it down, and he took several other names and addresses as well.

And then Henk was arrested. The man he had spoken to in that little cafe was Gestapo; the real contact had been arrested shortly before, and the Germans had learned the password sentences, probably by torturing him. So they set their trap and arrested everyone who came to the Hilversum cafe.

But for all of us in Group HEIN — and for all of those people with whom Henk had contact — he had suddenly disappeared on November 14 or 15, 1940. Nobody knew where he was. People began to phone to try to find him. They called The Hague — his brother Hein's apartment and the Eman household — because he was often at our home. But, of course, he wasn't there. When Henk simply wasn't to be found, his Uncle Kees, Dominee Cornelius Sietsma, a prominent Amsterdam preacher, investigated more deeply into his disappearance and discovered exactly what had happened at that cafe in Hilversum, that Henk had been arrested.

One evening, soon after all of this, we came back from a meeting at Platteel's, and Mother seemed very agitated.

"Hein," she said, "you shouldn't be here. The Gestapo came to look for you here tonight."

We phoned his boarding house immediately, and the Gestapo had been there too, so he couldn't go back there either. At that point we still didn't know the reason exactly: we had no idea that Henk had mentioned Hein's name in Hilversum. But the Gestapo had come looking for another friend as well; fortunately, he wasn't home that night either.

What this meant, of course, was that by November of 1940, only six months after the Germans invaded, the men Henk had mentioned that day in the cafe had to go into hiding. That night, so early in the war, so early in the Occupation, was one of the worst experiences of my life, even though there was so much more still to come. A curfew was being enforced by then, so everyone had to be off the street — especially if the Gestapo was looking for that person. That night I went to many Christian friends and family, and no one would take Hein in. I was on my bike, and curfew was at eleven; Hein, of course, had to get somewhere before curfew. Wherever I went, I heard nothing but excuses, lame excuses in my eyes.

The Gestapo wasn't really that powerful yet, but that night — which was early in the Occupation and still fairly quiet —

many of my best friends, my best Christian friends, wouldn't take him. Not even my grandmother, whom I later asked to take him in. My grandmother was, in my youthful eyes, an old lady. Because she was old and had a big house, I felt she could easily take some risk. Besides, she, like everyone else in my family, loved Hein. I asked her if Hein could be hidden there. He had to have some place to stay, even if it was only for one night. But she was afraid, like everybody else. I was very upset with my grandmother because I thought, "So what if it happens to be dangerous! You've already had a full and good life — and you love Hein." We all loved him.

I remember that I was riding on a main avenue in The Hague, Laan van Meerdervoort, which goes from one end of the city to the other, tears streaming down my cheeks. Nobody wanted to take in my beloved Hein. People would remind me of their little children at home, and they would say, "We don't know what the Gestapo might do if they find him here." And they were all so busy, and they had to have other guests. They were all fake excuses, lame excuses!

That night, right there on the street in The Hague, I made a vow that if ever people were being persecuted and needed a place to hide or something to eat, I vowed I would help them. What had happened that night to me was horrible. I was so upset with all those so-called Christians.

This is exactly what I thought: "What are *words*, really? I mean, if you say that you have faith, then you have to apply it to the life you're living." I was angry that night, very angry. I was searching for a place for Hein for only *one* night, after all, not for a year — one night, to get him off the street. When we couldn't find a place, we went to the home of Platteel, who himself had two little children and had held many Resistance meetings in his home.

Hein was supposed to stay only one night at Platteel's because of the danger to those children. But he stayed there two weeks before I could find him another place. He couldn't go to his office anymore, of course, because the Gestapo had been staking that out too. At times, already that early in the war, Hein and I didn't see each other frequently.

▲   ▲

December 25, 1940

Christmas in occupied Holland. Hein on the run with the Gestapo after him.

Help me, O my God, for I cannot take any more. I have the feeling that the cross I have to bear is ripping my shoulders, and I cannot take it any longer. I *know* that I don't have to carry this alone and I *know* that everything is for our good and to bring us closer to you. But, O God, whatever happens to us, whatever is taken away from us — liberty, peace — you will stay with us until eternity.

Guide us according to your counsel and if possible bring us again together here on earth. Be close to him, O Lord, and let him experience your nearness all the time, O Father. Shine your face over him and give him peace.

from the diary of Diet Eman

▼   ▼

For a time only one man knew where Hein was hiding: it was in the home of a mother and a daughter, and the daughter was engaged to an Italian man. The mother and daughter were very nervous about Hein's staying there, so he decided that he couldn't stay very long or he would be in danger. The Italian man who was dating the daughter was very friendly and told Hein that he had another place for him, a better place. But at the same time, Mattijsen, the Jew from Scheveningen we'd been working with, found a place for Hein with the Versteegs, a charismatic Christian family. Then Mattijsen suddenly discovered that the Italian man was in the SD (*Sicherheits Dienst* —"security service"). The SD was not as sinister as the SS, but it was also a kind of secret police.

When Hein heard this, he immediately knew that he was in danger. Although he had not yet been picked up, the SD knew that he had been with the mother and daughter and was now staying with the Versteegs. The Italian man with the friendly face had said, "Oh, I'll get another place for you." And when Mattijsen found out all of this, he knew that Hein was in serious danger. In his haste he sent a very disreputable person, a guy who looked like a thug or a crook from the underworld, to the home where Hein was, the home of those charismatic Christians. Mattijsen told this character to get Hein out of that home no matter what, to bring him instead to his own house. "Just get him out!" he told the tough-looking messenger. "He is in grave danger."

So this man rang the doorbell at the home of this Pentecostal family. The mother, a wonderful Christian woman, took one look at this unsavory character at her door, and said, "I'm not giving Hein up to you. I don't trust you. Besides, he was just brought here."

But the man had been commanded by Mattijsen to insist that Hein go with him, and not to take no for an answer.

"He has to go with me," he said. He wouldn't let her shut the door in his face.

Mrs. Versteeg was frantic. She turned away for a moment and called every one of her children to the door.

"Children," she said, "come here and fall on your knees. And Hein, you too — get down on your knees." And then she prayed, "Dear Lord, if this man is evil, punish him severely. We don't want anything bad to happen to Hein, and we just don't know. If he is evil, punish him." That's how she prayed. She was really something.

Then Hein accompanied the tough-looking guy, once she had laid the long condemnation on him. The man must have been surprised by all this, because he was a communist and thus probably an atheist. In any event, Hein left that home, and he was barely out the door when the Italian man showed up there. Hein just scraped by that time, just missed being caught. Mattijsen and his scruffy messenger had saved his life.

Later, we hid a Jewish man in the Versteeg home. That woman was always on her toes, any time anyone stayed there with her — always vigilant. One day a traitor neighbor saw a strange face in her window and told the Gestapo, who immediately came to arrest him. But her house had rooms that had two doors, front and back entrances. So while the Gestapo were at the front door, she pushed him through the sliding doors; and when they went to the other side of those doors, she pushed this Jewish man out into the street. He ran away as fast as he could because he understood what was going on. We didn't know where he had gone, so we searched all over. In the end, he knew my parents' address and came to their house.

Meanwhile, Mrs. Versteeg was arrested for helping a Jew escape, and the whole affair went to court. The Versteegs were a very devout family, and like Corrie ten Boom, they absolutely refused to lie. But their refusing to lie, of course, was not only very dangerous for all of us — Hein had brought this Jew there himself—but this poor, hard-working family could easily go to jail for hiding the Jewish man.

"If the judge asks us, 'Did you know he was a Jew?'" Mrs. Versteeg told Hein, "we have to say yes, but we will not say that you brought him."

Hein told her that we didn't want her poor family to go to jail simply for helping us. So he said, "If they ask you who brought him, and you will not lie or say that you don't know, then I'll come forward and I'll go to jail for you."

That trial was very scary for all of us because none of us knew what would happen. My father's best friend was a Frisian who was high in The Hague police, in the *recherche*, the detective squad. We had a talk with this uncle, and we said, "Is there any way that you can influence somebody?" Because if the Versteegs refused to lie on account of their faith, and if they mentioned that they had *known* the man at their house was a Jew and that they *knew* Hein, then everything we did would be in jeopardy. We didn't want Hein simply to give himself up either. We were in a terrible position; all the possibilities were bad. Everything would depend on just exactly how the questions were phrased and how the family members felt compelled to answer.

My uncle may have known the judge before this case, and my father was in the back of the courtroom that day. I was not there, but I was praying. The judge — probably one of the good Dutch judges was presiding that day — never asked the questions that would have forced those people to tell the truth. It was simply providential. They didn't have to lie because they weren't put into a position that made it necessary, and they were merely sent home with a warning: "Don't do this anymore" — a little slap on the wrist.

Some of the police, like my uncle, were having a horrible time, working under real pressure, because the Germans were more or less supervising everything. But if all the good people had left government positions, life would have been much worse for all of us. A fair number of noncollaborators stayed, though it sometimes looked to many of us as if they were collaborating. Theirs was a terrible life, a balancing act, and not just between life and death, although that was part of it. Theirs was a delicate balance between what they had to do for the Germans and what they couldn't do to their own people. They performed this balancing act to help the cause of those who were loyal to the Queen, even though many who didn't understand what they were doing despised them for what appeared to be their collaboration.

The Call to England

After a few weeks, Hein left The Hague and went to stay with some of his family in Friesland, because nobody wanted to take him in The Hague. In Friesland the Gestapo did not yet know the whole story of his brother Henk in the Hilversum cafe. They hadn't yet pursued all the angles, nor had they interrogated all the relatives. So Hein was safer there living with his maiden aunt and his *pake,* his grandfather, in Tijnje, a very small place north of Heereveen. He had been there many times before, of course, so the neighbors did not think it at all strange to see him there again. But he did have to take a false name.

▲   ▲

January 1941

I long so much for you to put your big strong arms around me, and hold me. When I am in church I feel so envious of all the couples who can be together, but even so I would not want to change places with them, because the end for us will be good, everything will be good.

from the diary of Diet Eman

▼   ▼

Not long into his stay in Friesland, Hein met a man named Louis Chaillet. Even then, early in the war, it was difficult to trust anyone, as his brother Henk's experience had shown, but he trusted Chaillet very quickly. Chaillet got him a job in Amsterdam at the National Luchtvaart Laboratory, even though he knew Hein had false papers. One day Hein said to me: "Diet,

I have met someone who is either really terrific or else a very, very dangerous person. If anything happens to me, I want you to see that this man, Louis Chaillet, is eliminated."

Chaillet was the director of a laboratory where many experiments were done. He had previously held some high position at Shell in The Hague, and Shell had lent him out to be in charge of the Amsterdam lab. Through him Hein got a position there in Amsterdam and even received new false papers and a new name, Jan Sybrandy. In Amsterdam there was a great stockpile of gasoline for research experiments, and the Underground badly needed gasoline for many illegal operations. Hein became very good friends at the laboratory with a young Frisian named Gosse vanden Berg. Gosse's girlfriend, Corrie, was also working for someone deep in the Underground, and together those two stole a lot of gasoline for the Resistance. Nobody ever asked any questions at the research facility; and no personnel ever questioned them, even though Hein had a fake résumé. In addition, any time he needed to go somewhere and do some Underground work, he could do it. The people who worked in that lab had a great deal of freedom through Louis Chaillet; we found out later that he was very high up in the Resistance.

Living in Amsterdam and working at the Luchtvaart Laboratory, Hein had a chance to see me every few weeks or so. Sometimes I rode to Amsterdam on the bike, and sometimes he came to The Hague to see me, but never at our house. My home address was not Hein's address; the Gestapo had simply found out from someone in his former boarding house in The Hague that he was often over at our house (the owners were elderly people and probably afraid). But at that point the Gestapo wasn't as strong or well organized as they would become; they hadn't yet begun the raids on the Jews, and they couldn't yet stake out suspect addresses. There were so many people who did things

— listened to radios and so on — that the Gestapo couldn't possibly have kept track of every little infraction.

I was riding my bike to Amsterdam more and more often at that time. There was a man in my office who had a girlfriend in Amsterdam, and so on Saturdays we often biked there from the bank together. When I visited Hein, I could stay in his new boarding house, where an elderly couple had many extra rooms. They took in young working men and always cooked for them. On weekends many of those working men would go home, and there was an agreement among the men that if I wanted to stay there, I would get the room of someone who had left for the weekend. I paid the old couple for it because, after all, the boarding house was their bread and butter.

By that time, Hein's brother Henk was out of prison. All the work of his Uncle Kees, the famous pastor, had apparently paid off, and at a certain point the authorities simply let him go. His name was still Henk Sietsma, of course, because he had been in prison and had no need to disguise his name. But Hein was no longer Hein, and he wasn't Sietsma. The problem was that Hein and Henk looked very much alike. Henk was already living at that boarding house, as a regular boarder, when Hein came in under his false name, Henk de Jong. The two of them told the family who ran the boarding house the whole truth about the situation, but no one else knew it. The men who boarded there were constantly commenting: "Gosh, you guys look so much alike, it's amazing." Hein would say that the two of them were amazed themselves.

One weekend when I was there, it was really hilarious: Hein and Henk's father had come to Amsterdam for a weekend to visit his brother, the preacher, as well as his sons. And Father Sietsma stayed over at the boarding house too. There we all sat at this big table for dinner: Henk Sietsma, with Father Sietsma,

Henk de Jong, and Henk de Jong's girlfriend. I had stayed in the Sietsma house many times, of course, but that day I was officially introduced to Henk and Father Sietsma: "This is Diet Eman, and she is the girlfriend of Henk de Jong." We were all introduced very formally, and we had to act as if we had never met each other before.

The idea of going to England was very important to us until the Germans started taking Jews. Up until that time, our Resistance work had consisted of little more than printing and spreading the news around and getting messages to senders, none of which meant a lot of time or real danger. Hein was already fully involved, because he was already living under a false name and with false papers, and he was constantly being looked for. And he still wanted badly to go to England.

One day he met a man in the Resistance who was called "the general," an important man, or so it seemed to Hein, with snow white hair. Hein always called him, in Fries, *"grieskop,"* the gray head. The *grieskop*, he was told, had been in the French Underground but was now working in the Netherlands and was in charge of many Underground operations. In early 1941, he said he would see that Gosse and Hein got to England safely.

Hein's name had been on several lists and yet each time the opportunity fell through. Then, all of a sudden, Mattijsen, who was also trying to get Hein to England, simply vanished. No one ever found out what happened to him. That happened very often during the war: people would simply disappear. And whenever someone would suddenly be gone, we always knew it was very dangerous: was the person who had disappeared arrested? And if he was, would he, under torture, give out all kinds of information?

Hein had a feeling then that his time to go to England was coming close. "Diet," he said one night, "before I go to England,

I'd like to be engaged. I'd like it if I would have your ring, and you would have mine. Why don't you come to Amsterdam next weekend? We can pick out our rings, and have them engraved."

So I biked to Amsterdam, along with my friend from the bank, on Saturday, March 29, 1941. Hein and I went to a jewelry shop, picked out our rings, and told the jeweler that we wanted a Latin phrase, *Omnia vincit amor* (love conquers all), engraved on them. We faced so many obstacles, but we believed, truly, that love would conquer everything. We also had our names engraved on the rings, after the Latin phrase. So in Hein's ring it said "Diet," and in my ring it said "Hein"; it's an old tradition in the Netherlands.

We paid for our order, and the jeweler said we could pick up the rings in a just a few days because it would take some time to do the engraving. When we got back to Hein's boarding house, the hostess told him that a big manila envelope had been delivered for him. He opened that envelope and looked at me. "These are my instructions," he said. "I have to leave for England right away."

I was glad that I happened to be with him just at that moment, but I said, "What about the rings?"

"Do you remember where the shop is?" he asked.

I didn't know Amsterdam very well, but Hein explained how to get there. He had a few things to get together for his trip, he told me.

"Go back to the shop," he said, "pick up the rings with this receipt, and never mind the engraving. Then hop on the tram — Line Two. Get on the back *balkon* of the last car."

Each tram had two *balkons*, the open space where you get on and off and where the conductor stands. If the tram was crowded, you could stand there on the *balkon*, although most people wanted to go inside.

"In two stops the tram will pass here and I'll hop on," Hein said. "We'll be able to say goodbye to each other."

So I galloped to the jewelry shop. The proprietor was very surprised, but I said, "It doesn't matter about the engraving — I have to have the rings right away."

He gave them to me, and I hopped on the *balkon* of the last wagon of the tram, Line Two, in Amsterdam. Two stops further, just as he said, Hein hopped on. And on that tram we put on our rings. It was the moment of our engagement, just a few minutes on the *balkon* of that tram in Amsterdam, as it clattered noisily through the city.

He had to go to the big station in Amsterdam, the Centraal Station. I wasn't allowed to go any further with him, he told me, because I wasn't supposed to know anything about how he was going to get to England. Before he disappeared, he said, "Now you go and have that ring engraved in The Hague, and I'll have mine engraved in London."

Then we kissed, he disappeared into the station, and I thought that would be the last time I would see him for quite a long time. There I stood in the station, tears streaming down my cheeks again, just as they had that night in The Hague when I couldn't find him a place to stay. He was going to England, where it would be safe; but I knew that just getting there could be very dangerous, that he could easily be killed. So there I stood, staring at the space where he'd just disappeared from my side.

I took the tram back to the boarding house and picked up my little suitcase and pedaled back to The Hague on my bike. That was the weekend I was supposed to be with him, the weekend we were engaged. And I was very afraid of what might happen to him.

▲ ▲

March 30, 1941

Father, I have to write down your miracles and your great love. While we so often forget you and gripe, through all our troubles you have listened to our prayers, and answered in a way we never dreamed of.

I had been praying, "If you are really God, bring Hein to safety and when you hear my prayer I will glorify you and love you." That was wrong, for really, out of myself I cannot even love you, and I should not have prayed this way, like I reward you with my love, if you do what I want. And instead of punishing me, you made me speechless by your benefits. That I could be there when it happened. And that I still got Hein's ring! If I did not know that you do this out of grace, it would nearly scare me to receive such blessings.

Lord, we now put our lives in your hands for the future. We know that you brought us together and now you part us and you will bring us together again in your time and in your place. Help us now and live in us that we both do whatever you expect from us, and protect us from sin.

Die ons bewaart waar wij ook gaan,
Al schijnt geen zon, al licht geen maan.

(He will protect us, wherever we go,
Even when the sun doesn't shine,
Nor the moon give light.)

from the diary of Diet Eman

▼ ▼

During all those months the Germans were still searching for Hein in The Hague, even in the bank where I worked. You never knew who were spies. There were pro-Germans in a bank that size, just as there were anywhere else. I didn't want people talking about Hein or asking about him anymore. Already a few weeks before he'd left for England, I knew it was too dangerous for him to keep returning to The Hague, to risk being seen when I couldn't trust many of the people I worked with. So to make it safe, I had spread the rumor to all my friends that Hein was already in England. Many people had gone there, and once you were gone, the pursuers stopped looking for you.

Now, suddenly, I had a ring, something I'd never had before. It was a simple ring with no diamonds, because in the Netherlands an engagement ring was considered symbolic: it was supposed to be round and smooth — no sharp edges — a symbol of what marriage should be. Of course, I wanted badly to wear my ring, so I did. Right away people in the bank talked about it. "What is this we hear?" they said. "You're now engaged, but your fiancé is in England?"

"Ja, I was so lucky," I said. I made up a story. "You know, the Red Cross sometimes gets letters through, and I got a letter and look what I found inside: I got my ring." I don't know whether anyone believed me.

When I left Hein there at the station, I thought that it would be the last time I would see him until Hitler was gone. But it wasn't more than two or three days after that departure that I got a letter from him saying that I should come to Amsterdam because he had so much to tell me about what had happened.

Gosse vanden Berg, Hein's friend from the Luchtvaart Laboratory, it turned out, had also received the note telling him

74

how it was his turn to go to England. The instructions said they had to go by train from Amsterdam to IJmuiden on the coast. A large sea channel, dug from Amsterdam to the North Sea coast for ships, named the *"IJ,"* comes out at IJmuiden. There were many *hoogovens,* blasting furnaces, in the area, foundries where arms were being manufactured.

By that time already, all the houses on the coast had been evacuated. The Germans had simply taken them. Later, when the Allies thought that war materials were being built there, they dropped their bombs in that area, and they weren't always on target. Many homes in that area were heavily damaged. So Hein and Gosse and some others were directed to a bombed-out house in the *Sperrgebiet,* the forbidden zone, where they were supposed to meet others at dark and hide in the basement. They had to be sure they were not followed.

They got there just at dark and found about thirty people waiting, as they were, to go to England. The place was close to the beach and the dunes, and the Germans had already been building fortresses everywhere. They were still pouring concrete; some of the fortifications were finished and some were not.

Once the Dutchmen were in this house, their instructions told them that there would be a speedboat along the shore, close by. They had been told that they would have to walk over the dunes to the beach, under cover of darkness, to a place where they would find a solitary guard. That guard, the instructions said, would have to be killed without making any noise, for close by was a guard house with more German navy men. Then they could take the speedboat to England.

But no one received a specific task. Hein and Gosse had thought they would be passengers on a boat that was going to escape — that's all, just passengers. The men all took off their shoes and crawled over the dunes, past the fortifications, some of which still had wet concrete that had been poured that day into deep holes. Finally, when they got to the shore, they found not one speedboat but two. And what was worse, they found not just one guard, but a double guard that marched toward each other, up and back. It was a whole different situation from what they had been told they would encounter.

"There is a guard house near," the instructions said, "where there are many more Germans, probably playing cards. You have to kill that guard in a way that prevents him from letting out a scream. When he's dead, hop in the boat and go."

There was a shed close by, so all of those men trying to escape went into it to discuss what to do next. Meanwhile, one of the two German guards wanted to smoke a cigarette, but the stormy night made it much too windy on the shoreline to light it. So he walked to the shed where the men were huddled so that he could get protection from the wind. Hein told me that he was petrified. Thirty men stood pressed against the wall in the dark — two rows of them — flat along each wall of this shed with an open front.

The German came in, lit his cigarette, and in the flash of his match saw one of the men. The man he spotted had terrific presence of mind: he walked out and said in German, "I am homeless, and I didn't know what to do —"

So he guided the German away from the other twenty-nine guys. When he walked away with the guard, the others were so petrified that they slunk around the corner of the shed and started running back. Everybody had his shoes off, and it was pitch dark. Off they went, first two, then the next two, the next two, and the next two, and so on. All the men ran, their footsteps muffled by the sand. They didn't have flashlights, and Gosse fell into a deep concrete pit. He didn't break any bones, but he was badly bruised and had open sores.

He limped along and finally, with the others, returned to the house where they had first assembled. The whole group started discussing what had happened, and what they discovered was that it was God's blessing the whole escape hadn't worked! When they began asking each other which of them was to navigate the boat, it turned out that nobody had any navigation knowledge or skills! Each one thought that the others knew what they were doing. Nor did anyone have the orders on who was to kill the guards. That was a good thing, because our group — including Hein — didn't really believe in killing at that time.

The whole arrangement was very poorly planned. It was only God's protecting hand that kept them all from death.

▲ ▲

March 31, 1941

Please forgive me, Almighty — what I said to you in my bitter disappointment. The heaviest to bear is not even the fear about his safety, but the worst is that my trust in God is now shaky. This is really ridiculous! — this last sentence. That I dare to make an accusation to him whose eyes do not see anything else than my unfaithfulness as opposed to his faithfulness, and that I dare to say this to him, who has blessed us so much.

Please forgive me my thoughts for the sake of the Lamb. My attitude is totally wrong. It is as if I give you an ultimatum to do this or that miracle and then (how ridiculous) I tell you I will be so "good" as to thank you! And that while I can hardly be thankful myself. What an idiot!

This morning, all the while I thought that our wish had been fulfilled, I was humming a song which now I will continue to sing. It was Psalm 46.

De Heer, de God der Legerscharen
is met ons, hoed ons in gevaren.
Wij werden steeds Zijn hulp gewaar
In zielsbenauwdheid, in gevaar,
Dies zal geen vrees ons doen bezwijken,
Schoon d'aard' uit haren stand mocht wijken
Schoon t'hoogst gebergte uit zijnen stee
Verzet wierd in het hart der zee.

Our fate is in your hands
We trust in you
For yours is the Power and the Glory.

from the diary of Diet Eman

▼   ▼

"We were scared to death," Hein said to me. "Even if we had killed the two guards, not one of us knew how to operate that speedboat. If we had taken only one boat, as we were instructed, and if the soldiers in the guard house had heard something, which would have been quite likely, we could easily have been overtaken, and the whole bunch of us killed."

With their lack of navigational skills, they would never have made it to England. They would very likely not have come close. Hein concluded that everything was very badly organized, and the whole experience really shook him up. He learned that these kinds of operations had to be organized perfectly — to the letter. At least the misadventure was beneficial in that way: after that, our group planned anything we did by trying to think of every last thing that could go wrong.

But there's a bit more to the story. Once they had escaped the Germans, those men were still in a forbidden zone, without shoes, and it was now morning. There was nothing they could do but try to get back to safety, so Hein and Gosse walked barefoot to Haarlem. By morning they were terribly cold, just freezing, when they stumbled into a little restaurant to have coffee. What happened next was another act of God. The man who ran that restaurant saw that they were in a strange and difficult position. It was early Sunday morning and very quiet in the streets. So he wandered over to them and began to talk.

"I see you're having some problems," he said, and he glanced at their bare feet. "Why don't you come into the back here with me —"

What choice did they have?

They walked into the back of the restaurant, and the man left them there for a while. When he returned, he had two pairs of shoes. On top of that, they didn't have to pay for the coffee. The owner of that restaurant — who, incidentally, turned out to be a relative of Gosse's future wife — simply understood that the activity those two guys were up to was the kind of activity he wanted to help.

Soon after that, the Jewish persecutions began in earnest, and we saw clearly what our task there in the Netherlands was to be. Later we were to hear from the people who had gone to England about their boring hours of standing guard and doing exercises — with nothing else to do. Going to England was much different from what Hein or anyone else had expected. Everyone thought the whole Occupation, even the war itself, would last only about a year, no more. We thought that our new army would be trained in England and that they would come back and liberate us. We never thought that all of this would go on for so long, with so much suffering. If we had known that it would take five years, we might have given up hope.

▲ ▲

April 2, 1941

Lord, I thank you that in your great wisdom you have *not* granted my prayer, or maybe I should say my *dwingen*. Now that I know what you protected them from, my soul is still in your presence, you who have spared his life!

We give our lives into your hands, Lord.

We *know* that you guide all things. Forgive us that for a moment we were in rebellion to what you in your great love did for us.

Help me to never forget that your way with us is Love!

How brave you are, Hein. I am so proud of you, for if I think of others, I don't believe that many would have done what you did. Still, I thank him that that horrible thing [the murder of the guard] was not necessary. And I am grateful that he sent his angels to protect you as he has done all this time.

Why is he blessing us so much above so many others? And that while often we are griping because things don't go as we in our stupidity and shortsightedness want it.

Hein, I am so proud to have your ring on my finger, but what a strange engagement we had!

Well, we happen to be a strange couple! And I can be

curious about how our wedding will be because I have the feeling that that won't be quite normal either!

Now, darling, I am going to sleep and thinking of you and of Him, who again spared you from death, and who is with us.

from the diary of Diet Eman

▼   ▼

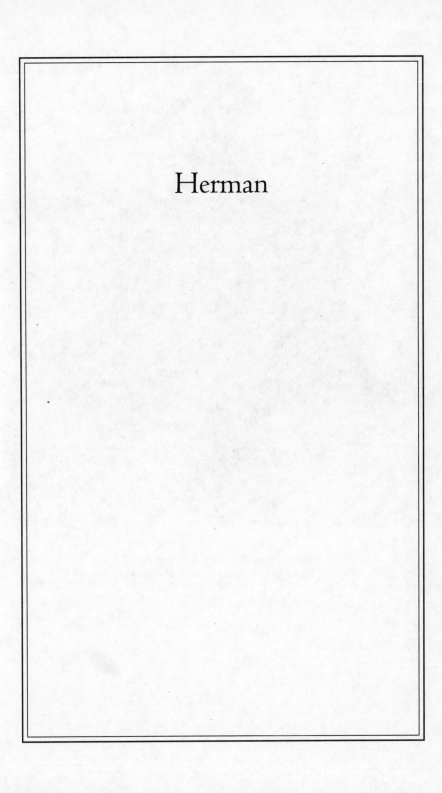

Herman

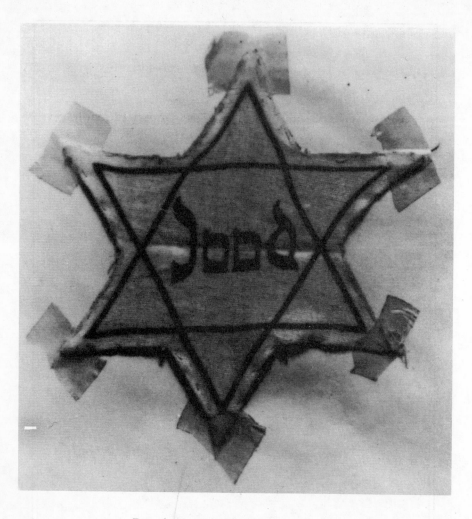

From the National Archives, Washington, DC,
courtesy of the United States Holocaust Memorial Museum

▲   ▲

July 1941

Last night we walked past the synagogue. Horrible: on the doors was written with large letters "Jude Süss." On the pillars a swastika and a large *V* and horribly drawn Jewish faces. In the street on the boarded-up shop windows, "Jew," "Pest Jude."

How long still, O Lord?

September 16, 1941

Yesterday the paper had a "short" summary of the places where Jews are not allowed! I can better mention where they are still allowed: "in their homes and in the streets!" God, punish those who are persecuting the people you chose and to whom Jesus also belonged.

from the diary of Diet Eman

▼   ▼

There came a day when my Jewish friend Herman, who worked with me in the bank in The Hague, began to understand that for him, as a Jew, life could not go on in the same way anymore. He thus became the first Jewish person that we helped during the Occupation.

First the Jews weren't allowed on the trams anymore, or on the buses, in parks, or in shops. Rules like that were printed in the newspapers, and they were displayed on the trams and in shop windows. It was an enforced limitation of freedom for Jews in all kinds of ways. Next, Jews weren't allowed to visit most places in the city anymore; they had to stick to their own Jewish areas and shops. And though Herman and his family did not live in the Jewish area of the city, they, like all Jews, were no longer allowed to visit non-Jewish people. It was terrible.

▲   ▲

May 6, 1942

It is again some time since I wrote, and much has happened. The Jews have to wear a yellow star with the word "Jew" in the center. Seventy-two Dutch men have been executed. From last Saturday till Tuesday, six-thousand people have been arrested. Ex-military, pastors, all people of the first and second chamber [the Dutch parliament], etc., etc.

The worst is, I remain so stone cold. Does this war make you an "alive-dead person"? Is it not possible to remain yourself in this chaos? How long still??

Will we ever, after all this, return to be "sensitive human beings"? All the nasty names we call the Germans, which we now think normal, will that all pass again?

And later, after all this, will I have to reproach myself that instead of getting closer to you, I have turned away from you as far as possible so that my soul is dead? It seems that the only thing that keeps me close to you is suffering. If that is so, I nearly would pray for sorrow, for most important is that I stay close to you.

from the diary of Diet Eman

▼   ▼

So Herman could no longer come over and play his violin with us as he so often did before all the regulations came out. My brother Albert played beautiful cello, and I could just make do on the piano; so when Herman came over, we often played trios. It was a wonderful experience for me, because both Herman and Albert were very good musicians. Even after the new rules, Herman would sometimes sneak over anyway.

The next law the Germans made was that non-Jews could have nothing at all to do with Jews. Even after that, my mother and father wouldn't have minded Herman's coming over, but at that point he did not want to endanger them. Actually, the Germans might have punished my family a little bit for breaking the rules; but Herman would have gotten into major trouble. So he stopped coming over to our house. My parents loved him, but suddenly he couldn't come anymore.

- Much of what had preceded the Jewish persecution had seemed an annoyance to most of us — no display of the royal colors, prohibitions against listening to the BBC — and for the most part we simply put up with it for a while. No one liked the restrictive laws, but in many people's eyes these relatively trifling laws were something we could tolerate. But when signs and notices suddenly appeared saying that the Jews had to leave their homes and could not live near us because, as the signs said, they were infectious (the Germans called them lice and rats and all kinds of names), when they were told they had to leave their homes in the Netherlands completely, then we stopped putting up with the injustice.

The Germans explained to us that the Jews were to be transported to East Germany from all the other European countries. There they would live only with each other, and that way they could harm only each other. When it started to go into effect, we knew we could simply not tolerate this horrible plan. We knew we had to do something.

According to Hitler, *we* were the great ones — the people with blond hair and blue eyes, the Aryan race. The Jewish scum, as the Germans put it, had to be quarantined, rounded up, and separated from the decent, blue-eyed people of what he thought was the super race. The Germans didn't come right out and say that at first, but we found out later that Hitler had given the order. We learned from both German Jews who had escaped Germany and from the propaganda we saw all over our country that this evil was the German way of thinking. And they were beginning to implement this kind of policy.

At first, the Jews would get notices at home that they had to report to such and such an address on a Tuesday night, say, after curfew. They were to report to schools, for instance, where the Germans gathered all of them and took them away in trucks. And they always did it after the curfew hours so that the rest of us wouldn't see what was going on. Or Jews were told they had to go to the railroad stations, and they would show up, very scared. Most people knew which of their neighbors were Jewish, even if the family itself did not practice the Jewish faith. I always knew, for example, that Herman was Jewish; there had been no reason for him to keep that from me. But the Germans had their way of knowing as well. They had their informants, like the NSBers (National Socialistische Beweging — the Dutch Nazis); and since they also ran all of the government offices, they had full control of all the records. The whole Netherlands is quite small, and every city and every village — even a tiny little village like Holk — kept town records in a town hall. A man and his wife and all their children would have cards somewhere in the town hall, which was full of important information.

If you were to move to another city, you had to go to the town hall and tell the officials you would be moving to a new address, and they would send along all the cards pertaining to your family to that new town. On that card was your birthplace, your spouse, your spouse's name, your job, and your religion, among other things. Most Jews, whether or not they practiced Judaism, were proud of who they were. So, where it would say *Gereformeerd* on my card and on my parents', their cards would say *Jewish*.

It wasn't just the Germans who went through those cards; they didn't have the manpower to sort through all of that bureaucracy. That's where the traitors came in. And those traitors often knew who was Jewish without having to go into the card system. If one had no conscience, that kind of finger pointing was something for which the Germans paid money, easy money. The people who did it were not only traitors; they were prof-iteers.

So at one point, my friend Herman's family got their notice to report. Like everyone else, Herman was instructed to take only one suitcase, small enough to carry. Can you imagine how difficult it would be to decide which of your precious things you would choose to bring along, and what you would choose to leave to the Germans? Maybe you'd pack some pictures or something, and of course a change of clothing. The Jews had to leave behind almost everything of sentimental value to them personally, not to mention goods of dollars-and-cents value. And they had no choice but to report; they couldn't just throw away the summons.

▲   ▲

July 21, 1942

A lot has happened again:
The Jews are walking with their yellow stars on, are

not allowed outside after 8 P.M., are not allowed to visit non-Jews, some streets are forbidden to them, etc., etc.

From Amsterdam many were sent to —— ??? Many are committing suicide!

O God, don't you see that they are touching the apple of your eye? Is it still not enough?

O let us, in the midst of all these things which drive us crazy, *still remember* that you are the ruler of everything and that the punishment you will give them for these things will be more just than all things we think of to punish them.

It is really ridiculous, if you think for one moment, that these people (if you still can call them "people") who are now harassing the Jews so much will themselves need a Jew to go to heaven. And it is unacceptable if you think that they are supposed to have been created in the image of God.

Please teach us Christians now to be true Christians and to put into practice what we confess, especially to these Jews. O Lord, make an end to all this, only you can do it. We know that you give strength according to our cross, but it is getting to be so very heavy, Lord.

from the diary of Diet Eman

▼   ▼

The people in my office at the bank knew where I stood concerning all of this: that I was very loyal to the royal family. But I still had to mind what I said openly. I also knew the sympathies of those with whom I worked most closely, at least some of them. But I kept my mouth shut when others were anywhere close. I spit out my venom only with people I could trust.

Herman wasn't working at the bank anymore at that time because he was not allowed to take the tram, the bus, or anything, and he was not allowed to enter that area of the city. So he asked me to come to meet him when he got his summons, because Jews were not allowed to visit non-Jews.

"If you were me, would you go?" Herman asked.

"I don't think so," I told him, "but I will see Hein tonight, and I'll ask him how he feels about it."

We had heard that Jews were going to the camp at Westerbork on the trains. And we'd heard that many trains full of Jews were also leaving Westerbork. "Where are they going?" we thought. The Germans kept everything very secret. The German newspapers said that the Jews were to blame for all the evil in the world, especially because they had all the money, owned the banks, and this and that. The Germans said they had to seize Jews' money because everything they had was either stolen or taken on the black market.

Herman's parents were middle class: his father was a decent man with a good government job. His parents really believed that this whole thing would only last a year. They figured the Germans would place them somewhere in Eastern Europe for a little while, a place where they might have to live a little more simply than they were accustomed to living at home. And then, when it was over, they could come back. That's what many people thought, Jews and non-Jews. *Nobody* thought they would be exterminated in gas chambers. Therefore, many of them went as meekly as sheep to their deaths.

German Jews who had lived from 1933 to 1937 or 1938 in Germany had seen how the Nazi system developed, had experienced *Kristallnacht,* and had fled to the Netherlands in the late 1930s.

Many of those people had committed suicide during the German invasion of the Netherlands. The night Hitler invaded Holland — and in the five days of war after the invasion — there was no place left for them to run: Belgium was overrun, and Spain was pro-Nazi. There was no place for them to go but the North Sea.

My father could not believe how evil people could be. I'm sure that at that time my parents' age group did not believe it could ever be as bad as it turned out to be. My father, like Herman's father and mother, thought it unnecessary to try anything resistant. But the younger people felt differently, most of them. Herman was only a year older than I, and we thought of the possibility that what was really happening was far worse than anyone had imagined. We thought about those suicides, and we considered Hitler capable of anything.

So that evening when I saw Hein, I asked him, "What do you think, should Herman go?"

"You remember what the German Jews did," he said. "They committed suicide."

So I said to Hein, "You say he shouldn't report, but what *can* he do? If he shouldn't go there, what else is there?"

And *that* moment was the real beginning of our Resistance work. Hein immediately said he knew plenty of Christian farmers around Holk — in the area of the Netherlands called The Veluwe.

"Any of those farmers I know around Nijkerk," he said, "any of them we ask will take Herman. He can work there on the farm. So what's the big problem?"

Maybe that was a bit idealistic, but we were young people. We both thought Herman would be safe in The Veluwe, and Hein was sure the farmers would take him in. In a year he could come back home to The Hague, take his job at the bank, and everything would be fine. So when I saw Herman again, I told him what Hein had said. "Hein thinks there's no problem," I said. "His father is a school principal over there, and Hein says any farmer he asks will take you for the duration of the war."

"That sounds good," Herman told me. "I'll think about it." He had a girlfriend, Ada, and they had some time to consider it before they were actually required to report.

When we talked again, he nodded his head and said, "Ja, I like that idea."

I don't remember where we talked. It was such a tense time because of all those stupid regulations. It certainly was not at his house: I did not want to cause any problems for his parents, and I would have put them in a difficult position had I come to their house. Then Herman asked if we could also find a place for Ada, his fiancée, and for Ada's mother, a widow who was also very scared. Hein said that he thought he could. So all of our work started with a request for just those three people.

Then Rosa, Herman's sister, wanted a place too. The whole business grew so fast that within two or three weeks we had over sixty people who wanted places out in the country, in The Veluwe. Sixty Jews in two weeks, and that was just the beginning. First it was just Herman and Rosa and Ada in August 1942. Hein went out to Holk on his own to try to find places, and he placed many Jews on the farms around that little town. But the list of Jewish people who wanted to hide kept growing.

Hein saw his close friend Ab van Meerveld regularly; in fact, whenever we went home to Hein's house, we always took our bikes out to see Ab, or Ab came to see us. Ab and his wife, Riek, had just been married, and the four of us would sit and discuss the war: what was happening in the cities, and what was happening in the country, and our hopes for liberty. Ab knew that we were hiding Jews, and he said, "I can find some addresses too."

And that's really how it started, how our group was formed: we simply got together and talked about what the Germans were doing to the Jews and the dangers that presented. Herman's uncle, Uncle Frits, who already worked with us and had been part of the group that met at the Platteels', added some names to our growing list. In fact, sometimes those meetings were held in Uncle Frits's home. He was a salesman and a very wonderful person — not a Christian but a humanist; his wife was Jewish, but they kept it quiet, so no one knew. Uncle Frits knew many more Jewish people, so when we started with his full nephew, Herman, he came to Hein with a list and said, "Can you help this one and that one? — and I have some more." And soon it was sixty people.

One of them was a man who became very important to our whole operation: Uncle Ben, a draftsman by profession, skilled in drawing and printing, who had wonderful talents and did mountains of work for us. At the very beginning of our work he would change IDs and ration cards for us — freehand. Certain numbers printed on those cards indicated certain things you could get — general numbers for general merchandise, and so on. But some parts of the sheets of ration cards were rarely used, and because he was so talented he could easily change those numbers so that all the separate cards would become useful — for instance, change all the threes to eights. Also, if we had stolen or pickpocketed ID cards, he could switch the wording and make it say something different. He was also very good at signatures and things like that.

During a *razzia* one morning, Uncle Ben and his wife had been literally pulled out of their beds and taken to the railway station to be deported. We were nervous wrecks about it, of course, because Uncle Ben was a friend and a valuable ally. It was very early in the morning: there they stood at the railroad

94

station, each with one little suitcase, in a long line of Jewish people. As others got onto the train, Ben said to his wife, "Let's stay at the very end — the very, very end."

The long line moved slowly toward the train. You could position yourself in the front or in the middle, but Uncle Ben and his wife were the very last ones. Along came six or seven Dutch fishermen. It must have been very early in the morning, perhaps five o'clock, and still quite dark. The Netherlands has many lakes and canals, and there was such a shortage of food then that those fishermen had bought a ticket to take the train to one of the cities that was close to a lake, perhaps Leiden or Utrecht or Gouda. They walked onto the platform, saw all those people in line, and never realized that this was a whole group of Jewish people waiting to be deported. They stood there behind posts, thinking they would have to wait in line, like everybody else, to catch that train.

Suddenly the Germans came up to them and said, "What are you doing here?"

"We are going fishing," they said.

"You don't belong here. Out! Out!" the Germans said.

Then Uncle Ben said, "We don't belong here either." And he and his wife simply walked off with the fisherman, as if they had no business there either.

The rest of their story is even more miraculous. Using the trains required tickets, of course; but at that time of the morning the railway stations themselves were working with a skeleton staff, and scarcely anyone was in the offices. You bought a ticket and handed in that ticket at your place of destination. That was how they counted passengers and administered the railway system.

Now the fishermen could show the tickets they had just purchased when they moved from one platform to another. All they had to do was go back and tell the official that they were simply at the wrong platform and show their tickets. But Uncle Ben had no ticket at all; the Germans did not give you one when they took you right out of bed and deported you.

I don't know whether Uncle Ben and his wife said a prayer, but the danger they faced was still great. When he came to the train official, he simply told the truth. Can you imagine that? He didn't even attempt to make something up. He said, "I have nothing." The man in the booth took one quick look at him and said, "Quick — go on."

That good man on the railway platform was someone who helped us more than he could have ever known. Who knows what went on in that man's mind just then? Uncle Ben and his wife simply walked away from deportation — and probably death. And just a short time later, we placed them out in the country with a wonderful family, Aalt and Alie Lozeman.

At first we thought that was all we had to do: simply help the Jews who wanted to be helped when they began to understand what might happen to them. But we immediately learned that if we were to move these Jewish people out to the country, we would have to get them false identification cards. It was simply too risky to put them on trains when they were carrying IDs, which were all marked with that big J and which the Germans required, to indicate the holder was Jewish.

The farmers would tell us that they'd be happy to have them and help them, but there were raids — *razzias* — which were very dangerous, and there were always neighbors around who didn't mean anything bad but were simply nosy. Sometimes people were betrayed by people who did not side with the Germans but were simply nosy.

The farmers who kept the Jews told us that they would

continue to shelter them, but they said, "Please, try to get these people IDs without a big fat J." That was a difficult problem for all of us who worked in the Resistance, especially in the beginning when everything was so new. But resistance begins at home, you might say.

Birthdays are very important events in the Netherlands. My father had a twin sister, and their birthday celebration would be held at our house one year and at my aunt's house the next. This year it was at our house and was just coming up when we knew we had to have safe, non-Jewish IDs. At least forty family members and friends came over for that big November birthday party.

All of those people were sitting in our front room, and the stove in the living room was pumping out heat, so those forty people all got hot. They hung up their jackets and coats in the hallway, and the ladies left their purses everywhere. What could we do? We needed to have those IDs — the whole operation needed them. So we looked at each other, laughed, and I said to Hein, "Shall we or shall we not?" We agreed we had to have them.

"Should we tell them now?" I asked him.

We discussed it, but we decided not to, because, we reasoned, if we asked them and they knew that they were giving their identification to Jews, some might find it very difficult to lie to the authorities when they went in to the city hall to get new papers the next day. Not everyone can lie well. "I lost my ID," they might say; then maybe they would stand there and blush or stutter.

We decided to simply grab the IDs, as many as we dared — about a dozen — and not tell my relatives. We decided that we would confess after the war. Of course, we had to be careful not to take IDs from people who lived near each other, or once they got home they would realize that something strange had happened at that party. We picked up some IDs that night, and helped a number of Jewish people, who suddenly and mysteriously became my uncles and aunts.

That helped a bit at the time, but later the whole operation became even more difficult because we had to get ration cards as well. So we had to start working with the *knokploegs,* the Resistance groups who robbed German offices. *Knok* means "sock it to them," and *ploeg* means "little group": this was the attack squad who executed the armed robberies. Every month they staked out an office and secured drawings of the layout of the whole building; they always had friends here and there who could supply them with that kind of information. A local government would have to receive enough ration cards for their whole population monthly, and these men would watch and wait for the new ration cards and new IDs to come in. The *knokploeg* would find out where the cards were being stored from the drawings supplied by someone on the inside. They always struck at little places where they knew someone who worked in that office, someone who could give them all the necessary information and draw the layout.

By 1943 the group we worked with needed over 800 cards every month. The men from the *knokploeg* did that work, and of course it was very dangerous. But they did it for good reason, not simply because it was high adventure. I went to a few of their planning meetings, and those men always got down on their knees first to ask God to protect and help them. They said: "Lord, this is necessary. We need those cards. Please protect us, and grant that there be no shooting — and that nobody gets hurt." After the prayer they executed an armed robbery. That sounds very strange this many years later: prayer and then armed robbery.

Once we had placed those first Jewish people, we knew we would need more places. Hein got on the train and went to see Ab van Meerveld again, to ask if he could find some more places. And Ab was able to find many more farms where Jewish people could be placed in the area of Barneveld, Terschuur, and Zwartebroek. Ab was a sales representative for a grain and seed business. Every spring farmers had to buy those materials for their farms, so he was always moving around Gelderland, very much on the go, a salesman who met and came to know many people. And he was, above all, a wonderful Christian man. Ab van Meerveld had a great influence on Hein.

Herman stayed out there around Holk for the whole war, as did Ada, his wife-to-be, and Rosa, his sister. They made it through the war. They were survivors.

There is one special story about Rosa. At one point we had to get her a new address, and our contact in Zwijndrecht was a man by the name of Adriaan Schouten. He and his wife lived in a giant house above a theater, and they had no children. They said, "Well sure, Rosa can come to us. We have this big house." So Rosa went there under the false name of Nettie.

Now the Germans were always looking for big houses they could confiscate, as well as phones. You couldn't get a new phone connection during those years. One day, without warning or asking, the Germans simply barged in and took over a large part of that big house, leaving only a very small part for Adriaan and his wife and the "maid Nettie," who was actually Rosa, the Jewish girl.

Adriaan did not have a phone at that time. He was very active in the Resistance, and we needed to contact him often, but he had no phone. So the Germans, who were establishing some kind of command post, installed a phone for their own use, and of course assigned it a number. Adriaan was very polite and kind to the Germans, but for all of that time he was being polite, he was up to his ears in the Resistance. Soon the Germans started using their phone, and sometimes Rosa would answer it for them. They had asked that the Schouten family answer the phone when they were absent. And Adriaan then asked if maybe he could use that German phone for his business once in a while; and they said it was okay with them. Not only did the Germans not know that the Underground was using that wonderful phone; they had no idea that it was often answered by a Jewish girl. In fact, they had that Jewish girl handle their calls and take many messages. So it was a wonderfully handy situation, and it went on for a long, long time.

Furthermore, it was a German phone, so it was never taken away, and it was never out of order.

▲　　　▲

December 3, 1942

I am just now reading what I wrote in my last notes of July 21, and *then* I was upset! And what is that compared to what happened after that!

Then the Jews had to wear a star. Now they are in Poland. "This is to protect them from the *barbaric treatment* the Dutch people give to the Jews," according to a German newspaper! And, "out of gratefulness the Jews gave all their homes and possessions to be used in the bombarded areas of Germany."

Has there ever, under God's heavens, been a bigger lie?? They drag women out of their houses, away from their children. Old people sent to Poland at the beginning of winter — without luggage!

Revenge!!! Revenge!!!

I *know* that I should not say this, but I feel it so much, and I *want* to feel it: "Damned barbarians!"

Jewish people are put out of their homes and into the street — without any shelter.

All of Scheveningen has to evacuate.

All the beautiful buildings are being razed! The coal [used for heating] has to be left behind, and when they raze the buildings this ends up under the rubble, while thousands are sitting without heat. All the government departments have to leave.

I think that Hitler is fulfilling his prophesy that if he goes under, he will drag all of Europe along with him. Now, if it is for this purpose, we will leave our homes with joy, you *vile ploert!*

And apart from this, maybe it is good for the Hollanders, for oh, they say, it is so sad, but few of them realize *what* it is to be sent to Poland.

"Be hospitable" is Christ's order, but this is rarely being put into practice, and what do nice words and prayer mean for Christianity? — *Deeds!!!*

And *now* it is time for that. But no, it is the same old story — "first let me bury my father." They find many excuses. And even if the Jews can go into hiding, it is still terrible for them, even if they have this advantage. They cannot take anything along, and when they close the door behind them, they have to start a whole new life. Even if they come through, it will be difficult to start over with nothing.

from the diary of Diet Eman

▼   ▼

Father Abraham and
Little Peter

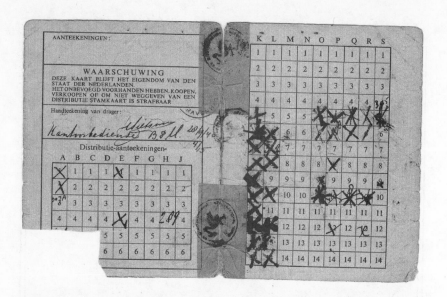

Ration book and ration card. The Jews in hiding depended on members of the Resistance to acquire stolen ration cards for the families who hosted them.

In grade school I loved those stories about the heroic Dutch resistance people during the Eighty Years' War with Spain. When I played with my brother and his friends, we often pretended there was war and we were spies. It was really hide-and-seek, of course, but I played that game so intensely at times that I wouldn't breathe because I thought the enemy could hear me. To me it was real war and my life was at stake, and I believe that all those clandestine spy games we played as children helped when the Occupation came.

But once we got fully involved in Underground activities, we often made mistakes when hiding Jews — especially in the early going. What did we know about it? Who did we ever have as teachers? We were really only a little older than the kids who had played at spying in our neighborhood in The Hague.

One of the first problems was the mail. Those farms where we hid the first Jews all had big families in those days, several daughters and sons, maybe the grandparents too — a full house. Everyone stayed at home back then: the oldest son, who probably inherited the father's farm; other sons who had become farmers; and even some daughters and in-laws who received only a piece of the land or had a place nearby. People stayed close to where they were born, especially out in the country where Hein was from. And if everyone in a family is close by, no one sends or receives any letters. Your brothers and sisters and aunts and uncles are right there with you. Plus, there was no junk mail in those days. It was a much different world.

But when Jewish people started living in those homes, suddenly mail started coming for them — letters from their relatives letting them know where they were. The rural mailmen would become very curious, of course, because they may have delivered mail to a single address for years, and that place only ever received the bank statement and another letter or two. Suddenly, there were handfuls of letters coming in addressed to names those mailmen didn't begin to recognize.

Such things make news in small towns. It was entirely possible for a mailman who meant no harm to wonder aloud how it was that people who never received any mail were suddenly receiving letters regularly. Someone must be on a long visit or living there, is what the mailman must have thought. Many people were arrested during the war because of the curiosity of neighbors, especially out in the country. Curious people often did not mean any harm, but someone would overhear that someone else had company at their home, then that someone would drop a word to someone else, and quickly the presence of a stranger in a home was no longer a secret.

Perhaps the mailman would say to the farmer, "You're certainly getting lots of extra mail," and the farmer would come to us immediately because he would be afraid.

"Hey," he'd say, "get these people out of my house! I'm scared stiff someone is going to find out."

So we had to make strict rules and rush them throughout the whole group. It was my responsibility to tell all the Jewish people we had hidden out in the country: "We have to do everything we can to avoid getting these people in trouble. You're endangering them by getting mail, because they never got any before, and now they're getting all kinds of it."

I became the new Underground mailman, or Hein would be the mailman, or whoever was working in our group would run those Jewish missives around. We told all the people we had placed in the country that we would carry their mail to them —and of course wouldn't read it. But we insisted that they could send nothing more via the public mail. Even after that, one time we discovered a couple who sent each other parcels around Passover — matzoh balls, of all things. How they ever got hold of matzoh, I'll never know. But the man on whose farm that package of matzoh balls arrived was so angry that we had to take those Jewish people out of his home immediately and find another place for them.

Incidents like that seem humorous today, but they were very touchy at the time. And they were extremely dangerous. Hein and I were scarcely over twenty, trying to make this effort work, and here we were scolding people who, for religious reasons, needed to have their matzoh. They apparently did not realize that they were risking the lives of that farmer and his whole family. In very little time at all, the work became very demanding and very difficult. Many times both Hein and I felt that we could not go on; and in addition to everything else, we were nearly always separated.

▲　　　▲

Sunday, January 23, 1944

Dearest,

Yesterday I screamed for you in a place where nobody could hear it — except me. I needed you so much, Diet, and even now I am longing so much for you.

If I cannot continue to do this, I will draw back and start on my own — with Ab, of course, and Piet. I won't have anything to do with certain persons anymore, and I won't do certain things so that I don't have to carry the continuous responsibility. Diet, I am asking myself, "Why did I ever start all of this?" Yesterday I could hardly handle it anymore. I wanted not to think of it, but I could think of only one good solution and that is not in my hands: the end of the war. Diet, do you know me and understand what I'm feeling? Please think deeply about it and tell me what to do.

In the background of all I do, I feel sometimes that I do it all for myself, and Diet, that's wrong. Do you know me well enough to understand what I'm saying? If you do, please tell me how it is! I cannot stand alone in this life. I need a break and I also need a help, a support. Diet, you can be that, can't you? I only want to hear "yes," for Diet, often you have been the one who let me make the decisions, but don't put yourself aside for my sake, okay? Oh, I remember so well what you wrote in your last letter and I will never forget that. And I also remember the text at the wedding of Bram and Nel: "That you take care of each other!" Diet, can you take care of me, even if I don't do that for you? Can you marry me, Diet — now?

I am always looking for that answer. If we see each other sometimes at night, I often don't have the opportunity to talk with you about this. I mean, what I look for in marriage, Diet — what's important: those things that will make us stay together. More than just the physical unity, and the children — what I mean is the knowledge that we need each other daily spiritually. Diet, I am longing so much for that specifically. I know that I've changed in the last couple of years, but I cannot think of anything more wonderful now than being strengthened by your words, your advice, your vision, and your eyes.

Please write back soon. Then I can pick up your reply next Wednesday.

Tell me that you too want everything I've written about here, and tell me you will always keep on pointing to our spiritual strength.

God bless us, darling.

Many kisses,
Hein

letter from Hein Sietsma to Diet Eman

▼   ▼

Just one of the many problems we faced was what to do about Jewish finances. One time, the Nazis decided to cripple the black market in scarce food and raw materials. That black market operated with huge cash transactions that were difficult to trace. So the Nazis announced that after a certain date, all thousand- and five hundred-guilder bills would be invalid. People had to take them to the tax office, where the officials would know if you had earnings that justified the number of large-denomination bills you were exchanging. This caused great difficulty for the Jewish families in hiding, many of whom had fled with whatever portable wealth they could carry: gold, precious stones, and large-denomination bills.

If such a Jewish couple was living with a simple farm family, for example, and that family came to their tax office with ten thousand-guilder notes — in a little village where people generally didn't have that kind of money — the officials would say, "Where does that come from?" Of course, the Germans would know immediately that something illegal was going on. We were trying to save Jews' lives first and foremost, and they had to trust us. But they also had to trust us with their finances at that time.

Many would ask: "Can you take our thousands and find people to shelter them?"

My father had a business, so he said he could take a certain number of those notes without getting into trouble with his own tax statements. He couldn't take in hundreds of notes all of a sudden, because he would get into trouble himself. My Tante Truus, whose business was fashion design, was willing to cover some of the money as well. And I went to every business person I knew who could shelter some of that money, anybody we could trust.

"Can you please shelter some money — even if it's four or five or six thousand?" I would ask. They had to promise, of course, that the Jewish people would get the money back, often quite soon because they would need it once they would be hidden at another place. But the people who sheltered that money were also at risk, with regard to taxes and other financial laws.

We had to smuggle all those people out of the cities and into the country on trains, which was difficult and always dangerous. Naturally, they all needed false IDs. Besides the farms, we had found an old hotel in the woods of Uchelen, near a monastery named Caesarea, that would take people in. Nobody went on vacation anymore at that point, and the hotel owners were practically going bankrupt. We had heard that that couple was willing to help, so we asked them if they would be interested in taking in some Jewish people. We told them that we would pay, or else the Jews themselves would pay — whoever would have the money. This place was way back in the woods, far out of the way. The couple consented.

At that time there was a very dangerous place on Reinkenstraat in The Hague, a little apartment that had twenty-seven Jews in it! We were working feverishly to get those people out of that apartment and into the country. Among that large group was a Jewish couple who were very wealthy: the husband owned a large chemical cleaning and dyeing factory in Zutphen. Their oldest son had already escaped to Switzerland; Martin, the boy with them in that tiny, dangerous apartment, was the youngest.

Now this man wanted very badly to get out of that apartment, but he also wanted to leave that place for just one day: he said he had to attend to some business that required him to see a man in Amsterdam. Constantly, he begged us if he could leave just once. But one problem would certainly be his appearance out on the streets or in the trains. If you were to open a children's Bible and look at a portrait of Father Abraham, you would see a perfect picture of this man, so typically Jewish-looking was he. By the end of the war, I could pick out Jewish people almost as if I had a sixth sense about it, even if they had blue eyes and blond hair. I would have been a very valuable Gestapo person. But this man's physical features would have given him away to just about anyone — that's how much he resembled an Old Testament prophet.

At about the same time, I was asked to go to a rather rundown section of The Hague, a working-class neighborhood that had smaller, simpler homes where hard-working people lived. I was asked to go there to a small dry-cleaning business belonging to a Jewish man. When I got there and found this diminutive Jewish man, and explained who I was, the tears started streaming down his cheeks.

"Juffrouw," he said, "I have a wife and five daughters. We are all working in this business, but my youngest is a seven-year-old boy. Never mind if the rest of us get killed, but please, save my little boy."

He didn't ask for places for himself, his wife, and his daughters; he wasn't thinking about hiding everybody. He wanted

only a place for this boy to be safe. The son was very important
to this family.

"We were a good, hard-working business," he went on,
"and now nobody may come to us with their cleaning, so we
have no business and no money. I do understand that you'll need
money for my son's food and things."

"I'll find a place for him," I said. "And don't worry about
the money."

I knew that Father Abraham, the wealthy Jew in the dangerous apartment in The Hague, with one son already safe in
Switzerland, could help sponsor the one lone son of this poor
Jewish dry cleaner. So I asked him whether he would help with
what was needed for the little boy.

"Oh," he said immediately, "I have no money at all. We
can barely get by, you know."

I knew he was lying. Mies, the woman hiding him there,
had seen his money. The doors of that apartment were made
with a glass panel, so there was not much privacy. With twenty-
seven people in one apartment, you couldn't be too modest.
Father Abraham's wife was very fat, and she wore a corset full
of stays. Mies had told me that she had happened to be in the
corridor to see this Jewish matron take off her dress. Mies had
seen her slip a roll of bills, thousand-guilder bank notes, out of
her corset and count them. A thousand-guilder bank note was
the largest denomination of bills, and Mies saw the woman
count about a hundred of them.

Father Abraham wanted badly to get out of Mies's tiny,
crowded apartment; but even more, he wanted to get out for
one day to go to Amsterdam. I had already done so many
jobs for them — delivering mail and IDs and so forth — that
I thought they would have trusted me. I knew that the day
was coming when they would lose all their money: the Ger-

mans had announced that those large bills could be redeemed for only one or two months longer. And during that time I kept asking Father Abraham to support little Peter, the one son of the poor Jewish family. And he continued to tell me that he was very poor.

"I'll find you another place," I said, "because it's far too dangerous here." I had my eye on that hotel in the woods for Father Abraham and his wife and son, but we still had to complete the complicated arrangements to make that move. But then I approached him once again: "I have one request. You remember that little boy we need to find a sponsor for. You have enough money, and I would like you to pay only one hundred guilders a month [about $25] for this little boy."

That's all I wanted him to pay, and after all, he would be helping out fellow Jews.

"Oh no," he said, "we can't do that. We are too poor." And then he pulled me toward him. We were there in that crowded apartment, and he didn't want anyone else to hear. He whispered: "Juffrouw, we are all sinking ships. See, there is a sinking ship," he said, pointing at one person, "and there's another. . . . That's a sinking ship too, and that's another." He kept pointing.

"But somewhere there is a safe harbor," he continued, "and I don't care if that one sinks —" he pointed again — "or that one, or that one. I only care if *my* ship makes it to safe harbor."

All of this was in a whisper. I was furious, but we were surrounded by people, so I tried to speak calmly.

"I have to tell you something," I said. "All those sinking ships are just the same to me. And little Peter is just the same as your sinking ship." I glared at him angrily.

"And I'll tell you one more thing: if you are unwilling to pay for Peter, then I know of other people who have to be taken out of The Hague and hidden. There's a long list of people who want to go. I'll take other people out, and you can stay here and take the risk."

He had a place to stay, after all, even though it was in that dangerous apartment. Many Jewish people had no place at all. It was not like he was living on the street.

"Now, you think it over," I concluded.

"I can't afford it," he whined, shaking his head. "I have no money. You think I'm rich, but you are wrong. I'm not rich!"

He continued to refuse to pay anything for Peter. The day came when the German law prohibiting the possession of thousand-guilder bills was about to go into effect and make all his money worthless. Now it turned out that I was the one from our Underground group who was in charge of that apartment, of keeping it supplied. Mies allowed her Jews to do only what I said was okay to do. We brought them papers and ration cards, so in a certain way I was the one who drew up at least some of the rules: no Jewish person was allowed to leave her apartment. That was the most important rule, because if neighbors were to see anyone going in and out of there, suspicions would be raised and people would talk. It would be the end of the whole operation at that address.

One morning when I came there, Father Abraham was pacing like a caged lion in the apartment. He had heard, of course, about the new law the Germans had passed. He stood in the hallway of that apartment, tears in his eyes, even more anxious to leave than he had been before.

"Juffrouw, juffrouw, please let me go to Amsterdam," he pleaded. "I have a friend there and I have to see him."

I was sure that he wanted to get rid of his ninety-eight thousand-guilder bills; but he didn't want me to know because he knew I would jump him again with my demands for little Peter. So I said this:

"No, you cannot go to Amsterdam. Look in the mirror," I said, pointing to the face that was a dead ringer for Father Abraham. "Before you get to the corner of the street, you'll be arrested, and they will ask you where you come from, and they'll torture you. And then it's all over for all these people here. You are not allowed to leave this house."

"You have to trust us," I went on. "We're already taking care of you. You already trust us with your life, you have to trust us with your money as well."

But he kept swearing he had nothing, and he kept begging me — both he and his wife — to let him leave for just one day to go to Amsterdam. They were in tears, but my mind was not going to be changed. I could not let him go. I told Hein that I was really curious what they would do in the end, what would win — his fear of paying me that little bit for Peter or his fear of all his thousands going down the drain. What would he say?

In the end he let almost all of his money rot. He gave me four of those thousand-guilder notes to place with businesses, and he finally agreed to pay for Peter. I think it was because he finally began to realize the depth of the danger.

Then I had to get this family out of The Hague and, by a circuitous route, to the old hotel in the woods near Uchelen. And that was the most dangerous, even foolhardy, thing of all. I ended up on the train with this stubborn rich man and his wife and son, all of whom looked very Jewish.

"Now listen," I told them, "you don't know where this place is, so I'll have to lead the way. I'll be in front." Then I gave Father Abraham the latest newspaper and told him to sit in the corner and keep the newspaper in front of his face.

"Don't *ever* take the paper away from your face or you will be grabbed by the Gestapo on this train. We'll have to pray that no Gestapo are on this train to check papers, because the moment that newspaper is down, everybody will see that you are a Jew."

"You and I will sit in one car," I went on. "Your wife will sit in a whole different section, and your son will sit in still a different section. You will follow me, but keep a good distance between us. In Utrecht we have to switch to another train, just across the platform. It will be standing there. We have to set these rules right away: if you are arrested — any of you — the others must go on. We cannot stop. We can't help you anyway, and at least two of you will have a chance to survive."

That's how we traveled. Father Abraham hid behind his paper the whole way. I had to take them from The Hague to Utrecht, an hour by train, where we had to change to another train, Utrecht to Amersfoort; there we had to change to yet another train that went from Amersfoort to Apeldoorn. Then we had to walk twelve or fourteen kilometers out into the woods near Uchelen.

Before they had left, they had packed a giant suitcase. But it was dangerous enough for them to be even glimpsed on that trip, let alone be lugging something that size, which would surely draw attention to them. I tried to lift that suitcase — and I was strong — but I couldn't. I don't know whether it had solid gold bars in it or what.

"You can't carry this suitcase because it will certainly draw attention to you," I told Father Abraham. I don't even know whether he *could* lift it. His wife couldn't for sure, and the son was too young. I prayed: "Lord, this is all these people have left in the world. You have to give me the strength to lift this thing."

And I did. I think that strength comes to you sometimes in your greatest need. That's what happened to me with that monstrous suitcase.

Father Abraham was an Orthodox Jew, and he was carrying his tsitsit, which was made of strings of leather.

"Oh, my tsitsit!" he said to me suddenly as we were crossing from one train to another in Utrecht. He had had it in his pocket or somewhere, but somehow, running, he had lost it.

"I *have* to find it," he said to me. "I can't go on without it."

"Run ahead and get on the train, and I'll find it," I told him.

I ran back, looking furiously, and thinking to myself that maybe the Gestapo, if they saw it, would think the tsitsit was a dog leash or something else made out of leather. But they knew what those things were, of course. I was so young that I didn't even know about those things myself at the time. That was a hurried and scary search, but I soon found it near a post on the platform.

Then we rode a second train, then a third, and finally we arrived in Apeldoorn, where my sister Fanny was living with the family she had joined after her fiancé was killed. I borrowed a bike from Fanny, to which I strapped the suitcase for the twelve kilometers we still had to walk from Apeldoorn to the woods of Uchelen. I walked with that bicycle in my hands, and a long distance behind me was Father Abraham, a long distance behind him was his wife, and then Martin, the boy, way back on the road. Even though we'd made it off the three trains, and were now a long way from that apartment on Reinkenstraat in The Hague, I was still worried sick. It was late Sunday morning, and people coming home from church or sitting on their little porches with coffee, or even in their living rooms, could easily see that we were strangers out in the country. It was still very dangerous.

But there wasn't much traffic that day, and nobody stopped us all the way out to that hotel in the woods. Out there at that old hotel they were far enough away from people that they would even be able to go out in the big woods from time to time. It was actually a wonderful place for Jews to be hidden, much better than most places, where entire families had to stay inside for the duration of the war. So Father Abraham's family was finally out of The Hague.

In the first month or two, it cost Father Abraham a hundred guilders to keep Peter sheltered. The next month I came with coupons for food rations and whatever mail they had, and Father Abraham said to me: "Now I'm here, and I *know* where I am, and I won't pay another penny for Peter!"

I was furious, but what could I do?

Not much later, when I returned to the hotel in the woods, I found that Father Abraham and his family had left. Martin, their son, had hated it all by himself in the country, and had talked his mother and father into returning to Mies's apartment because there were more people there and more things to do, even though there was so much less space. They'd remembered the address of the apartment, of course, so the three of them had returned in the same way, I imagine, that we'd come out to Uchelen, under cover of the newspaper. And they made it back to that dangerous apartment, the three of them. But they weren't safe there. No one was safe at Mies's apartment.

▲   ▲

March 4, 1943

We are still not at the end of their repertoire!

Tuesday, February 9, we got a phone call. Everywhere in the city groups of auxiliary police in black uniforms with red bands on their sleeves were seen, and they arrested all the young men in their homes. They had come to Tante Ida's house already at a quarter to six in the morning. The sons of the middle class and rich were the special victims; but all young men in that age group were taken in the street. They also went to offices and took men there. Hein and Bram promptly phoned in sick!

That night hardly a young man slept in his own house. Hein and Bram stayed "sick" for a week. All the time new rumors: "Now it is the girls' turn!" Father had put a ladder in the garden so I could flee to the roof, but fortunately it was not necessary.

Don't go to church on Sunday, for they will catch you there, it was advised. Father said there was hardly anybody in church. Saturday afternoon we celebrated Bram's birthday at Hein's address, and we played Monopoly. In the evening Mother and Albert had planned to go to *Hamlet,* but they could not because curfew was 8 P.M.

The wildest rumors are circulating. Hitler has not given a speech in two months, so of course he must be dead. Van Ravenswaay also should be dead, etc., etc. Many young men have already returned from Vught. However, Mussert and Hauptdienstleiter Schmidt give big speeches all the time from which you can smell that they want all young men to go to Germany. Monday, March 1, all young men who had (before the war) applied for the Dutch military for officer training had to report in Utrecht to become POW's!

The English are carrying out nonstop bombardments which they explain over the radio is the beginning of the invasion! Also recently the Green Police are searching people in trains and trams and even in the streets!

And still it is not the end . . .

Cheer up! Every day brings us closer to that which we are yearning for.

LIBERTY!!

How lucky that we cannot look into the future. Otherwise, how would we have been able to hold out this long?

from the journal of Diet Eman

March 5, 1943

Van Zuylen told me this morning that Mrs. van Rantwijk also had been searched when she was in the train in Haarlem, and at that time there was a young man who had a weapon! Oh, if you think for a moment, what must have been in the thoughts of that guy when he discovered they were searching and knew that it meant his death! And his parents, who probably did not know their son even carried a gun or that he was even arrested and who will not see him come home again! O God, please bring an end to this war.

What must the end of the world be like, the time of which it is written that "if the days would not be shortened, nobody would be left"? *This* is already so nervewracking, all this fear and uncertainty.

Now that all the things we lean on around us are breaking down, now that we don't have "certainty" anywhere anymore, we should be "rich" because our homes are built on a Rock and they can never be toppled. Very deep inside I am completely at peace, even if the very worst should happen. But still, now and then, fear bubbles up in me because right now, at this time, it seems as if Hein and I are completely happy. If something should happen, I know it will be so much more difficult to bear.

But it is wrong to be worried, for in the first place, God has always protected us up until this time, sometimes by miracles. And, secondly, *if* something would happen, we have to remember all we had together, and how rich we are, and that would be a consolation. I nearly believe that this is the richest time in our lives. I would not want to change with anyone, even though we have our problems. But I can be grateful, every day again, for everything you have given us in each other and for each other.

from the journal of Diet Eman

▼　　　▼

The Apartment
on Reinkenstraat, Spring 1943

Cartoon of Mussert, the leader of the NSB (the Dutch Nazi sympathizers), announcing in 1943: "Because on the 10th of December the Führer told me that he wouldn't treat our people as enemies." Juxtaposed, on the bottom, is a reference to the 12th of March, 1945: "A large number of innocents were murdered in Wetering park [in Amsterdam] by the 'Green' troops," the German military police.

The Apartment on Reinkenstraat, Spring 1943

In May 1943 my life took two sharp turns, one of which I had anticipated joyfully. That was, of course, the day that Hein and I decided to get married: May 4, 1943. We went to the town hall, took out a wedding license on that day, and filled out all the appropriate forms. Every bit of information about people in the Netherlands goes on the card system. That day, it said on my card that I was licensed to be married to Hein Sietsma, and vice versa. Then we had to set our date: it would be months later because we needed to get coupons for sheets and towels for our new house or apartment. The day before we went to city hall, we had been talking.

"You know," I said, "I just can't imagine that we will get married. I don't know if it's because it seems too beautiful to be true, but it's just very difficult for me to imagine that we will ever really be married."

"It has to be true," Hein said, "because otherwise there is only one alternative — either I die or you die. Maybe that's the fear that you have?"

"No," I said. "It's just that I can't believe we are going to get married."

I knew very well that our relationship could never break up, so I told myself that the reason I couldn't imagine our being together forever was that marrying Hein was just too good to be true. But inside me there was this strange feeling that it just wouldn't happen.

Inside city hall the next day we had to fill out the cards and other documents. We were planning to get married in September, but we couldn't really set a date. I remember holding this big bunch of red roses in my right arm, and my left arm was hooked in Hein's right arm. In his left hand were those papers and the wedding license: that's the way we came walking out, down the steps of city hall. Then he touched my nose with the license and said, smiling, "Now, you *still* don't believe we are getting married?"

That moment is in my memory: down those steps of the courthouse we came together, he with our marriage license in his hand. But I still could not believe it. He looked at me, and he was so happy. And yet voices in me screamed out that our marriage would never happen.

But I couldn't tell him that, so when he asked again whether or not we were going to get married, I said, "Yeah, yeah, yeah," because I couldn't say that something inside me was telling me loudly that it would never be. It was very scary for me to feel that way. I already had my wedding dress at home.

I knew it was the kind of moment at which I should have been absolutely ecstatic, the moment of my life I wanted to live for so long because I wanted badly to marry Hein. But I also knew that I *couldn't* feel that way, that I wasn't feeling the kind of happiness that I should have had at that very moment there on the courthouse steps.

It was something indescribable, really, this sense that as wonderful as it was to even imagine it while we were standing there on those steps, my being married to Hein Sietsma would certainly — almost certainly — never be. That was May 4, 1943, a day I had looked forward to for a long time, but a day that even today holds bittersweet memories. I couldn't tell him what I felt for a long time. But he told me what he felt.

▲   ▲

Somewhere, July 13, 1943

My darling,

Even before I take the train today, I will start writing you and if I don't finish the letter, then I will at least mail this part. I forgot to give you writing paper and envelopes, and I will mail that to you.

Darling, I am so happy that you told me what you did yesterday. You must never keep things from me, for that would mean we were not communicating with each other fully, and we are now nearly married, isn't that right? And it should be that we are already spiritually one. Or, should I say "one spiritually"? We took out our marriage license, didn't we?

I hope that what you told me you foresaw will never be true — I mean, that your intuition is incorrect. Every day I pray for you and I know that you are doing that for me. When I pray for peace I will also pray that you will soon be my wife and I your husband. You should not try to live without thinking and feeling, for then you are only a piece of machinery, not a human being. Even if it hurts. Even if the things you have to think of are sad, think them through; live them through and write or tell me. Only when we completely work through our thinking and feeling do we live a full life. I know that last night when you were in bed you had to cry — isn't that so? But you also prayed to God for strength. He will give you that, absolutely.

Always write me what you feel, darling, and what you think and also what you think about our being married. You know that I always was an optimist.

Do not be sad, for he will in his wonderful way give deliverance, even if the invasion doesn't come for another three years. And, if we never get the joy of being a family together, then still we won't be desperate, for our lives — each of our lives and our lives together — have not been lived in vain. He has taken care of us, and he who dwells in the shelter of the Most High will abide in the shadow of the Almighty.

That is our strength and our joy in war and in peace, and in life and in death!

Always trust in him, pray every day to him, and then you can always be happy, *Dieneke*.

Now I'm going to the train and will write soon again. One big kiss.

Your guy

a letter to Diet Eman from Hein Sietsma

▼   ▼

Spring 1943, however, held another event for me, one that I had also anticipated in a way, I suppose, but one that meant my living at home with my parents, even going home to them for a short visit, would be almost impossible. What made me have to leave my home was what happened at the apartment on Reinkenstraat, a place where far too many Jews were being hidden. I didn't know who had brought the Jewish people there, but it was not our Underground group; they were not the Jewish people we had been working with. A man named Bram, someone we did not know, seemed to be in charge of the place, at least he was the one who brought them food.

When I first showed up at that place, I had to give some code sentences to identify myself as someone who could be trusted. I rang the bell and said the correct words, and a woman named Mies, whom I had not yet met at that time, invited me in. Her dwelling was very small, a one-person apartment that was not very well insulated, on the second floor. And when I walked upstairs and into her apartment, I couldn't believe what I saw. She had a small living room, a tiny bedroom, a kitchenette, a shower, and a toilet. Just fine for one person. And in that little place, the first time I came, she had twenty-seven Jews hidden, right in the middle of the city! In the farms outside of the city, where it was much safer, we never kept that many in any one place.

The moment I saw how many people were there, I felt something tighten around my heart. It was fear. All those Jewish people were talking and talking, making all kinds of chatter. Mies had all the mattresses piled up against the wall to look like a divan so they could sit comfortably; and at night she would roll those mattresses out for them to sleep on.

There was Father Abraham and his family, an elderly married couple, and a young couple expecting a baby. There was a little of everybody in that place. I couldn't believe my eyes.

"How long have you lived here?" I said to Mies.

"About eight years," she said.

"And always alone?" I asked.

She said yes.

While I was standing there, I heard the hum of conversation in the adjacent apartment, and I knew immediately that the walls were anything but soundproof.

"Do you know your neighbors?" I asked.

"No, no," she said shyly.

"You don't know whether they're Nazis or NSBers?" I asked.

She had no idea.

"Well, listen," I said, "can you hear them talk?"

She turned her head. "Why yes," she said.

"You mean you've lived here all these years alone, and now you have all these people in this apartment — twenty-eight people!" I couldn't believe it.

While we were talking I heard the toilet flush next door and the water run through the pipes. "Do you understand how dangerous this is?" I said to her. "If I can hear them go to the bathroom next door, they certainly can hear you. When you are here alone, you flush the toilet — what? — maybe four times a day? With twenty-seven additional people here, that toilet must flush eighty or ninety times. Do you understand what you're doing? You want to help, and that is wonderful. But this cannot go on."

She didn't say anything.

"You're living on top of a volcano that's ready to erupt," I told her. I was extremely nervous just standing there talking with her.

So I told her that I would take as many of her Jews as I could and place them elsewhere in the country.

"I'll leave you with two or three," I said, "and then you can try to get those people through the war with you."

Mies meant well, but perhaps she never realized the danger of her situation.

"How can I reach you?" she asked.

This was such a dangerous address, I thought, that I really didn't dare to have *her* reach me. Besides, in Resistance work you never used your own name. The fact is, you didn't *want* to know anyone else's name. The more you knew during the war, the more dangerous it was for others, and the more dangerous it was for you too. If you were arrested, it was common knowledge that they would often pull out one fingernail, then another, then another, until you talked. The less you knew, the less could be tortured out of you.

"You can call me 'Toos,'" I said, "and listen, I'll call you three times a day: every morning before I go to work, and I'll call you an hour before my lunch break, and two hours before curfew. If you need me, I'll be here."

I went to that apartment three or four times a week under the name Toos. I took Jews away and placed them in the country;

I brought ration cards, and I brought IDs without the J. I don't know whether Mies ever fully understood how dangerous it was for her there.

One day when I came to take more Jewish people out, I discovered that she had taken in six new Jews! She had such a big heart, but it was becoming more scary every time.

"Mies, I am so afraid to come here," I said. "From now on, before I come, I'm going to call you from a phone booth around the corner, and if you don't answer yourself, I'm not coming. I have the feeling that one of these days I'm going to ring the bell here and I'm going to walk right into the hands of the Gestapo."

When Hein came to The Hague, I told him to go to that address because I knew he wouldn't believe what was happening there. He went there alone in the afternoon; I couldn't accompany him because at the time I could only go there during the hours when I wasn't working at the bank. When he came back that evening, Hein asked me if I had ever met the man named Bram when I was at Mies's apartment.

"No, never," I said.

"He must be from the Underground," Hein said, "because today he came with bags of potatoes and food and lots of supplies. And he asked how he could contact you."

"Are you sure he's to be trusted?" I asked.

Hein told me that Bram must be okay since he had brought all that food to the apartment. "I gave him your father's phone number," Hein added.

We both thought that Bram was okay: if he brought the food, we figured it was safe to trust him.

I could write a whole book simply on what happened in Mies's apartment. She could never really leave her place, because some of the Jews she was hiding constantly wanted to go into the street. Sometimes she would have to stop them, actually grab them by the shirt at the last minute. Those people were nervous wrecks, all of them. And you couldn't blame them, being cooped up like that. Sometimes Mies would even give them tranquillizing injections just to calm them down, she said (she had been a nurse). They'd go to sleep and wake up a little quieter.

On February 9, 1943, a man named Mr. van Putten died in Mies's apartment. We had to arrange a clandestine funeral, of course, so that the neighbors, who thought that Mies lived there alone, wouldn't notice anything strange. Getting the body out was very difficult: we rolled him in a rug and put him on a vegetable cart, then Hein drove him away. The whole event was very sad. His wife was not allowed to weep because the neighbors might hear it.

At another point Mies took in a young woman with a four-month-old baby, and the baby was not allowed to cry. And at that same time there was another young woman there who was pregnant. Mies simply could not say no.

One day I phoned Mies to ask if she needed any supplies, and a strange man answered her phone. I hung up. A few hours later I called again, and again a strange man answered. I didn't like it at all; in fact, I was very worried. I called one more time later, and again the man answered.

Across from Mies's apartment was a little grocery store, and I thought that perhaps the best way for me to get a sense of what might be going on at the apartment was to go to that shop and just listen in on what people were saying. If there had been a *razzia* at that address, the Germans would have blocked off the street, as they always did, and brought in trucks and soldiers with bayonets on their rifles. I was sure that if that had happened, the people across the street would still be talking about it.

So I took my ration cards and pretended to go shopping. Sure enough, the shoppers were all talking about the Jews who had been arrested in the apartment across the street, along with the woman who lived there. They all knew. It had finally happened, just as I had thought it would.

I immediately told Hein that we all had to disappear. In fact, that night, instead of going home, we all slept at the homes of friends. For a few nights I slept at a married cousin's house. But nothing happened right away. Weeks passed, and we began to think that everything would be all right. We eventually went back to our homes — Hein to his apartment, and I went back to my parents' house.

But not long after that, we discovered that the secret police were looking for me. They had found Mies's diary, and in it she had listed everything: "Toos here today"; "Toos brings papers"; "Toos has been here, brought IDs"; "Toos has been here, took Jews away." I had been there four times a week for months, according to the diary, and I had supplied ration cards, all of which had been stolen, as the Germans well knew. At that point the Germans knew that we were at least in contact with the people who had robbed their offices.

One day the Gestapo came to my parents' house while I was working at the bank. My brother Albert was home, and his being there when they came was dangerous in itself: Albert had false papers at the time, and he was in the age group that was required to go to Germany to work. Some young men could receive an exemption — they called it *Ausweis* — from going to Germany, but they had to have jobs in food supply or some other important area. In addition, there were exemptions for those with tuberculosis, and for those who were pastors or priests.

A neighbor, a young man who worked in food supply, had been able to get identification for Albert that said he was also in that field, even though Albert had never worked there or received any kind of salary. He was actually working for my father at that time, but all he needed was that piece of paper to stay in the Netherlands.

Two Gestapo officers came to the door looking for me, and Albert let them in the house. They acted as if they were Jewish, and they claimed they were looking for me because I could help them. They said they had heard that I was a person who did a lot of good things — helping people with problems and so forth. They did not say "Jews" or "Jewish people," but they acted as though there were an urgent reason for them to see me. One of them, a man named Lemke, spoke Dutch with a strong German accent; the other, a man I later learned was named Bolland, was Dutch.

Albert was afraid — and very suspicious. He knew there was something quite fishy about the two guys coming to our door, because it was not how Jewish people would operate. Once the men were gone, he immediately phoned my office. I wasn't there at the time, but he said to my boss, "It's really urgent that I get hold of Diet," without saying why.

"Well," my boss said, "she's gone to the printing office."

Now my friend Nel, the girlfriend of Hein's old friend Bram, was the receptionist at the *Landsdrukkerij,* the government printing office where I'd gone. Albert immediately thought of Nel, and he phoned her: "Get hold of Diet, because I think we had the Gestapo at our door. I don't trust them at all. Tell her to call me back."

So Nel alerted me by calling the office where I had stopped. After speaking with her, I left that office and I never went back to my own bank office for fear that the Gestapo would be there. But I did stop to see my boss. I knocked on his door and stuck my head in. Usually, you would say that you had to go to the dentist or something and that you'd be back in an hour. This time I knew it was something more dangerous than the dentist. I stuck my head in his door, and all I said was, "I have to go. See you after the war."

His mouth fell wide open; after all, I was his secretary. I phoned my brother right away, and he said, "Those men wanted very badly to know where you were. They said it was important — very urgent. They asked what time you would be home, so I said 7:00 o'clock."

I was always home at quarter after five, so that gave me some time to try to come up with a plan of action and get out of there. The men did come back that night, and this time they showed papers indicating that they were secret police. When my father said that he didn't know where I was, nor why I was late, they stayed until the 11:00 P.M. curfew hour, the time I was required to be home by law. But I didn't come home.

According to my parents' story, I should have been home by that time. So the Germans said to them, "What's the matter with your daughter? She should be home."

I was really quite an obedient daughter, but my father said, "That kid! You don't know what kind of trouble I've had with her. There's nothing I can say to her anymore." He acted as if I were really wild.

So the next night they came back again. "She didn't come home the whole night?" they asked.

"No," my father said. "That's exactly what we go through with that girl. Time and time again it happens."

"Do you know that she's taken out a marriage license?" the officer said. "Didn't she tell you?" They had discovered that information by checking into my name and finding the information Hein and I had just recently filed in the town hall. My parents knew about Hein and me, of course, but they acted as if they were shocked out of their wits.

"She's what?" they exclaimed.

"She's getting married to a man named 'Hein Sietsma' —
do you know him?"

My parents shook their heads sadly. They told those
Gestapo men that this Hein Sietsma had been the cause of all
their pain with their daughter, that he was shiftless and rough,
no one they wanted their daughter to chum around with, much
less marry.

"You'll have to help us find her," the officers insisted.

They came back every night for almost a week. Then they
came every other night, and after that they started coming in the
afternoons and at other unexpected times. They became exas-
perated.

"Isn't she coming home?" they would say, and my father
would only shrug his shoulders.

We knew, of course, that once they had my telephone
number, they could collect a lot of other information very easily.
It wasn't long before Hein's residence also received a visit. His
landlady, Mrs. Overvelde, told them that Hein was really something of a wanderer, a man who still owed her money for staying
at her boardinghouse. She told them that she wanted nothing
to do with that wastrel. In the meantime, of course, the Gestapo
officers were still coming to my parents' house. One of them
asked my parents who this man was that their daughter was
planning to marry. My parents told them that I wanted to marry
a man who was absolutely no good, a man they had forbidden
ever to come to their house.

"He is a horrible influence on her," my father said, "and
sometimes she doesn't come home for days when she's with him."

"I know just what you're going through," one of them said,
patting my father on the shoulder. "I have a daughter just like
yours. Listen, here's my name and phone number. If she comes

home, don't tell her I was here. Just call me — my name is Lemke."

So my father said that was exactly what he'd do. And the dumbbells believed him.

But they didn't give up. They visited my parents at intervals for the next two years until the end of the war. And we began to realize that their constant concern meant they were after me for something very serious.

One morning at breakfast the phone rang and Mother took it. It was for me, and Mom said I was not home. Just a moment later a car came racing up the street and those two Gestapo stormed in and screamed at my parents that I was actually home and they knew it. Then they counted the breakfast plates and saw it was the right number, so they disappeared — again without results.

In those days I often felt like King David when he had to flee from Saul and live in caves. All I could do was hide, nor could I stay long in any one place. I knew right away that it was Mies's apartment, that apartment on Reinkenstraat, that had gotten me in trouble. I suspected something had leaked from the raid there. I had always thought that that place was my only weak point: Mies simply seemed unable to control the situation.

In a normal situation, if the Gestapo thought you were hiding or helping Jews, they would try to catch you maybe once or twice, and then quit. They did not really pursue you endlessly because so very many people hid Jews. They were aware of that because of the great number of Jews who simply didn't show up when they were ordered to report — who simply disappeared. The Germans knew that hiding Jews was something of a popular movement. They thought we were stupid to do it, of course; in fact, it was beyond their comprehension that we would risk so much for Jews.

I don't believe the Germans ever really understood the Dutch people. As small as the Netherlands is, it has many different small religious denominations, for example. For centuries the Dutch have said, "If we don't agree with what you preach, then we'll start our own church." Some people, even in the Netherlands, think of such splintering in the church as wrong. But it also means that the Dutch have a long tradition of thinking for themselves, not just swallowing what officials tell them. They have a tradition of not being merely followers, as the Germans seemed to me to be. Our not following orders made life difficult for the Germans, more difficult than they had thought it would be. They had to treat us as if they were balancing on a tightrope. A German named Seyss-Inquart, the Nazi in charge of the Netherlands, tried to convince us that we belonged to the great Aryan race and that we should be overjoyed that we'd been accepted. But, quite simply, many Dutch people never followed orders.

What was a mystery to us, however, was how on earth those Gestapo officers would have come to my parents' house. We could not understand how they had made the link between Mies's apartment and Diet Eman, because I'd never used my real name with her. Then we learned from someone who had an inside track with the SS that the man named Bram, whom Hein had met bringing food to that apartment, had been arrested too. He had been there at that fatal time. He was the only one who knew my phone number. We heard that the Germans probably promised to let him go if he would tell them who "Toos" and "Dick" were — our aliases. He didn't tell them right away, not until they threatened to deport him to Germany, leaving his young wife at home alone. Then he talked. We didn't know that then, so we didn't understand — at least at first — exactly how dangerous it was. But I knew enough to hop on my bike and go straight to

Hein's office at Shell the moment my brother told me about the men, one of them with an accent, looking for me. I thought that if they were looking for me, they would be looking for him too. If they knew where I worked, they would be coming to where he worked too.

"We'd better disappear," he said when I told him, "because this doesn't sound good."

The raid on Mies's apartment was on March 23, 1943, and all of this happened at the end of May, so there were a couple of months in between. We had been lulled into a kind of complacent feeling that we were not in danger. But once they came to my house so regularly, once they clearly would not give up, we were sure they had found something. We knew that they would not have kept coming if they believed we were merely hiding Jews. We knew from our inside SS informer that they knew we were supplying Jews with all those false IDs and ration cards, which we were getting from armed robberies.

From that moment on, I could never go home again during the war — not safely. Sometimes I would sneak in, but only much later, and only at night when no one could see me. From then on, and for the rest of the war, I saw my own parents very little.

Hiding at Eindhoven

THE LOW COUNTRIES

0   10   20   30   40 miles

0   10   20   30   40   50 km

North Sea

Frisian Islands

Emden

Leeuwarden
Harlingen

Groningen

GRONINGEN

Den Helder

FRIESLAND

Assen
DRENTE

NETHERLANDS

NORTH
HOLLAND

Alkmaar

IJsselmeer
(Zuider Zee)

Zwolle

OVERIJSSEL

Almelo

Haarlem

Amsterdam

Bussum

Hilversum

Apeldoorn
Nijkerk

Deventer

Enschede

Leiden

Amersfoort

Utrecht

GELDERLAND

Zutphen

IJssel

Doetinchem

Scheveningen

The Hague

Gouda

UTRECHT

Arnhem

Delft

Rotterdam

Wageningen

Neder Rijn

Schiedam

SOUTH
HOLLAND

Dordrecht

Nijmegen

Rhine

Schouwen

Overflakkee

s' Hertogenbosch

Wesel

N. Beveland

S. Beveland

Vught

Walcheren

Bergen op Zoom

NORTH BRABANT

Maas

Westkapelle

Middelburg

Breda

Roosendaal

Tilburg

Essen

Flushing

Goes

ZEELAND

Eindhoven

Duisburg

Düsseldorf

Breskens

Krefeld

Terneuzen

Hulst

LIMBURG

Ostend

Bruges

Antwerp

Mönchen-
Gladbach

Ruhr

Dunkirk

Ghent

Cologne

Scheldt

Brussels

Louvain

Maastricht

Aachen

Bonn

BELGIUM

Liège

GERMANY

Namur

FRANCE

Map [altered] originally drawn by David Hunter for *A Liberation Album: Canadians in the Netherlands, 1944-45* (Toronto/Montreal/New York: McGraw-Hill Ryerson Limited, 1980).

▲   ▲

How much has happened again since I wrote the last time. And how wonderfully have we been protected again. If I just think back on it all I can say is, "My soul is quiet unto thee."

I can go on quietly now, even though the first days here were a little difficult. Tomorrow I will be here a week and I now am starting to feel "at home."

Up to this time, I have been with family and friends and with Hein, but now that I am alone among strangers and have to do totally different kinds of work. I was a bit nervous. But now it begins to go better.

Every night between 1:30 and 3 A.M., there are heavy bombardments by the Allies. We all feel so droopy for lack of sleep. I probably won't have any excitement here, but a little bit of "rest" after all the emotions of the last couple of months is welcome!

from the journal of Diet Eman

▼   ▼

When I first had to go into hiding, it was in the city of Eindhoven. I took the false name Dineke de Jong and became the maid for a family named Bakker. Mr. Bakker worked with the mayor on the Eindhoven City Council, and Mevrouw Bakker was a sister of Platteel's wife, Truus.

"I could ask my sister to put you up," Truus had said, because she knew that their maid had just recently left them. "But you know, you'll be a maid."

I told her that was okay, even though my training had really been in business and I was not particularly adept at things in the household. "I'm not a good maid," I told her, "but I'm willing to learn."

At home, Mother had always done her own laundry, sewing, and ironing; and Fanny, my sister, was so perfect in the household that there was never any need for me to do any cooking or housework. I didn't even know how to do the laundry. I had two left hands around all that kind of work. And since I felt I wasn't worth much in that kind of a job, I told Truus I didn't need a salary.

"If I have a place to live, and they feed me," I said, "that's fine."

At the Bakkers, everything was *Mevrouw* this, and *Mevrouw* that — very high class. After all, her husband was a counselor to the mayor. They both had a very good sense of humor, and I could see that it was a very good marriage. But often Mevrouw Bakker made me really feel like nothing more than a maid.

"Normally our maids have to eat in the kitchen," she said to me, "but your situation is a little bit different, so we'll allow you to sit at the table with us." I thanked her very much — to be actually allowed to eat with the whole family.

They had three children, and the youngest, Rudy, had a form of *ketonuria*, an illness whose progression meant that he would become severely mentally retarded unless his system received heavy doses of fat in the form of oil and butter. Those were just the kinds of foods you couldn't easily obtain during the war. Little Rudy was only three years old, and he would gag severely on all the grease that he was forced to eat. But as long as he was on this diet he was fine. All during that time, no one else saw butter; it was a commodity that was very rare. But the Germans agreed to supply the Bakkers with it, once they could produce the doctor's statement. The family received special rations for him because it was so important that he ate a certain amount of fat, all of which was measured exactly by the gram. It was such a strict diet that his mother was busy with his menu the whole day — breakfast, lunch, and dinner. The Bakkers worked very hard to keep Rudolf healthy.

But that darling little boy couldn't stand to eat all that butter and grease: he would get a little slice of bread with so much butter spread on it that he would actually vomit. And I had to force him to eat it. I loved him very much and felt very sorry for him. Every one of the Bakkers' maids had left, perhaps because of the difficult situation with Rudy — or perhaps because Mevrouw Bakker was sometimes a bit moody.

Rudy and I slept on the second floor of that house, and the rest of the family on the first floor. There were air raids nearly every night, because the Philips plant, a very important radio and electronics factory the Germans had taken over, was in Eindhoven. It was terrifying when the Allied planes came over and dropped bombs.

"If there is an air raid," they said, "and we have to flee, you grab Rudy, and we'll grab the other two kids."

Rudy really took to me. In the morning I always woke him up with a Dutch wake-up song — "The sun is already out" — by singing his name in the song. He loved it so. He would be smiling and laughing because he loved singing. And once we got to know each other, he didn't want to eat for his mother anymore. He would eat only if I fed him. Sometimes children get into a power struggle with their parents, and I think Mevrouw Bakker was a bit jealous of that really close tie between her little boy and me. Of course, I *was* responsible for him if there were air raids or anything else, and I grew to love him dearly.

I had come to Eindhoven in June of 1943, and I never got a break from my domestic work at the Bakkers. I went to church, but I did not dare to go to anything like the Young Women's Bible study then. I lived in total isolation. With work that was strange to me and Mevrouw Bakker's moods and her husband working all the time, I became very lonely there. At a certain point I was even miserable.

▲   ▲

Sunday, September 14, 1943

When will it be the end? It's now 11 P.M.

How will it be exactly a year from today? Will I then be with Hein in our home? Will Jan be free again? Will we have heard from my brother?

You know the answer to all these questions, Father, and we have to wait quietly, even though we are longing so much to know.

My peace is in your hands, Immanuel.

Break our chains and make all things well.

Tonight I would have loved to walk into the St. Gerardus Church just to pray quietly alone. But it is always busy, always something to do, never a quiet moment here. And when at long last I go to bed I am so sleepy, and in the morning again it is always a hurry. Still during the day, in my work, I am praying and singing.

from the journal of Diet Eman

▼   ▼

During those few months in Eindhoven, Hein never came to see me because he was very busy and there was no place for him to stay. But he wrote me faithfully.

I never took a day off: what would I do with a day, or even an afternoon, off? I didn't have any money. Once in a while, the Bakkers gave me perhaps ten guilders for stamps or something. But you couldn't buy anything in the shops anyway.

Their home was on a village square, and I remember there was a big Catholic church with chimes. Sometimes I was in such despair — and the Catholic church was always open — that I just went in there and prayed. They didn't even know me, but I sat way in the back. It was really a rough time for me, a bad time, when I think about it now: I was alone, a maid, doing a job I wasn't really trained for or good at, in an occasionally unfriendly house.

Finally, I got a letter from Hein asking me to meet him.

"Diet, come," he said, "we have to see each other. Take the train to the station at Geldermalsen."

Since I had never had any time off, I said to Mevrouw Bakker that I needed to get away for a day, because I had to meet Hein.

"Have to go?" she said. "You can't. I have invited people for coffee after church."

I couldn't believe it! Her precious coffee time was just an hour after church. That's all. And because I had to serve the silly coffee, she was saying I couldn't meet Hein. I felt that her demand was totally out of line. The Bakkers didn't pay me a salary, after all, and while I was grateful that they were hiding me — anyone who hid a fugitive would be equally guilty — her demand was ridiculous to me.

I told her that I didn't even dare to write Hein that I was not coming; I knew that he wouldn't begin to understand.

"Ach, so childish," she said. "What would he do, throw a tantrum?"

"He will be very angry," I told her, "and he is not easy when he's angry. I mean, he's a Frisian."

She said, "Well——"

"I don't even dare to write him and tell him no."

Finally she said, "Well, you may go meet him at that station, but then you must come back on the very next train."

That Saturday, Hein was to come from Friesland and I was to come from Eindhoven. His plan was that we would each take a train, we would meet in Geldermalsen, and then continue together and stay with friends in The Hague. I knew Hein was looking forward to this, and I wanted to be with him. We hadn't seen each other in months, and I didn't know where I could reach him because by that time he was always traveling around, working and staying out of sight.

So I said to Mevrouw Bakker: "I don't know where to reach him. He will be there at that station at such and such a time and he will think——"

"Then you can ride to Geldermalsen," she said "and you can tell him that you can't come with him, and you can come right back on the next train."

I gave in. But I felt really stupid about it. I had done all that Underground work for others, and I was so grateful to everybody who took me in because I always thought the Gestapo was right behind me. I knew that if people took me in, I was putting them in danger too. I felt as though I had no rights, that I was just a big risk for people. So when Mevrouw Bakker said that I should go to Geldermalsen and tell Hein that I couldn't come, I said that I would.

I hopped on the train and went to Geldermalsen. Hein's train was to arrive there first, but I had to go back on the very next train.

We met there in the station, and we had just a few minutes to make a connection. It was wonderful to be with him again, of course; but I hadn't told him that I couldn't go with him. "Come on," he yelled to me as he was off to the next train. "Come on!"

"I can't," I yelled back. "I can't come along."

"Come on — it's leaving . . . it's leaving!" he said and pulled me physically, but I was pulling away. Meanwhile, the connecting train was moving away.

"Diet," he said, "what's the matter with you?"

So then I told him the whole story.

He was angry, as I knew he would be. He was very upset with Mevrouw Bakker — and with me for not speaking up.

"How dare she not permit you to come?" he said. "Now don't just say, 'I have to go back there.' You're leaving that place!" He was adamant. "You're not staying there."

"But I can't leave," I said. "What about Rudy?"

"What about *our* work?" he said. "It's getting more and more urgent now, and we need you very badly."

I was so torn. I felt that I owed the whole world and I really had no rights. And I felt so close to little Rudy. In addition, it was safe at Eindhoven: no one was searching for me there. It was the first time I had been in hiding, and I felt deeply grateful that the Bakker family had hidden me. I also realized that even though Mevrouw Bakker could be tough, times were hard for her too, and sometimes she took her nerves out on me. It was difficult for everyone during the war.

"Well, you will leave there very soon," Hein said. "You listen to me." His stubbornness gave me the feeling that I had no choice.

"What happened?" Mevrouw Bakker said to me when I returned that evening.

I told her that Hein was very angry.

"Well," she said, "that's too bad."

"He was so angry that he wants me to leave."

"To leave? To leave this house?" She sounded somewhat anxious. "You can't just leave."

"I'm sorry," I said, "but he explained that there is so much work to be done in the Underground, and he says I need to be doing more traveling around to help the guys."

"What about Rudy?" she asked.

That hurt me very much.

A little later, we talked again, this time with her husband. I told him it would be only a matter of time before I would have to leave them, because the Resistance work was getting more and more demanding, and the men would be needing me. Hein had explained that it was increasingly dangerous for our men to be out on the trains, on bikes, and on the roads. The Germans were after all the young men for forced labor; no men were really safe out in the open. Women had to do more of the work. Mr. Bakker understood, I think. But I got the feeling that he also understood some things about his wife that I found difficult to live with.

When I left the Bakkers, I traveled from place to place where we had Jews hidden. I again distributed ration cards, because those families hiding Jews or *onderduikers* naturally needed more food if they and their families were to survive. The ration cards we received were always stolen by the *knokploeg* that operated out of a base somewhere between Rotterdam and Zwijndrecht. When that group broke into a government office, they stole thousands of blank IDs as well. That particular group was our source for much of what we needed to keep our operations going, but there were many others.

By the summer of 1943 there were so many Resistance groups operating that a number of those groups met and merged to call themselves the National Organization, the *Landelijke Organisatie* (LO). A lot of groups who did not have their own source of ration cards and IDs were naturally happy to join the national organization, which not only pulled off its own robberies but had its own press to communicate all the messages from the queen, the government in exile, and other resisters.

That organization, in turn, asked our group to join, which prompted a complex discussion for us. In the end, our leadership decided not to join. We were totally self-sufficient anyway, so we didn't really need to join. Our reasoning was this: the more people there were on the inside, the more danger there would be all the time. In addition, each member of our group was a Reformed Christian. The motive that prompted us to do Resistance work was not merely one of adventure.

Some of the other groups not in the LO did terrific Resistance work, but they also killed collaborators and blew up train lines. One time, all the men of the small town of Putten were taken away and locked up in terrible prison camps (of the 600 deported only 49 came back alive) just because an inexperienced group had killed a German officer on a road just outside of that village. We felt that some of the activities that precipitated such reprisals were not called for.

After I left the Bakkers in Eindhoven, my base of operations was at Barneveld, in The Veluwe, at the home of Jo and Dries Klooster, who had seven children. I was doing mainly Resistance work, but there was always mending and household work that had to be done when I was around. The arrangement was that I could stay in that house, almost as a base of operations, but

I would also help out with the work around the place — without pay, of course. But then, no one had any money. It was only December 1943, but already at that time no one had anything. And things would only get worse.

Watergoor, 1944

Above: Watergoor Farm, home of the Lozemans and a refuge for many during the Occupation.

Right: Symbols that Diet recorded on maps to indicate the position of German fortifications and troop movements for the Underground.

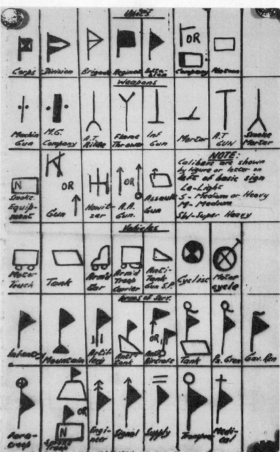

In February of 1944, under the name Willie van Daalen —
"Willie" was short for Wilhelmina, the name of our queen
— I moved my base of operations to the home of Aalt and Alie
Lozeman, a beautiful small farm just west of Nijkerk, Gelderland, on a quiet two-lane road that led to Bunschoten and
Spakenburg. The farm itself we called "Watergoor." It had a
very long sandy driveway; tall trees stood a short distance away
from the house, and there was a beautiful hedge of bushes
alongside. It was a wonderful place, not fancy at all but always
loving, a place that became not only a base of operations but a
home for me.

With the generosity of the Lozemans, that house was open
to anyone — shot-down pilots or *onderduikers* or Jews — anyone
needing a place to hide. During that time Aalt and Alie risked
their lives continuously, because the Germans had said that
anyone aiding enemy flyers would be shot on the spot. But Aalt
and Alie always told me, "Whoever you bring here — if you
vouch for them — those people may sleep here."

Aalt and Alie taught their two young children how to talk
about all visitors: they never mentioned names of people in the
house to those young kids. Farmers call their neighbors the
buurvrouw, the neighbor woman, and the *buurman*, the neighbor
man; when they use those terms, there is no need for names. So
those little children, Frits and Rietje, two and three years old,
always spoke of Uncle Ben and his wife Marie, for example, as
the *buurman* and *buurvrouw*. That way, if they were ever with
others who didn't know that Aalt and Alie were hiding people
on the farm, no one would suspect anything: the children were
merely speaking of the neighbors.

Aiding downed pilots was especially dangerous, but we
believed that if Allied pilots were risking their lives for us by
flying bombing missions, the least we could do would be to see

that they didn't fall into the hands of the enemy when their planes were shot down. After all, those pilots could have been sitting at home safely on the other side of the ocean. But they were trying to help us.

Those downed pilots would often hide in haystacks or barns unbeknownst to the farmer; once morning came, they would gamble on communicating with the farmer who came out to do his chores. Most of the people in that area would certainly know some member of the Resistance and knew how to contact a member of our group. We gave those pilots civilian clothing and hid them; then we handed them over to another Resistance group, who could get them to Portugal (a neutral country), where another group would help them on their journey back to England or Allied territory. Once we had delivered them, our part was finished. We had no idea what would happen to them; but we hoped, of course, that they would escape successfully.

One night, when Hein was at Watergoor and we were hiding some pilots, Hein's brother Henk happened to stop by. Hein had already told those pilots that his name was Pete (you never gave your real name). So when Henk came in, those pilots took one look at his face and couldn't believe their eyes. "If this is 'Pete,'" one of them said, pointing at Hein, "then this guy is 'Repeat.'"

Aalt and Alie kept a radio, which we listened to almost every night. The BBC always carried the news we wanted to hear, but in addition it often relayed messages to the Underground. In the middle of the broadcast we'd hear some odd phrase like "the apples are green," a message meant for specific listeners somewhere in occupied Europe. Three or four weeks after those pilots had laughed about Henk's resemblance to Hein, we were listening to the BBC broadcast one night, when suddenly we heard, "Regards to Pete and Repeat." We immediately thanked the Lord that those men had made it back to England safely.

People were coming and going all the time at the Lozemans' farm. But in addition to those who stayed for just a little while, Aalt and Alie were hiding Uncle Ben and his wife, the Jewish couple who had simply walked away from their own deportation more than a year earlier. All of the time Uncle Ben was in hiding at Aalt and Alie's, he kept working at falsifying the documents we would bring him. His wife learned to spin and knit; and she peeled potatoes and worked on the pears during canning time. Everyone helped out at Aalt and Alie's, and there were always people in hiding, sneaking in and sneaking out again.

Uncle Ben and Tante Marie had lots of work to do in that house, which was good, but they sometimes got on each other's nerves. Of course, most couples in that kind of cramped situation for two or three years — never seeing other people, locked up in a little room — would almost strangle each other in the end.

One day, while Uncle Ben was working hard at all of those documents and Marie was knitting and peeling, I brought him more things to do, and I found him very desperate.

"She!" — and the poor frantic man pointed at his wife — "this woman? She has this *lap hangen* [a piece of cloth]," and he pointed at her tongue, making flapping motions with his hand " — and all day long, she yaps and yaps and yaps. I'm going absolutely crazy here!"

The two of them could not, of course, leave that house at all: they could leave that room during the day only to go to the toilet, and that was something they could do only at certain times. On many Dutch farms the animals were right in the back of the house during the winter, in an area whose doors are always open, called the *deel*. No farms had toilets back then. In the winter the *deel* is like a barn, with stables, where the cows are chained in their stanchions. All the manure falls into a trench and is then pushed out into the *grup*, a manure pit.

At the end of that trench is a little space like a small bathroom. In that space you would find a wooden cover that you lifted up, and that was where humans did their business. Uncle Ben and his wife had their own little room, but they did not have a bathroom. Sometimes, when nature called, there would be neighbors in the *deel*; perhaps Aalt was making a sale or trying to buy a horse or pig. The Jews would then have to hold back and squeeze because they absolutely could not go when somone else was in the *deel*. It is easy to realize how hard that was.

One day Uncle Ben had to go to the bathroom, and there he sat at that little end of the stable, far away from the room where he was supposed to be hiding. To get back to his hiding place, he would have to go through the whole *deel*, and then a little doorway, through a roomy kitchen where the women did all the housework, including sewing; and then he had to go through the door to what was called the *heerd*, the big, beautiful room in the front of the house that was used only for weddings or funerals. In the *heerd* there were two doors that went to two small rooms: Uncle Ben and Marie had the left room off the *heerd*, and I had the room to the right when I slept there.

That day Uncle Ben was on the toilet, a long way from the *heerd*, out in the *deel*, and a neighbor came! Ben must have sat there in the *deel* for hours, because he had strict instructions never to come out if a neighbor was there. In the end he got very nervous. I went outside because I could move around, and I went to the little ventilation window in that cubicle.

"Can't I get out of the window, and run out of here?" he said.

"No, you have to stay there until he leaves," I said. We always had to keep our eye on people, always had to be very careful during the Occupation. Uncle Ben was ready to climb out of that window, even though it was very small. And if he were to get stuck or something, the commotion would certainly draw the neighbor's attention.

In that little room where Uncle Ben and Tante Marie stayed, Aalt and Hein's brother Henk had made a big opening in the floor: with a hook and a ring, they could lift a trapdoor on hinges, which opened to steps going down into a space where there was dry sand, a mat or a piece of linoleum, chairs, and a flashlight. There are no basements in the Netherlands, so no one would suspect a space there. If it became dangerous upstairs and they had to disappear quickly, Uncle Ben, Marie, and whoever might be in hiding at the Lozemans' farm just then, could go down into that square hole and hide. Occasionally, we would all do a drill.

"Go, go," we would say. "Danger is at the door."

Because it was imperative for them to hide quickly, we timed the drill. (I didn't have to hide, because it was widely known around Nijkerk that I was the maid at Aalt and Alie's. Everyone knew I was from The Hague, but few there knew that I was a friend of Hein Sietsma. To most people I was simply the maid who helped Alie with her housework.)

Uncle Ben's wife had been eating more and more the whole time she was there, getting heavier and heavier, her hips growing wider. All she did was spin and eat, sitting all the while — no real exercise at all. When she cleaned the potatoes, she didn't overeat; but when she peeled pears and apples, she ate very well. Eating was the only joy she had, and you couldn't blame her. And it was good food compared to what the rest of Holland was eating early in 1944.

So it got more and more difficult and time-consuming to get her down the steps quickly and into that hole. And when she finally did make it, she hated it down there. Anybody would!

It wouldn't be two or three minutes before we would hear her call, "May I come out now?" Perhaps she had claustrophobia, and who could blame her?

"No, you may not come out yet," we said. "And you may not yell, because some day it won't be just a drill, and then if you call out like that, it will be all over — just like that. You may not yell."

We were very serious about the test, but often smiles would cross our faces then.

Watergoor was a wonderful place to stay, but it was very confining for the Jews. Life was like that for every Jewish person we hid — very difficult. But at least they were alive.

Late in the evenings, when the outside doors of that farmhouse were finally locked and the children were put to bed, Uncle Ben and Tante Marie could finally come out of their little room, their hiding place. Then we would all sit under the lamp around the big kitchen table and eat pears or, in the winter, apples, all of us in socks or slippers. Alie would read a little meditation while we were eating fruit, after things had grown quiet and seemed more safe. It was a good time for our devotions. She would read something wonderful in the glow of that lamp. For all of us there — Aalt and Alie, Ben and Marie, other men and women there in hiding that night, and me — those were beautiful moments, safe in that warm farm home.

One Saturday night, after I had been there only a short while, we had to have our baths. There was no shower, of course; we all bathed in the warm kitchen, the only heated room. We took turns, and others stayed out of the kitchen while we bathed.

"We have so many people," Alie said, "and we need to conserve as much wood as we can to heat the water with. Would you mind if we heat just one big tub, and if the two of us take a bath together using that water?"

I had just arrived there and felt somewhat self-conscious. Later I thought of Alie as a sister, and I still do; but I will never forget that first time we bathed together. There we sat, each on our knees with that big tub of hot water between us. We first washed our faces and hair, and then our shoulders, and then down a bit further, and down further. We went slowly — first this part, then that part. But we were in this whole odd business together. Later everything became natural, and everyone became very much like family in her home. But that first time it was almost funny. I have to laugh thinking about how we washed and scrubbed in stages, not looking at each other.

This young wife took loads of risks, especially with her two little children and a third on the way. She often gave away loads of provisions to those who stayed at that farmhouse, some of whom she didn't even know. She was — and still is — a wonderful woman.

During that period I was needed in the Underground work because of the danger for men to be seen anywhere on the road. So I was almost constantly on the go; but whenever I was at the farm I helped Alie. With her husband and two children, Uncle Ben and Tante Marie, two of Aalt's brothers who were helping out, and me, there were often ten or twelve people, not to mention those Resistance people who might be hiding or staying for just a night or two. I said to Alie when I first began my stay there, "You have the neighbors and the *buurman,* and you have pilots here, and you have me. Now listen, you tell me what a maid would do if you had one that you paid, and I'll do it. And if I don't know how, you teach me."

"I'll remember what you said," she told me. "But why don't you start with the laundry? That would be very helpful."

There was very little soap, only what you could receive on your ration card. That meant a lot of scrubbing, because the loads were huge and there was no washing machine, only big wooden tubs that held hundreds of liters of water. Alie usually let the laundry pile up to try to conserve what little soap she had. Today, if you are sweaty, you change clothes; and if you sweat every day, you change every day. But at that time we kept clothes on for a week, and socks too — sweat or not.

I was still a novice at housework. I had learned some city housework at Eindhoven, but when I got to Watergoor I learned the real ins and outs of a household, and I loved it. On those mornings when I did the laundry, Aalt woke me up when he went out to start milking — around 4:30. I had to go out and pump water from the spring in the *deel*, then carry the yoke on my shoulders, balancing two pails, just like you see the Dutch girls doing on postcards. I had to carry that water to an outside furnace to heat the water. Aalt had cut some kindling and started the fire already; then I stoked it with twigs, and when finally that water was practically boiling, I had to carry it inside to the tubs on the *deel*.

In the meantime, I grated soap from the big lumps of brownish stuff they had made; it had to be grated or otherwise it wouldn't dissolve. Because there were so many people's clothes in that wash, we had to churn the heavy load with a large wooden paddle. Alie taught me every step. I had to start with all the white things, churning those clothes two hundred times to melt the soap and get them clean. Then I had to plop it all into the next tub, the rinse water; in the meantime I had to get more water warmed up. Then I repeated the same ritual with the medium-colored clothes, then the dark clothes, each load getting darker and darker, and finally the stinky socks. By that time, the water was dark and dirty.

The whole long job went in stages: first you churned and then you rinsed; then another rinse; then the white clothes went into the bleach — and it was real bleach — and then into something to get it whitish blue, *Reckits blauw* it was called. In March and April I had to spread all the sheets and everything on the meadow. That was to make them whiter still, but it was done only in certain months of the year because the ozone in the air during those months would bleach the wash. I learned a lot from Alie.

I worked and worked until breakfast, which was around eight o'clock. As a city girl, I had always eaten a couple slices of bread for breakfast. On the farm, at eight o'clock, after all that work, I came to breakfast with my stomach craving bread. But my stomach sometimes had to get accustomed to heavier stuff, like *zuurkool* (sauerkraut) with potatoes, leftovers from the day before (which was called *muisje*). That kind of breakfast often felt as heavy as lead in my stomach, though to the men, who'd also been working for hours and were accustomed to that kind of breakfast, the meal was wonderful. There were many in the Netherlands who suffered hunger during those years; but I was never hungry at Watergoor.

In the spring, when all the cattle went out into the meadow, the stable walls were caked with cow manure and laced with cobwebs. So Alie said, "Yep, Willie, now we start." The two of us wore our babushkas around our heads, and we hauled in the garden hoses and the pump, and we cleaned all the walls and whitewashed them. Work, work, work. Alie was pregnant, so I tried to help as much as possible; sometimes her sister came to help as well. And it looked great after everything was clean.

Occasionally, the men would slaughter pigs and we would all make sausage. Even *I* did that, a city girl taking meat and pushing it into the intestines — but even worse, scraping those intestines clean! All through the period that I was staying at Watergoor, from February to May 1944, there was always work to do on that farm, hard work. Most of the time I worked for our Resistance group; but whenever I was needed on the farm, I worked with Alie and the men, and I loved it.

That Aalt and Alie would take in a city girl for a maid was rather surprising to some of those farm folks. After all, I didn't even speak their dialect. People probably thought that I was a poor city girl who had come to The Veluwe because at least in the country there was enough to eat. To them I was Willie van Daalen, Alie Lozeman's help.

That spring their horse was expecting a foal. You can leave cows alone when they're calving, unless there is a specific problem; but the men on the farm told me that you have to watch a mare to make sure she bites the umbilical cord properly. The mare was about to foal at a time when the men were all busy with planting, so I told them I would sit with her at night. There I was out in the barn playing midwife to a pregnant mare. I remember sitting there, spinning yarn in the light of a little oil lamp, a city girl who knew nothing about farming, sitting on the *deel* beside that mother in pain, already beginning the birthing process. All around me there was darkness and perfect silence, except for the mother's pain. It was as if the war didn't exist in those hours. When the colt's time got very close, I had to wake the men up. The foal was born safely that night, a little mare foal that they called Kia.

Those everyday things happened in the middle of the war, in the midst of the danger I faced from day to day, while I was walking all over the country keeping our families supplied, playing mail carrier, and always lying. I loved some of the things I saw and felt and heard on that farm: the clothes in the tubs, the darkness on the *deel*, the meadow grass full of white sheets. When I did the laundry, I wore an apron, and that colt, Kia, loved to nibble on the knot I had tied in the back. She'd keep taking off that apron, just as if she didn't want me to work.

I remember the men talking about a *neurende koe* (in their dialect, "a cow in heat"). To me *neurien* meant "humming" — singing without words. I wondered how a cow could hum. What they were talking about was a cow that wanted to be with the bull. And they laughed their heads off when they found out that I was listening for the cow to hum but didn't hear a thing. The whole world of the farm was wonderful and strange, and I loved it dearly because it was such a relief through those months.

When I think about that time now, on the farm with Aalt and Alie, with Uncle Ben and Tante Marie cooped up in rooms off the *heerd*, when I remember whitewashing the walls of the *deel*, then it seems odd that at that very time both Hein and I were getting deeper and deeper into the Resistance, working harder and harder out there in the country. Somehow, even though we were still in constant danger, Watergoor gave me a sense of safety and strength. It was a beautiful place, and Aalt and Alie were wonderful people.

During that time a lot of Resistance work had to be done regularly, certain things on certain days, and it involved walking all over the region. What I did was most often up to me because I was in charge of that part of Gelderland, and I knew where the Jews were; they were *my* Jews, so to speak. There might well have been other places in that area hiding Jews, but I knew only where the Jews that we had placed were in hiding. When we got the ration cards from the guys who had robbed the supply offices, and earlier from the men who were falsifying cards, then my job was to get those cards to the people who were in hiding for whatever reasons.

One day Hein told me about a family in Nijkerk, a wonderful Christian family, who he thought would help us. We had two Jewish sisters who had been at Mies's apartment on Reinkenstraat and whom we needed to hide. So I went to this fine

Christian family, and the father, a very prominent man and a pillar of the church, met me at the door. I identified myself. He knew the Sietsma family, and he knew that Hein was engaged to me. I told him that we were desperate to get a place for these two Jewish girls. We *had* to find them a place.

"No," he said, "I don't want anything to do with it."

So I started working on his status as a good Christian, and that this was part of his obligation to serve the Lord. I really pleaded with him. I begged.

Still he said no.

I was desperate. I came up with every argument I could, but he was adamant. He wouldn't budge. He wouldn't take any Jews, he said.

"Please, I beg you," I said.

"No," he said, and he shut the door of his house in my face.

When I left, I was furious with this supposedly fine man, a well-known Christian, a man of God, who wouldn't help us.

After the war I found out that this man already *had* Jewish people in his home, people whom he must have taken in from some other group working to hide Jews. But he wasn't about to tell me that the reason he wouldn't take those two sisters into his house was that he already had some Jews in hiding. I had not grown up in Nijkerk and I was not an oldtimer in the area, so he might have thought that he couldn't really trust me totally. I didn't know it, but I put him in a terribly difficult position. And why should he tell me he had Jews anyway? Even if he could trust me, what he would tell me would only add to what I knew, and the more you knew about the whole business the more dangerous it was. That man of God might even have thought that it was in my own best interests not to know. So he lied, perhaps even to protect *me!*

It was stupid of me to go on with my argument and not to think of that possibility. But I was a young girl, even though what I did through those years made me mature very quickly.

As our list grew, the people who were hiding Jews were no longer just farmers. Many of the addresses I had to supply were city addresses. Those families were also suffering hunger, and they would have been hungry even if they hadn't chosen to hide Jewish people. It was a starving time. We *had* to get those people ration cards; it was a matter of survival. It was risky enough, such a sacrifice, simply to hide Jews; and then there was often no food either. So we had to get them supplied as best we could.

But they also had to have money. At first, some of the Jewish people still had some money, but later there was just nothing at all; they had used it all. We had to keep our people supplied. We couldn't just send them out into the street with nothing. So we got into fundraising after some time, because there were many Christians who said to us: "Sorry, we are scared of taking people in, but we will help—here's five hundred guilders."

So my job was to deliver ration cards and money when I could, but I also had to pick up stolen ration cards from addresses given to me, along with false identification. We didn't know where the robberies would take place, because we didn't pull those robberies ourselves. Our getting our hands on new ration cards depended on how close we were to the site of those robberies. Sometimes I had to hop on the train and take a bunch of ration cards along; sometimes Hein would come to the Lozemans' and bring a couple of hundred. Often I walked. During the war I walked all over the Netherlands.

Those ration books had to be distributed every month, so I made that the occasion for postal delivery too. Because the Jews were in such danger and, often as not, their families were broken up, they wanted to exchange letters with each other to find out how their loved ones were doing. For example, Ada, Herman's future wife, was hiding in one place, and her mother was in another. They needed to correspond with each other.

Usually I could make my own arrangements on where to go and what to do, and as a rule I did not feel that I was in real trouble all the time. For the men, the kind of traveling I did would have been much more dangerous, but for women it was not so. As a rule the Germans would not stop girls and start searching them. Nor were the Germans rapists, at least not typically; there was very stiff punishment for that kind of thing. Hitler wanted a pure race, of course, and while his soldiers may have raped Jewish girls in the camps in Germany, as far as I knew, such things did not happen in the Netherlands. It may have been because the Germans valued Aryan women, such as Dutch women, too highly. Even though we were their enemies, in the Netherlands they didn't have the reputation as rapists.

The worst indignity I ever suffered in my travels was that they would confiscate my bicycle. Five times German soldiers stole my bike from me. If they were walking and they wanted to bike, they would simply stop me and steal it. But at least one time, I wasn't about to give up my bicycle to that rotten Hun. My hair went up that time. I was more timid if I had a lot of dangerous stuff on me, because if I were to give them some trouble at a time like that, I might risk a confrontation. Then they could easily search me and find all the illegal papers or whatever it was I had with me. But that time I had nothing dangerous on me, and I wasn't about to part with my bike.

"No, that's mine," I said when one of them commanded me to get off my bike. But the man had a revolver, and he fired a shot right next to my foot. In other words, he was saying, if you don't give it to me, the next bullet will go into your foot. So I gave it up.

After my bike was gone, I had to go to Amersfoort one time on foot to try to get some money from a wealthy family named Pon, people who owned a bicycle factory. By that time you couldn't get shoes anymore, so I was walking all over on the crummiest shoes. Your shoes wear out when you walk all those distances. When I got to the address, a beautiful house in Amersfoort, at 11:00 in the morning, Mrs. Pon said, "Come in. Come in. We are going to have lunch, and you can eat with us."

Now I didn't know the people very well, even though I had been there now and then to ask for contributions. They were so wonderful and warm, and they had a lively family of young kids. I heard Mr. Pon say something to his wife, and then I heard her say, "Ja, ja," and then disappear. When she came back, looking at my feet, she carried in her hand a pair of the most gorgeous leather mountain-climbing shoes. It was her own pair of lined hiking boots, made of leather with thick soles.

"Are these your size?" Mrs. Pon asked. "They are my mountain shoes, and they're just standing here doing nothing. We are not going anywhere. You put them on."

They fit perfectly.

"You keep them," she said.

Walking all over the Netherlands, even outside Gelderland, after that was a whole different experience with those new boots. I wore them until the end of the war, and they were a wonderful blessing.

Because I was seeing so much of what was happening in our little country, I began to work at times with a man we nicknamed "Klein Jantje," a man who did a lot of espionage for the Underground and for the Allies as well. (*Jan* is a very common name in the Netherlands, and *klein* means small: "Little Jan.") I respected him very highly because when the South was liberated he would cross from occupied territory to liberated territory in the south, across big, dangerous rivers, and back again to occupied territory. I used to wonder whether I was strong enough to do such a thing. I imagined myself free, somewhere in Belgium perhaps, and I found it very difficult, even in my imagination, to be strong enough to come back again into Nazi-occupied Netherlands when I could have put it all behind me. But Klein Jantje, one of the finest men I've ever known, risked great danger and did it several times, back and forth.

Sometimes I gathered information for him. He would give me maps plus descriptions and photos of military equipment — tanks, artillery, etc. — and the flags that referred to troop movements and the rank of the commanding officers. I would locate these German deployments on my trips and record what I saw on those military maps. I recorded, for example, what the Germans were building, their fortifications and troop movements, and coordinated on the maps how far apart they were in meters, in degrees and minutes, and so forth, so that the intelligence planners could draw it all out. I would take the map of Amersfoort, let's say, and draw out what I had seen around that city and return it to Klein Jantje and his spy network. The men in espionage would ask me to collect that kind of information because they knew I was walking all over the country by that time.

It was always exciting, but it was also always dangerous. And fear takes a toll finally: when you live in danger from moment to moment, the constant tension becomes very wearying. Every step I took on the roads of Gelderland was nerve-wracking, because I was secretly carrying the very material that could turn out to be my own death warrant.

Watergoor, 1944

▲   ▲

April 25, 1944

What shall I write? That I am so very unquiet for the last couple of days, and that I yearn so much for the end of all this? I long so much for the end of the war, but I do not deserve it for lately I have not been praying for it. Still I cannot live without you, Lord. And when I hear now that a lot of action is happening again, the Allies making progress, I should be grateful for everything you're doing.

from the journal of Diet Eman

▼   ▼

Leeuwarden and
Zwijndrecht, 1944

Top, in both German and Dutch: "For the German army only."
Bottom, in German: "Careful what you say — the enemy is listening!"

In April 1944, I was doing my daily work, Hein was traveling through the whole of the Netherlands, and we had in our possession stolen ration cards and loads of false IDs. We kept a post office box where we would hide that material when we had simply accumulated too much. We didn't want to endanger the lives of the people we were staying with. If we were discovered with all that stolen stuff, we were sure that the people we were staying with would likely be shot, just as we would.

Hein and I had spoken often about our coming wedding. We were engaged and had already received our wedding license, though we'd never set the date firmly. But the work we were doing didn't seem likely to stop until after the war. We really wanted to, but one obstacle was that both of us were now operating under false names. We knew the mayor of the city of Kamerik, near Utrecht, a good man who was himself working in the Resistance. He told Hein we should come to Kamerik — it was right on the routes we traveled — and he would marry us. "If you want to get married under your false names, that's no problem," he said. "I'll marry you. Then after the war, you can change your false names back to your real names."

We let our parents know about our feelings, but they were very much against it. Father Sietsma felt that we should not get married because . . . well, nine months and two days later we would probably have a baby. That would make just one more to hide. He himself had twelve children, so that was the first thing that came to his mind. My parents felt that as long as the Gestapo was still keeping an eye on our house, they themselves would be unable to attend our wedding, no matter where it would be, because they would perhaps be followed. And we also felt it wouldn't be safe for them.

We discussed it, and we finally decided that with the years already behind us, we might just as well wait and get married when the war was over, which we thought would be soon. If we had known that the Occupation would go on as long as it did, I think we would have gotten married. But no one ever thought the war would take so long to end. So we simply assumed that when this whole business was over, we could marry each other the right way — with our own pastor, our own ceremony, and with our parents and all our friends in attendance. It would be such a happy day, we thought we certainly would want to share it with our parents. And we wanted so badly to be free.

One day Hein sent me a note: "Diet, we haven't seen each other for weeks and that's not good. We should keep in closer contact." We were both very busy, in constant danger, and I was often away from Watergoor.

"See that on Saturday night" — that was April 22 — "you are at Aalt and Alie's. Be there, Diet, because I'll come to pick you up on Sunday morning, and we'll have that day for ourselves. We'll go to Amersfoort to church and there is communion, and then have Sunday for ourselves." Ab van Meerveld and his girlfriend Riek had been married and were now expecting a baby. He said we could have Sunday dinner with them. "Then we will have time to talk," he wrote.

There were some places where Hein could not go during daylight by this time because the authorities were searching for him so carefully. He could not visit towns where people knew him, such as Nijkerk; I could still visit Nijkerk because I was the city girl under the false name.

So he picked me up, and we went from Nijkerk to Amersfoort on our bicycles, about forty minutes away. This was a large city, where few people would know us. We went to church, and had communion, and then after church we biked to the van Meervelds' in Barneveld.

After dinner most farmers take a nap on Sunday afternoon

because they have to get up so early every morning. But Hein and I left and went for a bike ride through the beautiful tree-lined countryside around Barneveld. It was spring, and The Veluwe was wonderfully green, with fruit trees in bloom. We talked about serious matters, and it was as if Hein had a feeling about the future. He talked about what I should do if he were ever to be arrested, how the Resistance work should go, and then at one point he read John 14 to me: "In my Father's house there are many mansions; if it were not so I would have told you."

We talked seriously, but we had fun too. And then it was evening. Hein had to go back to Friesland, and I had to go back to Aalt and Alie's because the next day there was work to do again. We could not take the main routes, so we traveled on inside roads that passed by meadows and very close to a woods. Hein was very tall, so when we talked while riding bikes, I had to look up at him constantly.

It was right at that moment, when we were on our bikes on that lonely road with no one else around, that I clearly heard a voice say, *Kijk nog maar goed naar hem* ("You'd better have a good look at him"). I heard the voice so clearly that I thought someone nearby had said the words. I looked around, but there was nobody. I thought I had dreamed it. Then I heard it again, a second time. I cannot explain it, not even today. I didn't dare to tell Hein what I'd heard, but I did look up at him, because that's what the voice had commanded me to do. I must have been staring, and he must have been bewildered. He said to me, "Why are you looking at me that way? Tell me why."

I didn't dare to tell him.

"Nothing. Nothing at all," I said.

We talked about other things after that and laughed as we biked past the places that had become very familiar to me out in this area where he'd grown up, the farms and the pastures.

The rest of that trip back to Watergoor went fine, both of us full of anxiety about the future yet so hopeful and confident when we were with each other. Sometimes I would look at him on the bike and smile. He would see me and break out laughing. But I will never forget that voice that spoke to me twice, telling me to look at him closely.

He brought me to the farm, and we said goodbye. We said we would try to meet more often, just as he had said in the letter. We said we should take more time for ourselves. I walked back into the house with Alie, and watched him bike up the long path back to the road. He was on his way to the places in Friesland where no one knew Hein Sietsma, places where he could operate under his alias. But we nearly always had in our possession some kind of dangerous contraband, and that Sunday as he left Watergoor, Hein was loaded down with illegal stuff.

A few days later the man I was to marry was stopped by the Gestapo on the train and searched when he was near Leeuwarden, the capital of Friesland. The authorities checked him over very carefully because he was of the age to be sent to Germany. He had false papers, of course, that identified him as a pastor, so he was safe in that respect. But that day, April 26, when they searched him, they found ration cards, IDs, and so forth, documents that were plainly stolen, and lots of recent photos of our royal family, in exile, which clearly had come from England. That instant he fell into deep trouble, the deepest he had ever been in.

While I was with Aalt and Alie, still reminiscing about our weekend, fearing the voice that had made me so apprehensive as Hein rode along beside me on that lonely road in The Veluwe, he was being put in prison in Leeuwarden.

He was held there for a few days and interrogated before they moved him on to the prison camp at Amersfoort. His guard during that transfer was a Dutch policeman. His situation must have seemed to him to be very dismal at that moment, so he understood that he had only two chances with that guard. The guard might be very happy to collaborate with the Germans in that prison; several Dutch people there did collaborate. On the other hand, this Dutch prison guard might be someone who had decided to stay in that position after the Germans took over just to see how he could help other people loyal to the royal family. There were those who did that too, and those very brave people — because they could not reveal what they were doing — were often shunned and despised by people from the Underground, people like us, since we didn't know what they were up to.

Years before, Hein had known a girl named Hieke Pars who lived in Leeuwarden. He had told me about her, and I remember feeling jealous about his former attraction to her. He could not remember the girl's address exactly, but in his cell he wrote a note to explain to this girl how she should let Ab van Meerveld know what had happened to him. The guard would have to try to find out where that girl lived. Of course, he did not write everything out explicitly; instead, he disguised what he wanted to tell Ab in a very cryptic way.

When the guard came, Hein gave him that note, hoping and praying for the best. That Dutch guard turned out to be a good man who happened to have some knowledge of the young woman because they were of the same church affiliation. So this man saw to it that Hieke Pars received that note. And she warned Ab. I think that she may have known before that time that Ab was Hein's best friend. There was some church connection between the three of them: they had attended a convention together or a retreat for young people, and Hein and Ab may have stayed at the Pars home in Leeuwarden. Perhaps Hein never even mentioned Ab's name in that note;

I'm sure that he wrote that note in such a way that if that guard would have been a Nazi sympathizer, he would not have been able to discover who Hein was referring to. Life would have become very dangerous for Ab if the guard could have figured out the whole arrangement.

So that message got to Ab, who didn't know anything about what had happened, on April 30, 1944. That same day, I received a message from Ab, who was the leader of our group. "Diet," it said, "I want you to come here immediately." I hopped on my bike happily that Sunday, a week after my Sunday with Hein, and I went to Ab van Meerveld's home. It was my birthday that day, and I thought this would be such fun. Perhaps Hein would be there too. Perhaps it would be a surprise party.

But when I entered that place, Ab was very serious.

"Diet," he said, "I have to tell you that Hein was arrested last Wednesday." And when he told me that the Germans found him carrying stuff, I knew immediately how serious it was for him, and I knew what might very well happen to him. Of course, one can hope. One can always hope.

Hein had also given Ab instructions to empty the post office box. He had been carrying a key when he was arrested. Ab had a key too, and so did Pete Hoogerwerff, another member of our group in Zwijndrecht, and my brother Albert.

The instructions were to warn everybody that Hein had been arrested. Then Hein had a special warning for me: "Please know that they will be looking even more closely for Diet because I had papers on me that pointed to her work under the name she is now using. Under no circumstances should Diet come to Friesland, because they are looking very hard for her."

The Germans were already looking for me under my real name, so now they could be looking for two of me — Diet Eman and Willie van Daalen.

"Be very careful," Hein's note said. "Warn everybody that they must use extreme caution because of my arrest."

Ab still had his own work, of course, and none of that could be halted. My brother Albert offered to empty that post office box in The Hague, which was extremely dangerous because the Germans could very well catch him there. At that point, we didn't know exactly what information the Germans had. If they had found that key on Hein, then tortured him into giving more information, they could well have staked out the place, waiting for someone to show up and empty that box of its contents. Albert went there with Bob, another young man who worked with us and was our contact with the LO (the national Underground organization).

Ab assigned me the task of going around to tell all of our Resistance people what had happened, and for a week I traveled all around the area on my bike and by train, telling all of those who needed to know that Hein was arrested and in prison in Friesland. I also had to pick up new ration cards and IDs for distribution elsewhere. And because Hein had also left explicit instructions that I had to get another new name, I spent some time creating another new alias as well.

Then, on the morning of Monday, May 8, I packed up all the material my brother had taken from the post office box and given to me. I was to travel around, warn others in more distant places about what had happened, and carry the contents of the post office box to Bob Visser in The Hague. That morning I had such a strong feeling — I don't know how to explain it — that I was going to be arrested that day.

I loved Hein's ring on my finger, of course, but I thought that if I was arrested, then it could be used against me and against everyone else as well. It said "Hein," after all, and the Germans would surely ask, "Okay, Willie, who is this 'Hein'?"

Hein had been arrested under a false name, Hendrik de Jong, but if the Gestapo started torturing, you just never knew what they might learn. So I took my ring off. I'd never done it before, and I just hated to do it. But I did, and I gave it to Alie. I told her what I had so clearly envisioned.

"Alie," I said, "I have a feeling that I am going to be arrested today. Will you keep this ring?" I slipped it into her hand. "I'm sorry, but I just have these very strong feelings."

"Willie," she said, "you're nervous — that's all. With Hein arrested, you're just extra nervous."

"Sure I'm nervous," I told her. "I know that."

She thought it was all in my head, and she tried to console me. But to me, even when I was getting dressed, it was very clear that I was about to be arrested. Almost all the underwear I had was light blue, but I had one pair that was black. I was so sure I was going to be arrested that I had worked it out in my mind: if I go to prison, at least I won't see all the dirt on black. So I put on black underwear. I had knitted myself woolen knee socks that were very warm, and I put those on; plus those good shoes I had received as a gift from the Pon family. So I was dressed well. If I was to be arrested, at least I'd be ready for prison.

Off I went that morning, the envelope I was carrying full of stolen documents, but my ring safe with Alie. I stepped onto the train and took it to Zwijndrecht, where I was to meet Piet Hoogerwerff and get more papers.

When I got there, it was about lunchtime. They had an organ, I remember, and I sat at that organ and played a Dutch hymn that expressed total reliance on God. I felt just shattered by what I had learned about Hein: everything I'd hoped for in the future, all of the plans I'd made — we'd made — for what was going to happen after the war, when ordinary life and freedom would return — all of that was now in jeopardy because he had been caught.

When I left Piet Hoogerwerff's, I put all that stolen material from the post office box, as always, in my blouse.

"Are you going to The Hague?" Piet asked. When I told him I was, he gave me more papers. Inside were our orders for a couple of Allied pilots who'd been shot down and some photos to enable those pilots to get IDs. There were blank IDs inside as well, some falsified ones done by Uncle Ben, and loads of ration cards. There was also 500 guilders donated by someone who didn't dare to do things with the Resistance. All of it was extremely dangerous material, especially the pilots' false identifications.

That afternoon, May 8, 1944, I walked to the Zwijndrecht railroad station, which wasn't far. The train I was supposed to take wasn't leaving for forty-five minutes, and it was practically empty when I got on, so I took a window seat. I had a book — I still remember the title, *Toen De Herten Riepen* ("When the Deer Called") — and I sat and read while the train slowly filled. At quarter to two or so, the train suddenly lurched forward, jarring me from the book I was reading. It had finally filled up, and it was departure time; automatically I looked out the window.

Walking along the moving train, as it was already gathering speed, were six Gestapo. I hadn't consciously counted the cars on that train, but there were six Gestapo and six cars. So they jumped on and started checking everybody's ID. They often did what we called *steekproeven*, random checks, on whatever train they happened to choose, just here and there, hoping to come up with something. We never knew where, or how, or at what time.

As soon as they hopped on that train, I thought, *O Lord, what's going to happen now? Maybe these officers are just passengers.* But they spread out through the whole train, each taking a car. One of them started checking identification right across the aisle from me.

"*Ausweis Papiere!*" he said. I was fluent in German, but I had made my vow never to speak German while they occupied our country. The woman across from me showed her ID, and he gave it back — then the next and the next. He was moving fast, really fast; so I thought that maybe I would be okay.

My heart was going *bump, bump,* noisily in my chest, because the Gestapo had already been searching for me for more than a year. They had been searching my parents' home in The Hague every two or three weeks — sometimes at three in the morning, then again maybe at four in the afternoon. And they were still looking for me. I now had false papers, which identified me as Willie Laarman, my fourth false name, and I had this envelope with all the stolen stuff, plus 500 guilders, plus orders for IDs for pilots.

I kept my head down, pretending I was engrossed in my book, but I was so scared that the words just danced before my eyes. Finally he got to me, and I had to give him my new ID. He had looked at all the other IDs very quickly and then given them back. But he did not give mine back.

"*Wann haben Sie das bekommen?*" he said to me.

I told him in Dutch that I didn't know what he was saying because I didn't speak German.

He looked away, hardly concerned, and went on jabbering in German. I told him again that I didn't speak German, and this went on for a while, even though I knew very well what he was saying. Then a helpful passenger said to me, "He wants to know when you got this ID."

"Oh, the date of issue is on it," I said in Dutch. "Everybody my age got it in November 1941."

He looked at it, and then he wanted my stamp card and my ration card as well. In the meantime, the other five officers had finished checking their cars and had all come to my car and were looking at my ID. They all started laughing their heads off.

In 1941 the Germans had handed out millions of IDs to the Dutch population, to everyone sixteen years old and over. By 1943, the original supply had run out, and they printed hundreds of thousands extras. Those printed in 1943 had the word "Nederlander" printed in black instead of the blue used in 1941. My age group had received their IDs in 1941, with "Nederlander" in blue; but what I had in my possession was an ID from a batch printed in 1943, with black ink, and thus clearly stolen in one of our last robberies. In the chess game that the Gestapo and the Resistance were playing, I was one of the people who walked right into their trap.

Now I had to come up with a reason why I had a plainly false ID and was nevertheless innocent, which was very difficult. What happened next was probably the greatest miracle of my whole war experience.

The train stopped at the Delftsepoort station in Rotterdam. The six Gestapo officers, one or two of whom wore civilian clothes, made me get off the train and sit on a bench in the station. In the busy Dutch railroad stations there are benches on both sides of the tracks, and they are often full of people, sitting on them or standing beside them. So there I sat, with the six guys around me. I opened my blouse, even though it was a chilly day. I hate to be cold around my neck, so I always take my scarf to protect my neck against a chill. But that cold day I opened my blouse buttons as if I were hot. As a matter of fact, I felt as though there were flames shooting out of me, because those papers in my bra would be enough to kill me, possibly a number of others, and risk so much of our whole operation. I was looking for a chance to pull the envelope out and throw it away.

I knew from many friends who had been in prison that,

once you got there, they would have you undress completely and then they would certainly find what they were looking for. It would be "up against the wall" for those found with the kind of things I had that day — the firing squad.

I was still hoping to get married to Hein; my wedding dress was already hanging up at home. I didn't want to be arrested, and I didn't want to die. I prayed on that bench in that station like I've never prayed in my life. I pleaded with God: "Lord, if it's necessary, then we will give our lives, but if it is at all possible, grant that those six men give me half a minute so that I can get rid of this envelope."

But if one wasn't looking, another one was. If it had been only one or two, I think I would have had a chance; but six men in a half circle around me was just too many. But miracles still happen, even if we don't think they do. The tallest of those men — he was well over six feet — had on a shiny gray plastic raincoat. We had never seen plastic in our life before: it had just been discovered as a material for things like clothing. This tall man's raincoat was a very long military coat made of plastic.

One of the others said: "Is that one of those new coats? Is it really waterproof?"

Of course, I could understand what they were saying to each other. "Yes," the tall one said, "I've been in a terrific rainstorm and it's waterproof."

"Oh, what a great coat," another said, "and it has so many pockets."

"You think that it has a lot of pockets on the outside," the tall one said, "you should see the inside."

At that he opened his coat, spread it out wide, and all the heads looked inside to see the pockets — every one of their heads. While those men stood there peering inside that long coat, I pulled the envelope out of my bra and hurled it as far as I could. I certainly didn't want the stuff inside to fall right under the bench.

Now in that Delftsepoort railroad station there are several platforms from which individual trains depart. The bench I was sitting on was not close to the tracks, so my throw would not reach the rails; they were too far away. So I threw it with all the force I could to the right, because there were people all over that area, going up and down the stairs, and those Gestapo men would never have known who dropped it. They could not arrest all of the people walking on that platform. I just had to get the envelope far enough away from me so that its contents had no clear relationship to me.

Even after it was out of my hands, I was still very nervous, because that big envelope was glittering, like something bright, against the concrete platform. They could have picked it up and claimed it wasn't there before. Once it was down there on the platform, though, it could be mistaken for anything — a bill or a receipt someone had dropped in a traveling rush. People lose their papers all the time. So once I had gotten it out of my hands, I knew I had a much greater chance of escaping with my life.

This one single moment changed my whole attitude at the time. It was such a miracle to me that I thought of it later, when I was quiet in my cell. It says in the Bible, "Before you have prayed, I have already answered." I believed that already that chilly morning when the German put on his raincoat, God knew that I would need that plastic raincoat.

I was still nervous, because I was so afraid that one of them would pick up that envelope and somehow link it to me. I had a very suspicious mind at that time, and I knew the Gestapo had a very suspicious mind as well. But they never paid any attention to it. I wanted to get away from that spot very badly, just so they wouldn't find that envelope. It was raining outside, so I told them I was chilled. I wouldn't speak any German, but one of them could speak broken Dutch. He turned to me and said "Well, what are you trying to tell us?"

"I am so chilly," I said again. "Would you mind if we stand in the tunnel there, where it's a bit more protected?"

Then I heard him say to the others in German, "Leave me alone with her. I'll get it out of her myself."

The others said it was okay, and he walked with me to the tunnel. Through all of the Underground work, one picked up an ability to read human character and understand people very quickly. What I read about this Gestapo soldier was that he was a big mouth and vain: he wanted to show off to the others — all of them — what he could do.

When we got into that tunnel and he started talking, I began to act really stupid. I thought to myself, *Diet, your best chance is to be really dumb. You haven't the slightest idea how you could have received a bad ID.*

So I said, "You know, sir, when you search those trains, what exactly are you looking for?" I talked to him as if I didn't have a clue as to what the whole business was about.

"Well," he said, "we're looking for spies and for Resistance people."

"Oh, I see," I said. "And do you do this every day?"

"Yes, we do this every day," he said, really proudly, as if he were an important guy.

"And . . . and do you catch many?" I said it as if I had absolutely no idea what was going on.

"Oh, yes," he said, "we just caught a spy from England, and he had all hidden negatives of pictures — "

"Really? . . . and you shot him?"

"No, he tried to run away," he said.

"And then you shot him, of course," I said, "like you do with bandits."

"No, we caught him," he said. "I can run fast."

And then I said, "I can run fast too — should we try it?" I kind of joked with him, as if I weren't nervous at all. "How about we race — can I have a head start?"

Then the train pulled in, and he had to go back with me to the others. In all that time he had written nothing on his yellow pad. He had taken the lead in the tunnel, but that whole time we were away from the envelope lying there on the platform. And that was my aim.

When the train pulled in, they put me in one of those cars with a sign *Nur für Wehrmacht* ("Only for German Army"). There was not a soul in that car.

I heard the one man again tell the others to leave him alone with me, because he could get it all out of me by himself. But by that time I was so relieved that I had gotten rid of all those dangerous documents, that I could play the little chess game again, and I could see some light at the end of the tunnel. I was still scared, but I humored this big-mouth German, even laughed with him. In that tunnel he had gotten nothing from me; and when he talked to me on the train, I told him I thought it must have been very interesting to catch an English spy. I was still playing dumb.

They were taking me to The Hague, only a short distance from the Delftsepoort station. When we arrived, the others came to the compartment, and still there was nothing written on his yellow pad. He'd gotten nowhere. The whole thing between the Germans and us was really a game. We had to find a tactic, a strategy, and then we had to have the nerve to carry it out. I saw right away that this guy was boastful and vain, so I played the fool.

But when we rolled into The Hague, I was again petrified, because I knew so many people there. I had already been in hiding for a long time, and here I was being brought back into the city where I was born and had worked for years, into the very neighborhood where I knew so many people. It was 4:30 or quarter to five, the time when the afternoon trams left downtown with office workers; and there we were at the railway station that was just around the corner from my old bank. This was precisely the time that the bank was getting out, so I prayed that no one from the bank would step on this tram and say, "Hi, Diet, how are you? We haven't seen you for years!"

The Germans took me to the Line 8 tram, which goes past the bank to the *Binnenhof,* the inner city with all its old government buildings that the Germans had confiscated, to the headquarters of the Gestapo. They were smart. Some of the men who had arrested me were in uniform, but others were not. They deliberately spread themselves out. Those in civilian clothes sat in my row.

The moment I stepped onto the tram, the conductor came for my dime. I don't know where I got the courage, but I looked right into his face and I said, "I'm not paying."

He seemed shocked. "Then you get off," he said.

"Yes, please," I said, "that's exactly what I want. I'm here against my will."

All the people were looking at me, and the conductor said, "But you should pay."

"No, I am here very much against my wishes, and that man" —I said and pointed to one of them, the man who wore the *NSB* (Dutch Nazi) pin — "that man and that man have put me here, and I don't want to be here. I won't pay."

Every passenger stared at the sourpuss with his NSB button.

"If you want money from me to ride on the tram," I told

the conductor, "then you should get it from them because I don't want to be here."

The conductor looked around a bit. "Oh, you're being arrested?"

"Yes," I said.

At that moment everybody on that tram knew who was Gestapo, *and* they knew I was being arrested. The Gestapo always much preferred that no one know what was happening. They never wanted to draw any attention to an arrest; but I had to be assertive because of the bank and its closing time. Of course, they had no idea that I had ever worked there, but I wanted everyone to be aware of what was happening, and to be wary.

I also thought that I might get a chance to escape. If the rest of those good people in the tram knew what was going on, and if there had been an accident, let's say, then I might be able to simply get lost in the crowd. I wanted to take advantage of anything I could.

The conductor went directly to the sourpuss. "If you want her to ride, you pay the dime," he said.

The sourpuss paid the dime. That was another little moment that built up my morale, and I needed it. Once that envelope was gone, I had felt such inner gratefulness to God for that miracle that I wondered if some of my courage to be that cocky was attributable to that. But also, we in the Resistance had been told never to show fear when arrested: "Never be afraid, or you'll have a terrible time." So when I was arrested, I played dumb and I was not going to show that I was afraid.

When we got to the *Binnenhof*, I was told to get off the tram and go into that big hall. The Gestapo men had taken my overnight bag, gone all through it, and found some notes I had written to myself in a kind of code that was comprehensible to no one but me. I'd taken shorthand classes, but this was a system of signs and words beyond shorthand that would have been indecipherable to anyone. It was my own secret language.

"What is this?" they asked.

"These are shorthand notes," I said. "They're letters that I write to friends — but I make notes and then later write them. They are just private things, letters. When I think of something that I want to write to my friends in Paramaribo, then I jot it down." My new ID said that I was born in Surinam, whose capital city was Paramaribo, a place where there was, at that time, no mail connection.

"Read it," they said.

"These are just scribblings, not even complete sentences," I told them. "I have to sit back and think again about what it is."

"Read them," they said. "This is spy stuff — that's what it is."

So I made something up, something that sounded innocent. Of course, they couldn't really tell whether I was telling the truth or not, but there was nothing they could do.

Once they had gone through my suitcase and tried to pry things out of me, they quit and put everything back. There I was, sitting in the *Binnenhof,* the lion's den. They told me they would take me to prison, and then they left me alone. I was going to be carted to prison in one of those awful *overvalwagens,* "paddy wagons," special cars for prisoners. At that moment, however, all the *overvalwagens* were out making raids to pick up Jews. There wasn't a single car, not one, to transport me to prison; so I had to sit there for a long time. It was after five, and I was sitting there waiting beside a German who was writing reports on his desk.

I was relieved that so much danger was behind me; all of this was going to be over for a while, I thought. Then suddenly

I remembered something. My mother had always worried about my nourishment during the four years I had been in this Resistance work. She had been to our family doctor for herself, maybe her nerves, and she had told him that she was terribly worried about the toll the work was taking on me. She could confide in him because he had been our family doctor for many years. "Is there anything that you have that she could use?" she had asked. "Diet has such an irregular life." The doctor had given her a little bottle of iron and vitamins, on which he had written "Mrs. Eman," my mother's name. Mother had given it to Bob, our Hague contact, and he had given it to me. For some stupid reason, I had not taken the label off, and this little bottle that I had just received was in my suitcase.

Oh God, I thought, *they have been looking for Diet Eman for more than a year already. They've searched our house, and I have my real name right on that little bottle in the suitcase. I have to get to that suitcase and get that label off.*

The Gestapo officer was sitting behind his desk, writing furiously on documents and reports.

"Sir?" I said. He looked up. "It's been hours since I've had anything to eat. I am terribly hungry." I pointed at my little suitcase. "There is a little sandwich in that suitcase. Would you mind if I eat that?" Piet Hoogerwerff's wife, Mijntje, had packed me a sandwich before I left.

"Go get it," he said.

It was a small suitcase with hard sides, a weekend suitcase. I flipped it open with the lid toward him and took that sandwich out. I was so nervous that I didn't have a drop of saliva in my whole mouth. Eating that sandwich was like chewing pure sand. But while I was chewing it, I was scraping my mother's name off that bottle of vitamins with the fingernails of my other hand. And I got it off!

Forcing the sandwich down was the hardest part. And when that pill bottle label was off, I wondered whether there was anything else in the suitcase that might reveal my real identity. When I closed the suitcase a paddy wagon had come for me. Once more, the same cocky Gestapo officer, who had been doing other things, climbed in, thinking he could break me. He was the one to take me to prison, and he sat next to me.

"Well," he said, "it's too bad what has happened. You have not told us anything, and now you have to go to prison. There isn't any way I can avoid that for you. I offered to help you, you know, but you didn't take it. Now the big boss has said I have to take you to prison."

But then he said, "There is one thing: if you tell me why you have false papers — and you do have false papers, you know — then you will get preferred treatment in prison. Every day you may choose what you eat, and you always get a drink before your meal."

I wasn't about to admit that I had false papers. At that point I had no idea what I was being accused of, so I thought I'd listen to him to determine why they thought I should be trudged off. I hadn't said anything yet because I didn't know what kind of story I would have to make up. His proposal was really an insult to my intelligence. If I were an actual spy, I wouldn't betray anything for a glass of water or a glass of wine. If I were innocent, I couldn't say anything anyway. He thought I was a moron; but, of course, that was how I had portrayed myself.

I knew there was no preferred treatment in prison. He thought that I might fall for that stupidity, but I had had too many friends in prison already, and I knew there was nothing like "preferred treatment." You learned to think and react quickly during that time. I realized then that I had convinced him that I was really stupid, so this is what I did. The Dutch word for applesauce — *appelmoes* — seems to me like a kind of silly-sounding word. I looked at that cocky guy, and I thought, "Okay, brother, if you believe I'm that stupid, then I can play a game with you." So I asked him, "Really, sir, do you think I could even have *appelmoes?*"

If he'd had any brains, he should have known I was pulling his leg. I couldn't think of anything more stupid to say than — *appelmoes*.

"Sure, sure," he said, very happy. He couldn't see that I was being idiotic. That little conversation was another inside victory for me. I thought to myself, "Brother, you are really the end!"

When we got to the prison at Scheveningen, I stood there in front of the gate, staring up at the big wall. There was a little door there, and you had to press the button to get response from the inside. There we stood, but this man waited for a moment before pressing the button. "Well — " he said and held his finger there, "I haven't yet pressed the button. You can still tell me why you have that false ID. You can still tell me. I haven't pressed it yet, you see?" I remembered the principle of never giving them the feeling that you are afraid when you are arrested, or they will despise you. After throwing away all the evidence, I had thought, *Well, Lord, you've helped me here.* I was in good shape: I knew that whatever was still in front of me could be really tough, but I had confidence by that time that I had a chance.

So I looked at this cocky German, and I took his hand and I pressed that button myself! He immediately slapped me, but I had asked for it. It was as if I'd said to him, "Come on, brother." I had mocked him right to his face, and he knew it.

I felt peace, even though I was still scared to death. I thought that, whatever would happen to me — I could still be killed, I didn't know — and in what I'd already been through, God was in control.

The Prison at Scheveningen

Illustration by A. van den Heuvel from E. P. Weber, *Gedenkboek van het Oranje Hotel*
(Amsterdam: Uitgeverij H. Nelissen, 1947).

When I first arrived at the Scheveningen prison, I had to stand with my face to the wall, all cells behind me. I was horribly frightened to be inside a prison where I knew cruel things had happened. When the guards stepped out for a minute, I could hear voices: "What's the latest news on the outside?" "Have you heard the BBC?" "What does Radio Orange say?" I wanted to tell them what I knew, but I was standing very close to the German offices, and I thought the voices might be the Gestapo and not real prisoners. If I were to tell them the latest news, it would be clear that I listened to the BBC. I didn't know who it was who wanted to know; so I didn't say a thing.

Then I was ordered to undress, and they searched me, straight up and bent over. Thank God, I had got rid of everything. Then I was sent to cell 306 in the A-corridor, where I was the fifth prisoner in a one-person cell, three meters long and two meters wide. I don't remember all the names of the other four prisoners who were there that first night; but there was only one bunk, a hard bed in the back with a thin mattress, and an old Jewish lady was lying on it. She was in her seventies, and her name was Mrs. Speier.

One of the prisoners, Lies Karel, was a nurse who had done a lot of good Resistance work before she was arrested. I eventually grew to trust her, though at the very beginning I trusted no one. I had heard that there would be informers, and there were criminals in the prison too, not just political prisoners. We were a strange mix. The Jewish lady was there simply because she was Jewish; Lies the nurse was a political prisoner; I was there because of my false identification. Another prisoner, a young girl, had been arrested with her boyfriend, a black marketeer and therefore despised by the Germans, who wanted all the Dutch money they could get for themselves.

Every Tuesday and Thursday night, Jews were sent from

the prison at Scheveningen to a concentration camp in Westerbork, where they were kept before they were shipped to Germany or Poland. If Jewish families or children were caught in
hiding, the Germans brought them to Scheveningen — fathers,
mothers, and little children — before shipping them out to a
concentration camp. On the nights the guards brought Jews in,
we always heard the children crying all through that place. It
was bad enough for us to have to suffer through a place like
Scheveningen, but it was terrible to hear those poor, innocent
children crying.

At Scheveningen our only light other than a small lamp was
the daylight that came in through a very small window up high
toward the ceiling. When the sun was shining, that light was
wonderful. We also loved the sound of the waves breaking on
the coast, close by, behind the dunes. The prison stood in the
dunes, right at the end of the last road of The Hague, the van
Alkemadelaan, at the North Sea, where the constant rush of
waves could be a consolation, as could the cry of the seagulls.
The sound of natural things was wonderful to us. In the middle
of all the suffering, it seemed pure, untouched.

About quarter to six or so the guards would start yelling
in the corridors, waking us up. They would open the door just
a bit, and each of us would be given a little bucket of water,
the size that children play with on the beach — five of them
per cell. We had no washcloths, no towels, and no soap; we
simply had to splash the water on. Nor did we have anything
with which to dry ourselves. It was May, a time of year when
it is very damp and chilly by the sea, and staying wet the way
we did was very uncomfortable. Sometimes I used my *onderhemdje*
— something like a vest or underwear — and took it for a
towel.

That small bucket of water was supposedly enough for our

bodies *and* our clothes. No one had clean clothes, so we took turns washing them in what water we were given. After I washed out my underclothes, for three days afterward I had nothing to wear, it took that long for them to dry. For all that time I walked around in nothing more than a dress. It seems awkward to have to live that way, but in such tight confinement nothing is private. Our menstrual periods could have been a terrible problem, but poor nourishment kept most of us from being healthy enough to menstruate. I was having my period the day I was arrested and did not have one again during my imprisonment. That's the way it was with many of us. I can't remember any of us in our cell ever having a period.

After we washed, we would hear the guards yell, "Coffee, coffee." There we stood with our rusty cups behind the *luikje*, the peephole or shutter on the door. The guard opened it from the outside, and we immediately shoved our cups beneath it, because guards would simply pour the liquid they called "coffee" over the floor if our cups weren't there to catch it. If they were especially nasty that morning, half would go in our cups and half of that hot liquid would scald our hands. Then they shoved a single piece of unbuttered bread through that peephole for each prisoner.

We had to do a number of jobs ourselves, but the worst was emptying the drums in the corner, our toilets. Actually, prisoners volunteered to do it because whoever did it received double rations. It was only one of the ways the Germans used us.

After that piece of bread, a long, boring time began. We tried to make conversation, and at one point I remember we agreed that having nothing to do wasn't good for us. So we decided to do calisthenics. I always tried to stretch backwards to the floor; I was trying to keep in mind how agile and healthy

I wanted to be when I was released. All we could think about in prison was what would happen when we would get out. Inside those walls, life seemed unreal.

We did exercises for at least an hour. Then we talked, while some of us scratched marks into the wall to count the days we were there. The others would keep an eye on the door, stand against it to cover the peephole, because it was supposedly a horrible crime to mar the walls. We would take turns scratching messages or verses into those walls too. I had managed to save a bobby pin in my hair when I was arrested, and I used it to scratch a Bible verse into the wall. It was a verse that always brought me comfort, even though I had no idea what would happen to us: "Lo, I am with you always, even unto the end" —Jesus' last words before he returned to heaven. I believed that promise, and I carved those words into the bricks of that prison wall for the others too, and for those who would come to Scheveningen after us.

Then lunch finally came. It was something like soup. We hardly ever got vegetables or potatoes, and meat was nonexistent. Lunch was a mishmash of something boiled in water. Prisoners were cooking it, and they did their very best, but it was awful. In the Netherlands, a weed called *brandnetels,* "fire nettles," grows all over. If you touch them, you get hives. The Germans often used the leaves of these *brandnetels* to make soup. Every day this lunch of boiled mush looked a little different, but it was always soup. Once a month the Red Cross provided a solid bean soup full of brown or white beans. For that day at least, we ate something of substance.

In the afternoon, we would do more exercises, and sometimes we would play a game of cards. A woman in the cell had ripped up a single precious piece of paper into tiny pieces, each of which we marked to become a full pack of cards. I had never learned to play cards, even though in our house, unlike many Reformed homes, cards were not expressly forbidden. The other women in that cell taught me how to play with those tiny pieces of paper, and I loved it.

At night we would receive another slice of bread, and once in a while a nick of butter. That was it. (Actually, the food supply in the whole country at that time was bad; many people were going hungry *outside* those prison walls.) Once darkness came, we would spread out the straw mattresses they gave us to sleep on. We were not allowed to sit on them during the day; they had to be rolled up along the walls so that we could stand in that tiny cell. During the day we were forbidden to lie down or take a nap. The Germans would often barge into the cell without warning, come booming in at any moment and start screaming. You had to stand at attention while they would search everywhere to see if you had something you were forbidden to have: a little stub of a pencil, a sewing needle, or those slips of papers we used as cards. To lose those things in a search was traumatic for us. They had become very valuable. When you have nothing, such little things become very precious; they are symbols of your defiance. So the moment we heard footsteps, we would start hiding anything that might be confiscated. We were constantly listening, constantly anxious, even in the darkness of the night in our sleep.

When I had been there for three and a half weeks, the guards told us that those in our cell would get an opportunity to take a shower. At certain intervals, each of us was called out. I was delighted. We had had no shampoo, no soap, only that bucket of water in the morning to clean both our bodies and our clothes. The opportunity to take a shower seemed wonderful.

I marched joyfully down the rug strip in the middle of the corridor, a mat that was there to mute the noise of guards walking outside the cells. I walked along so happily that one of the guards screamed at me to walk on the concrete, not on the mat: the mat, she yelled, wasn't meant for prisoners. When I got to that shower, a guard gave me a half-inch piece of something that looked like brown putty, only stone hard. That was the soap. And I received a rag: it looked to me like be a bath towel a hundred years old, all frayed and limp, but I didn't care because finally I was going to get a shower. *When I stand under the warm water*, I thought, *it will be wonderful.*

~ I undressed and stepped in, and just at the moment I began to turn the handle, I heard a loud voice: "Get out. Get back to the cell! You're finished."

I never got a drop of water on me! It was a game, a psychological trick.

New prisoners were coming into our cell all the time, and others were leaving. Soon after I came to Scheveningen, our cell took in a young Jewish girl who introduced herself as Sonjia Barzilai — a Portuguese or Brazilian name. She was, as the Dutch would say, very *mollig* — well-endowed, kind of juicy and sexy; she wore lots of make-up and had very beautiful skin. There were no chairs or sofas in those tiny quarters, so Sonjia and I talked late into the evening that first night sitting on the floor, our backs against the walls. She told me she hoped that if she would offer her body to the German men, she might get out of prison and that that sacrifice would save her. I felt very sorry for her.

When Sonjia was called out, another young girl was brought into our cell, and right away she came to my side, almost as if she knew me.

"It's a big mistake," she said to me. "I don't belong here at all, and I'm sure I'll be out in two or three days!" She leaned closer to me. "Do you have a message for the outside world? I can take it. If you want to tell anybody anything at all — "

"How can you know when you'll be out?" I asked.

"Oh, I know," she told me.

"Nobody knows when they'll get out," I said. "I mean, I don't even know why I'm here. I haven't even had my hearing. I've been here two weeks already, and I don't even know why!"

"Yeah, but I know I will soon be out again," she said.

"How can you know?"

"I'm engaged to a German," she said, smiling. "I'm going to get married." Then she looked at me seriously. "He's a *good* German."

To me at that time, there were no good Germans.

"I know he'll get me out real soon," she said. "You just wait. At the longest, I'll be in this place only two or three days, and then I'll be out — just like that. If you want to get a message out, I'll take it. I promise." But she never approached my cell-mates — only me.

I didn't trust her.

"No one really cares where I am anyway," I told her. "I'm not worth much to anybody at all. I have no family here in the Netherlands." I told her that I had already made many good friends in the prison, and I wouldn't know who in the whole country would be interested in seeing me outside the walls. "They might miss me where I worked as a maid," I said, "but only because now there will be more work to do." I told her I wasn't on very good terms with the woman at that house, so I had no messages for her to deliver. In other words, I didn't bite.

If she had been smart, she would have gone to the others in the cell and asked them if they had messages; then she might have convinced me she was telling me the truth. But she came to speak to me alone. She was in our cell for two days, and every so often she would come and ask me again: "Do you have any messages for the outside? I can deliver them." I believed she was a spy.

Often the Allies flew over at night to drop their bombs on Germany; and sometimes they dropped bombs very close to us, because the Germans were building fortifications in the dunes near the prison in anticipation of a North Sea invasion from England. The whole prison would tremble when the Allies flew over. But we would all get up and start knocking or rapping or banging on the walls, making all kinds of noise, as if to remind each other how great it was to know the fight outside was still going on. Our friends were flying over, and I always prayed for their safe return. To participate in that way was a thrill: even though those bombers were destroying buildings near where we were standing, and it was dangerous for us and Dutch people outside the prison, we knew that they were fighting Germans, and after what we'd already seen, we loved it.

One night while this young woman with the "good German boyfriend" was staying in our cell, our friends from England and the United States flew over and dropped a bomb really close by. Immediately, she ran to the front of the cell, which no one ever did, and began to beat on the door: "Let me out! Let me out!" she yelled. "You know I don't belong here, and I want to be released." She was hysterical. "Those rotten English!" she screamed. The guards opened the prison door and took her out. I said, "Thank you, Lord," because when that happened, I knew for sure she was a spy planted by the Germans, and I knew I had to be careful about anything I told anyone about myself. It was a blessing that I learned about spies such a short time into my imprisonment.

Not long after I got to the prison, in early May, the guards brought in another new girl, taller than I was and a few years older. She introduced herself as Beatrix Terwindt — "Trix" we called her. She had a little tiny fur piece in the shape of an animal around her neck, something that resembled a marten. She called it "Freddy" and sometimes spoke to it and stroked it. Even when she introduced herself, she spoke to this little fur piece. Her eyes seemed kind of wild and nervous, very sunken, and her facial features were pulled tight. She was very anxious.

That night, after the others had gone to sleep, I stayed awake because something inside me told me that this woman was special. Although I'd never met her before, my instincts told me I could trust her, and I knew there was more to her than the little she'd told us. We sat on the floor against the wall, just the two of us, and we talked the whole night while the others were asleep. She told me her story that night in cell 306.

She was from a very well-to-do family, so rich that she didn't have to have a job. Before the war she had studied at a university, but she became bored with going to school, she said. Air travel had just begun at that time, and she became one of the KLM airline's first stewardesses. She said that she flew only to challenge herself: she had been deathly afraid of flying, so she challenged herself to get on an airplane by becoming a stewardess, of all things.

When the war broke out, she'd made her way to England and was working for the Dutch intelligence service. When she arrived, Queen Wilhelmina invited Beatrix over for tea! It's difficult for Americans to understand loyalty and love for the crown, but I always loved our royal family. That night, when Beatrix told me that she had had tea with the queen, I was nearly overwhelmed with admiration for her!

Often the secret service in England would use the Underground in Holland to secure important information or to run "pilot lines," secret routes along which downed pilots and escaped prisoners of war could return to England. Occasionally, Dutch resisters in England would be dropped over occupied territory during the night. They would parachute out of a plane over some prearranged spot, where no one would be able to see them except the Underground, who would be waiting with flashlights to guide the planes and the parachutists.

Because the Germans might hear the planes, throw on their floodlights, and fill the air with flack, that kind of work was especially dangerous. If the men who were dropped were lucky enough to make it to the ground, the Underground had to slash away that heavy parachute as quickly as possible, then bury it or get it out of sight somehow, and whisk the man away before the Germans found the whole operation.

The pilot lines were a very secret operation. For a long time it went very well. Intelligence agents would sneak into Holland to help with the pilot lines and then leave. Sometimes they were picked up by seaplanes from one of the Frisian lakes. But at one point agent after agent began to disappear and never be heard from again. The intelligence services in London wondered what was happening, but they continued for a while to fly in agents, because the work of the pilot lines was essential. That kind of messenger had an extremely dangerous job, because not even the Geneva Convention protected those spies.

In the winter of 1942 one of the pilot lines suddenly broke off, and British intelligence asked Beatrix Terwindt to set up a new one. No women had yet been executed by the Germans at that time on Dutch territory; they thought that maybe a woman would stand a better chance of succeeding. So this person who had at one time been deathly afraid to fly volunteered to jump out of a plane in the dark of the night over occupied territory.

Beatrix received all her instructions: she was trained to jump out of an airplane, and she was told exactly which sentences to repeat to the people on the ground. She even carried an important message printed on rice paper, very fine paper she could swallow and digest if she feared being caught. She told me all of this that first night she came into the cell. We talked the whole night long, because she seemed very eager to tell her story. And I trusted her story, right from the start.

She was parachuted in, she said, and as soon as she landed the guys with flashlights found her and cut away her parachute. They were farmers, she said, not Gestapo. She repeated all the password sentences she had been instructed to give her rescuers, and they in turn responded with the correct answers. They immediately ushered her through the darkness. She said that while she was running along with them, she thanked God because it was such a relief to make it down safely.

When they reached the shed, they opened the door to a group of men sitting there in front of her. They were all Gestapo! The men who had picked her up and who had used the correct sentences were not Underground people. The Germans had infiltrated the whole plan, the whole way of communicating with England. And Trix was arrested.

After they had interrogated her, they took her to Haaren, near Tilburg, to a very old prison, St. Michielsgestel, a place with walls one meter thick and bars in the windows. There she sat in her cell, all alone; she wasn't allowed to see anyone. Three Germans guarded her. They brought her breakfast, lunch, and dinner — such as it was — but they rarely spoke to her. The whole time she was there she continued to undergo severe interrogations. She suffered immensely through a form of punishment the Germans called *einzelhaft*, solitary confinement. That was probably when she started talking to this furry marten, "Freddy," because he was her only friend. She had to speak to him in order to remain sane.

Whenever she was taken out of her cell, she had to wear a mask so that other prisoners could not see her face. None of the prisoners there was supposed to know who else from the Resistance was in that place. Occasionally, masked, she was brought to the inner courtyard by a German guard so that she could breathe some fresh air. Then she was returned to her cell. She spent fifteen months in that prison, in total isolation except for the times of heavy interrogation.

At one point, one of the three German guards took a kind of pity on her. He said: "You can't do any harm with a radio. Here, just have it." They had hundreds of radios since they'd confiscated so many from us. The German undoubtedly meant for her to listen to music, but whenever she could, she tuned in to the BBC and listened to all the latest news. It was 1944, and the Allies had already landed at Sicily and were marching up into Italy.

That old prison was heated by steam, and one day, out of sheer boredom, she started tapping out Morse code on the steam pipes. All of a sudden, to her great surprise, she received a message back. She did it again, and what she discovered was that there were other agents in that prison who had come from England! So they sent messages, back and forth, via Morse code. She never saw any of them, but together they communicated in code about when they were going to walk in the courtyard and how they had been arrested. Since she had the radio, she could give the rest of them all the news from the BBC.

After all these months of solitary confinement and terrible hearings, for reasons she wasn't quite sure of herself, Trix was taken out of the prison at Haaren and transported to Scheveningen.

"Willie," she told me, "I want you to know one thing: *if* they take me out of this place, the invasion will come soon. I don't know why the Germans moved me from Haaren, but I know they don't want me to fall back into the hands of the Allies. Just remember, my leaving here means that I will go to Germany, but it also means the invasion has finally happened."

The problem that I struggled with from the time I came to Scheveningen, from the moment I was arrested, was a problem in my conscience. I hadn't yet firmly resolved whether outright lying was a legitimate form of defense for me. I wasn't sure whether I could stand in front of those who would conduct my hearing and tell them a bald-faced lie. In the time that had passed before Beatrix came to our cell, I was often praying hard, asking for clarity: "God, you hate lies, but this time I can't tell the truth. I have to tell lies."

I had decided, in a way, on the following course of action: I'd try to be brave and simply keep my mouth shut. I wouldn't say anything at all, not a word. That way I'd avoid lying, but I'd also avoid having to give them information that would jeopardize our whole operation. I told myself that when my hearing finally came, I'd be silent as stone.

I told Beatrix my plan, because she had told me her whole story and I knew it was true. I could see the truth in her face. She was no spy. She wasn't at all like the young women I knew were snitches. I read the suffering in her face, even in the darkness of our cell in the middle of the night.

"I can't tell you my story because it's complicated," I said, "but I will face big problems in my hearing. They found false papers on me, but actually they have been on my trail for a long time. Now they have me here, but they don't know whom they have since I am here under a false name. I've decided I'm not going to say a thing. I've decided that I will simply be silent. What do you think?"

She shook her head. "Make up a story and make it good," she said. "If you don't speak, they will *know* you know more than you're telling them. And if they know that, they'll find a way to get what you know out of you. Believe me, they'll get everything out, Willie. Don't have any qualms about it — make your story good and make it believable. Silence won't work!"

This was an expert giving me the best advice she could. From that point on, I worked hard *not* to remember the people I loved, to try instead to create another life, a false life, the life of Willie Laarman, a maid who was born in Paramaribo, Surinam, to parents who were both dead. I tried to think like a maid, a woman with limited abilities and someone who really presented no danger or risk to the Germans. I tried to become a person concerned only with very simple things — and scared. I tried to become the woman I needed to be in order to live.

In just a few days, just as she had predicted, Trix was called out and sent to Germany. The following is a poem she wrote anticipating her transport to Germany.

Single Transport Berlin
by Beatrix Terwindt

O God, again the hour had sounded,
and I stood before you as on the night in February
when I could only stammer for fear
in that empty hull of the dark plane
on my way back from liberty abroad,
back to the oppressing Occupation;
for my task, my heart was full of insecurity
and my head full of black premonitions.

We were alone, you and I,
and I said: God, here I am now,
and I did not mean God the Father,
or God the Son, or God the Holy Spirit
of the Catholics, or the Christian Reformed,
or the Reformed,
who thought they alone owned you.
No, you know everything, that my heart was open to you
and my head did not hide any secrets.
I said: God of all people, yes, also of the enemy,
who crushes my country and tramples my soul,
and who in this dark night is lying in wait for me,
I said: God of all people and of me,
you know my black and my white sides,
you see my faults and my failings,
but you also know that I consciously risk my life
to form a tiny particle
in the giant machine that must oust
those foreign armies from our cities and fields.

They told me my chances were fifty-fifty.
It was up to you, O God, to decide
whether I would land on the left or on the right fifty.
God, you know everything: it's all the same to me now.
I was strong, healthy, and young,
and to die for a goal in which one believes
is not so difficult.
Didn't I know that my fate rested in your hands?

But it did not turn out to be a balance of figures,
neither to the left or to the right.
It became something nobody counted on:
being imprisoned . . . and God, I felt you had deserted me.
In my lonely cell,
with my fist clutching the Irish rosary,
my charm from a British Anglican,
I paced from wall to wall, from pail to door,
my teeth clenched, my eyes squeezed shut, my cheeks wet.
And I called, my head swinging from left to right:
God, O God, where are you. . . ?
God, where were you when the hours dragged and
insanity appeared tormentingly on the ceiling?
Where were you when a young woman in her cell
below me was being tortured and murdered
because she, standing on the table,
tried to see something of your sky
through the airslot overhead, in the bricked-up window,
to smell it and to search
for some contact with a fellow human?
God, where were you when her death agony's scream
faded out of her body?
When I pounded on my cell door and cursed the guards,

when I demanded accountability from the commander?
For even a hunter does not shoot a pesky hare
when it sits down.

Cowards! Cowards! Cowards!
I screamed in my fury and powerlessness
at that commander.
But it did not console me.
God was gone and the child was dead.

And later in Ravensbrück,
when we stood for hours for morning roll call,
work roll call, evening roll call,
or, out of nowhere, punishment roll call,
until our backs were breaking:
I was standing next to Sigrid from the far north.
Sigrid's look was serenity
as she gazed beyond the gray wooden barracks
and the stinking, black cinder paths
(paved with crematory oven ashes?),
it was as if she saw the most beautiful trees
with leaves and a wealth of flowers.
And I said: "Sigrid, what are you thinking about?"
And Sigrid answered: "I'm thinking about God."
My brain wondered how she could think about God
after they had put thumbscrews on her in Oslo
and had tortured her in other ways.

"Do you think about God?" she asked.
"No, Sigrid, no. God has gone away, God is dead.
Just smell the stench of the burned people,
look at the smoke rising day and night from the ovens,

look at the mountains of dead or nearly dead,
the skeletons waiting for incineration.
There is no God."

Had I still not suffered enough?
The dysentery, the hunger and thirst,
the wounds and no sleep,
the fleas and the lice,
the disease and the dirt,
the hurryings and the beatings,
the swearing and the cursing . . .
was it still not enough?

They told me I would be liberated,
what did I choose: Sweden or Switzerland?

That night I could not sleep.
Morning roll call came:
"Wo ist denn die Terwindt,
so was, die hier nicht bleiben will?
Was fehlt euch hier?"
(Where is that Terwindt woman?
What's wrong, don't you want to stay here?
Do you lack anything here?)

Macabre joke . . . or the truth?
How would they liberate me with fifty-eight wounds?
Wouldn't they nurse me before handing me over?
And the guard changed from a beast to a human being;
She still pulled up my prison dress
to see if I was not too dirty.
But we had remained Dutch,

and with the Norwegians had washed ourselves
under the spouts of water in the cold Waschraume.

Arrived in the front of the camp, where the big shots lived,
the seniors, the Poles, and the leaders.
They bandaged my pus-covered legs
with strips of threadbare cotton.
And I got jerrymade shoes with wooden soles
(for it was already 1944),
high shoes to hide the bandages,
but I counted my wounds from my instep
to my thigh and there were
not five but fifty-eight.
The bandages were pushed down into my shoes.
There was enough room in them — soldiers' shoes
are bigger than a woman's size seven —
and fresh air does not hurt wounds.

The female guard accompanying me was given a paper,
and the words *Einzelhaft Berlin* (Berlin Solitary)
caught my eye.
God, what a scare!
Yes, God, I called you!
You grabbed my shoulders,
You shook me awake and looked at me.
Because Berlin Solitary meant *death.*
Nobody had ever returned from there,
whether because of the gallows or the rifle.
No, this death I did not fear,
even though I preferred a firing squad,
I hurt so much and was so weak.
They would have to kill me with their guns —

they had not been able to crush me in the camp.
Was I too proud?
There I stood, God.
No . . . I walked, a slow-motion film just like
all camp skeletons move,
maybe a little slower because the
shoes were pressing on my swollen insteps,
and the weekend suitcase of the female guard
was so heavy.
I felt the lukewarm pus run down my legs.
Was she afraid that her suitcase would be infected,
or did she have some feeling for her wounded slave?
She pulled the suitcase from my hand
and yelled at me to hurry,
the train was waiting.
I staggered up the stairs
to the platform, and I called:
God, O God, heal my wounds before I die,
They hurt so much I can hardly walk,
Give me my last wish,
that I can walk erect and die a brave death.

Again I remained alive,
and there is no end to my suffering.
And still there is hunger
and torture and death in every country.

They say that you are dead, God,
what should I believe?
What can I hope for?
Where is the new God of love, neighborly love?
And the world that's been destroyed?

The Prison at Scheveningen

It's more sea than land
from all the tears and suffering
of all those people.

Barracks No. 4,
Vught Concentration Camp

Vught Concentration Camp, November 1944

Photo by Seargeant Laing, from the National Archives, Washington, DC,
courtesy of the United States Holocaust Memorial Museum

June 6, 1944, the day of the Normandy Invasion, came. That afternoon, all of the prisoners at Scheveningen, sixteen hundred people, were told to gather all the belongings we had because we were going to be moved right away. We had no belongings, of course, so I was ready in a moment. We were called out, cell by cell, and we had to line up in long rows and be loaded onto those trucks, some of which were covered with canvas. The soldiers were standing all around us, bayonets on their rifles. They moved us first to a railroad station, and then they put us on a train.

Even while they moved us that night, the Germans were very nervous. The invasion had begun, and they were scared. None of us really knew about the invasion, but I suspected it because of what Trix had told me. And I heard the Germans, while they piled us on the buses and the trucks, talking about it themselves.

I knew this area, and I knew that if we left the Scheveningen prison through the side door, as we did, we would be on the street at the very end of the city of The Hague, the van Alke-madelaan. On the left were the dunes, with all those German fortifications that the Allied planes had been bombarding; then there was the coastal strip with its big, expensive hotels. But there was nothing else around the prison — nothing other than the strip of dunes where Hein and I had often biked together, the place I could never forget because the little trees had their peculiar honey smell in the spring — the *meidoorn* trees. The place was called Meyendel. I had even biked there as a child with my friends Rie and Jet, and played cops and robbers.

When we left the prison, therefore, I thought we would go to the right, because the city had two railway stations: one to the south, the *Hollandse spoor*, and the other to Utrecht and the heart of the country, the *Staats spoor*. The stations were only twenty minutes from my parents' house. I told myself that we should be going to the right because there was nothing to the left except the forbidden territory of the dunes.

Instead, the buses took a turn to the left. The only destination to the left would have been Waalsdorp, in the dunes, and everybody was scared stiff of Waalsdorp. It was the place of executions, so I was terribly afraid too. The Hague prisoners all believed that if they were being taken to Waalsdorp, there would be nothing but silence for all of us. At the same time, though we didn't know where the invasion might have happened, we knew that there was an invasion somewhere. And an invasion represented, for us, the end of all our misery. The Allies had landed. Everyone expected it sometime, of course, like the coming of Christ: we all believed that at some point, somewhere, our Allied friends would come and we'd be free again.

But when those buses turned to the left, the prisoners from The Hague knew what was going to happen. The trucks followed a road where the dunes are high on both sides, an open area full of dry grass called *helm*, to Waalsdorp, the place of execution in the dunes. Some people on those trucks were so desperate that they were nearly out of their minds with fear. I think that God gave me a very logical mind; sometimes that is good and sometimes not. But in this case I had already thought that there was no point in jumping out of that truck: you couldn't really run in the sand, and soldiers were all around, so where could you go? Even if you didn't break your leg or get a concussion jumping off the train or truck, you couldn't run very fast up steep hills of dry sand in forbidden territory full of land mines.

But some were so desperate that they *were* jumping out. The buses kept right on going, so I never knew exactly what happened to them; but there were other vehicles full of soldiers right behind us.

Barracks No. 4, Vught Concentration Camp

At two in the afternoon we came to a tiny railway station that I had never known about. There all sixteen hundred of us were crammed onto the platform, arranged in blocks, and again surrounded by armed soldiers. We stood there in deadly silence for hours, except for the Germans who were talking to each other. And it was during those silent hours of standing there that Corrie and Betsy ten Boom (whose story was told in *The Hiding Place*) first saw each other. They hadn't seen each other for months, and their father had already died in our prison. I didn't know Corrie or Betsy then; I'd never heard of them. Although Betsy was only two cells away from me in Scheveningen, we had never had any occasion to speak to each other. It was only after we left Scheveningen that we got to know each other and discovered that during that whole time in prison we were that close to each other. Corrie was in another part of Scheveningen altogether. The Germans thought that she had tuberculosis, and they were very afraid of TB. So they had Corrie in solitary, not for punishment, but to be isolated from the others.

As we were standing there, the two sisters started worming their way toward each other, which you could do very slowly without being spotted in that mass of people surrounded by the Germans. Finally they stood beside each other and could whisper a few words when no one was looking. After several hours a train pulled up, and we were herded in. Corrie and Betsy were able to stick together, and once they were on the train they could actually sit next to each other. It was a passenger train with seats, not a cattle train. I happened to end up in the same compartment with them, and that's when someone who may have been in Betsy's Scheveningen cell told me the story of Corrie and Betsy. When I saw them sitting there for the first time, they were holding hands, tears streaming down their cheeks from happiness — and sadness too because their father had already died.

As we were being loaded onto the train, the Germans walked up and down very menacingly. For all those months, we had talked only to our cellmates; but here, all of a sudden, were sixteen hundred people on that train. It was maybe 6:00 or 7:00 by now, and getting dark. Every train at that time was equipped with blackout curtains inside, so that the whole train would appear perfectly dark from the sky — thus the Allied planes could not see them. As the train lurched forward, I was praying that we wouldn't go to Germany, because I knew that if we crossed that border our chances for survival were not good. I'd been initially overwhelmed by the fear that we would go to Waalsdorp and be executed; now that fear was removed, and the longer we stayed on the train, the more I believed we were going to Germany.

But I wasn't as afraid as I had been before we got to that tiny train station. The train ride seemed more safe. That we had even got on the train at all meant, to me, that there would likely be no executions. They wouldn't have gone to all the trouble of loading us up and burning all that coal to take us somewhere else to be executed. Besides, we were women, and up to that time at least, I had not heard of Germans executing women on Dutch territory. That also brought me some relief.

All of a sudden, the sound of the steel wheels beneath us changed. We couldn't see outside, and there were guards walking up and down through the aisles the whole time. But when I heard the sound of that train change, I peeked out quickly and saw water. I knew that we had to be at the Moerdijk Bridge, a very long bridge over a long waterway, the Hollandse Diep. Again, I felt a sense of relief. I knew then that we were not heading east toward Germany, but instead probably south to Vught, the big concentration camp in a wooded, sandy, and infertile area near Den Bosch. Actually, I had held out hope that we would go to Vught: of all the evil places, I believed, it was probably less bad because at least we would stay in the Netherlands. Vught did have a bad name — there were many executions there — but Amersfoort also had a bad name, and every camp had a bad name of its own. I knew that it was not going to be any fun.

At one point on that train ride a woman got up to use the bathroom, and she stayed inside so long that I didn't know what she was up to. But when the train took a little curve, and I saw that she had opened the window in that bathroom, I guessed she was going to try to escape. If the train had been going straight, I wouldn't have seen that. I thought immediately about how I could help her. I knew she was going to need time, so I tried to make sure that nobody would enter the bathroom right at that moment. Nobody else was in line right then, so I stood there as if waiting for my turn; meanwhile, I could be sure that nobody else would come and force the door open.

Then I saw her jump off the train. That woman must have known that territory like I knew the area around Barneveld — like the inside of my pocket. She knew there was going to be a sharp curve where the train had to really slow down. It was dark already, and I was keeping my eye on a little split in the door. And when I saw her jump, I said a prayer, *Lord, protect her.*

The rails there are situated mostly on the dike. German soldiers were sitting on the roof of the train with machine guns, but it was very late on the 6th or early on the morning of the 7th of June and quite dark. She knew that curve was coming, knew where there would be woods and shrubs, and she jumped at the right spot.

That escape gave me an indescribable feeling. *There!* — *one got out. Thank God!* I said to myself. All during that prison time I really lived by prayer. Be in prayer always, we're told, and back then I was. I prayed that this woman wouldn't get hurt, and that she would roll over and away from the guns. And she made it! I'm sure that she made it.

We arrived at Vught in the darkness of early morning, and there was roll call immediately. About eight had disappeared. So, apart from the woman I had seen jump, there were other escapees. I was very happy that eight had gotten away during the train trip alone. I heard that report because the guards often spoke to each other as if we weren't even there; to them, we were just like cattle. Sometimes that was a good thing because when they discussed what was happening in the war, those of us who could understand German picked up a lot of information. When your life is at stake, your ears are like radar. Whenever I heard them discussing anything — such as how many had escaped — I listened very closely.

When the train stopped and we got out, we were in the middle of a woods. The step off the train seemed very high — we had to jump down — and all around us were woods. No paths really, just woods. Many German soldiers were stationed all around, still with their bayonets mounted, holding Doberman Pinschers on leashes. We were told to form rows and march into the darkness because the train couldn't carry us any closer to the camp. If some fell — if they stepped in a hole in the pitch darkness, say — there was screaming and pushing and a couple of whacks. But people quickly got up and marched again on the uneven ground. After a while, we came to the front gate of Vught.

At the camp, we were all put in an enormous reception hall: it had no windows, except maybe a few very high up, and it was still quite dark. There was no place for us yet in that camp, and for a while they didn't know where to put us. Suddenly and unexpectedly the officials at Vught had received sixteen hundred people from Scheveningen — and perhaps from other prisons as well. The leadership did a lot of running around there, and the Germans left us standing in that hall with no beds, no blankets, nothing. But I had a rain coat and I put it over my head and got down on the concrete floor. I felt blessed: at least I had something. I was very tired, and I slept.

In the morning someone high up said that the prisoners all had to undress — the men gave us the order — and so we stood there naked. If you tried to keep your bra and your panty on, they got mad and yelled, "Undress! Undress!" There we stood, while those officers were passing by, when suddenly a whole bunch of male soldiers came into that hall. I was scared, standing there naked. Those soldiers started walking back and forth, laughing and making remarks about what they saw. So many young women, and all of them undressed in front of those guards and the other officers walking back and forth. There were female guards too, so it was not as if we were at the total mercy of those men; but I'll never forget the way they walked past and stared.

It was a very short time that we were absolutely naked because one woman guard came along and said, "Hey, get those people their prison dresses." Our own clothes were bundled up, except our underwear, and we all got prison gowns. We still didn't know what was going to happen to us. We finally got our underwear back, put it on again, and got into our prison gowns. They were the kind of gowns that could be opened a long way in the front: no buttons — only hooks and eyes, and very large pockets; no sizes, of course, just large and small; thick cotton, as heavy as denim, and gray with dark blue stripes. For a very long time after the war, I would never wear stripes — never.

They called off the list of names, and slowly we were all placed in the barracks. They had to find a place for us separate from the rest of the camp because our group had not yet had our hearings. It was very important to them that we be kept separate. We weren't to converse with each other; they thought we would plan strategies. They watched us like hawks that morning, and for weeks afterward.

When we came to our barracks, we found a big "4" painted on it. Around that group of barracks stood a tall barbed-wire fence, and outside lay a large open space, then another very high barbed-wire fence, just like you see in pictures of all the concentration camps. That fence was hot with electrical current. On the corners stood towers, and in the towers were guards with machine guns.

Right away they made a big announcement: "There is another fence with barbed wire, and there are mine fields between, and we have trained dogs. So don't ever try to escape. You will be shot, or killed by the current, or ripped to pieces by the dogs, or else you'll step on a mine."

Nakedness in front of those soldiers, the prison gown, and that warning — that was our introduction to the concentration camp at Vught.

In Vught we were called to wake up at quarter to six in the morning. Inside our barracks were rows of metal bunk beds, three high, with a little space in between. The beds were stacked so close together that you scarcely had room to move your arms. On the other side of this large room sat wooden tables and seats where we ate — lots of benches, but not enough for the 175 women who occupied our barracks. If you wanted to sit and eat, you took turns or sat cramped up together.

The door was in one corner — there were windows on both sides — and across the room was the bathroom with ten toilets, five on each side, no divisions between them. In another corner the guards had their place, which was closed off to us. They used it for an office; they could drink coffee there and keep an eye on us.

Outside the four corners of the building stood four soldiers with rifles. The windows were all open, and outside the windows the clouds looked so beautiful that I would stand there for a moment just to admire them. They were just clouds, but they were God's consolation to me, so beautiful in the sky. Below the clouds, the countryside was full of flowers, lots of purple shooting up to the sun. I would stand there at times and remember how beautiful God created this world, and then I would be reassured that he would certainly take care of me and all of my loved ones.

I was standing there one day, lost in my thoughts, when just like that — zzzhhhhhhht! — a bullet zoomed by! My elbow had been sticking out of that window, not far, but that bullet came so close I could hear it.

Those guards were probably not the best German soldiers, because Hitler's better troops were spread all over Europe by that time. One guard was an Austrian by the name of Krause, a very small man in his forties, a man who often had pity in his face. Some of the guards were younger, and they were moved around so we didn't see them every day. But Herr Krause was there often, as well as another man whose name was Hans. We knew these men by name because occasionally we heard the women guards yell at them, and sometimes we saw them when we were let out of the barracks to march around.

The pity on the face of Herr Krause came out especially when he saw a young prisoner, a very beautiful girl named Ansje Kropff, only nineteen years old and married just six months. She had big blue eyes, beautiful dark wavy hair, and a very nice face with pink cheeks. She was so happy and so deeply in love with her new husband, Herman, that she would talk about him constantly. But Herman had helped Allied pilots, and in those cases the Germans always took both husband and wife. So she had been arrested along with her husband.

Ansje was not in the kind of serious trouble her husband was, because the women were generally released after some time — usually after the Germans had executed their husbands. But she was so young and innocent that I was afraid she would just crack up. She was not a Christian, but her parents went to church once in a while — at Easter and Christmas maybe. I had great pity on Ansje, because she always acted very happy, but I believed that it was really a front. I could see through it. Inside she was crying because she was really very sad. You pity people like that — the ones who try to lie to themselves — because they suffer so much and don't face reality.

Herr Krause felt pity for Ansje Kropff too. As a guard, he probably got to know a little bit about most of us, and I think he knew that her husband was sitting across the street in the men's section. I knew what Krause felt because I saw how he always looked with pity at Ansje when we marched outside. I would see him smile at Ansje, not a mean smile from an evil thought, but like a father's smile: pity for that young girl who had to sit in prison, apart from her husband, someone she loved so much.

We were transported to Vught on June 7, and August 9 was Ansje's nineteenth birthday. The day before her birthday, I was standing at that window and looking at all that beauty of nature outside, all those purple flowers. Herr Krause was not the kind of guard who would have shot someone leaning out the window; he was on duty that day, and he was the only one I would dare to ask. When he walked past, I said, "Herr Krause? Herr Krause? Can you go pick some flowers for Ansje? Tomorrow is her birthday."

He did. And I don't know how he did it, but he also got a raw potato for us. We scraped out that raw, half-rotten potato with bobby pins and hollowed it out to form a small "basket" to put flowers in. Then we pulled threads out of our socks and made three little ropes so that the potato became — with the flowers in it — a hanging plant. It was tiny, but to us it was beautiful.

Ansje had a middle bed. While she was sleeping, we tied that little hanging plant to the bed above her. And when she woke up, there it was for her birthday.

I had not really gotten to know anyone deeply in Scheveningen, where there were only five women to a cell but there was also a frequent turnover of prisoners. I had talked intimately with a couple of fellow prisoners there, but hearings seemed to occur quickly and women moved on rapidly. In the concentration camp at Vught, on the other hand, I was able to form more friendships. Initially there were 175 women in our barracks; that population stayed quite stable, and the turnover because of hearings took much longer. At first, the guards wouldn't let us speak to each other because we were special prisoners — the ones who were yet to have their hearings. But later they must have assumed that the danger of our sharing information had passed, because after a while, once it was evening and the place was locked up, they began to leave us alone, and then we could talk. Watching us was their only duty, and they must have become very tired of it.

The only time they watched us closely was when we got our bread, because that was when resentments could grow and tempers flare. If you were assigned the duty of cutting margarine, you had to be very careful that all the lumps were exactly the same size. Margarine was all we had — no jam, no marmelade, no nothing — just bread and a little pad of margarine. You had to be very careful slicing it because the others would watch closely to be sure no one pad was any thicker than another. If one slice would have a bit thicker chunk of margarine, there would be bickering for sure; when you're hungry, such arguing comes up very easily.

When it was my turn to cut the margarine, I felt miserable, and I think it was the same for everyone. Whoever had that job received *two* slices of bread and *two* pieces of margarine — which was kind of nice, but hardly worth it. It was a miserable job because, with all those women standing there and watching so closely, it became very tense. And you had to cut those pads off a big chunk of margarine, so it wasn't easy to make certain that every last piece was exactly the same size. Besides, what you were given had to go all the way around; if you ran short, they weren't about to give you any more.

The washroom, next to the toilet room, was equipped with white wooden gutters lined with zinc. There was a pipe for water in that room, and faucets, but no warm water. We could go in, sixty or seventy at a time, put our hair under that cold water and splash our faces. There was no soap or towels at Vught, but it felt really good, much better than those dirty little pails at Scheveningen.

After roll call and a breakfast of bread and margarine, almost all of the women went to another barracks where they made twine out of wet paper: they twisted it tightly and, when it was dry, braided the twine into rope. I was hardly ever a part of that because I was Willie the maid. I had to scrub the barracks floor and do the guards' laundry.

Corrie and Betsy ten Boom, along with most of the other women in Barracks No. 4, always made twine. And they were real evangelists: they started evangelizing every morning, surrounded by a whole group of women who were, you might say, quite desperate. Some of those women were already Christians, but Corrie and Betsy told them *all* about the Bible and the faith, which was beautiful. But few women ever got the chance to be alone with them because they were always preaching to many others.

In a corner they had a little group in which Corrie actually taught a Bible class. She had her own Bible in prison, the tiniest little Bible, perhaps just a New Testament or a part of the Bible. At night the pages of that Bible circulated among the women who could be trusted; everyone got one part of that tiny Bible. You could have it for about five minutes of reading under your grey blanket, and then you had to hand it on to the next person. It was summer, so it was light outside for a long time, but under that blanket I had to squint to read the tiny print. Reading anything was precious.

We all knew that Corrie and Betsy had hidden Jews, and that their father had died in Scheveningen. It was a sad story that had become joyful now that they had found each other again, and it became known to all of us in Barracks No. 4 at Vught. I knew Betsy and Corrie for those weeks they were in Vught, but I really did not have close contact with either of them. Some women needed the strength that Corrie and Betsy could give them more than I did. Some were very weak, and Corrie and Betsy lent their strength to others — always with the gospel.

I had learned to depend on myself alone. I had had to. I depended on God, of course, but I didn't depend on other people. Besides, I didn't work with the women who braided rope while Corrie and Betsy talked and talked about the gospel. The two sisters were in the camp-within-the-camp at Vught for only about three weeks. Then they had another hearing and were sentenced. After they left, I don't remember reading that little

Bible anymore, so they must have taken it with them to the bigger camp at Vught. That was the last I saw of either of them during the war.

After a few weeks, I got to know practically all of the women because there were no radios or books and little to do but talk. Once I got to know others, I often wondered, What is *she* in for? What would *she* have done? And sometimes I did learn about them: one didn't do anything herself but her husband helped pilots; one hid Jews; one worked in the black market.

Those women who worked together making rope got to know each other quite well because of all the time they spent together. But because my false identification had indicated that I was a maid, I was singled out to mop and clean, along with two other girls who helped do the laundry. A guard was constantly standing beside us, except when she went away to get a cup of coffee or a beer. Scrubbing the floors was a job I did alone, so I didn't have the sense of community the others had. When they came back in the evening, it was obvious to me that friendships were developing between them.

I was an outsider, but I didn't mind it that way. I didn't want to draw any attention to myself, because in prison I was not the person anyone thought I was. In addition, I was still trying hard to convey the sense that I was backward and foolish, even moronic. I acted so stupid, in fact, that I became annoying to the guards. The Germans were so militaristic that they always wanted prisoners to stand straight, at attention — shoulders back, stomach in, and all of that. So I slumped deliberately.

"Willie! Stand straight!" a guard would yell at me.

"I can't understand what you're saying," I'd say. "Could you please speak Dutch?" That made them more angry at me.

In the Netherlands it is thought to be very bad manners if you have your hands in your pockets when you speak to someone in authority: custom declared it very impolite. If Grandma came, or uncles or aunts, and I was wearing a dress with pockets, Mother was always telling me, "Diet, take your hands out of your pockets when you speak to someone."

My prison dress had two giant pockets, so whenever the guards spoke to me, my hands would go into my pockets right away. I didn't want to pay any respect to them at all.

"Willie, Willie — *nimm die Hände aus die Tasche!*" they screamed at me every day.

"I don't understand what you're saying," I'd say.

Then someone would translate for me, and I'd furrow my brow a bit and say, "Oh, oh, yes, of course. I remember now," and I'd take them out. In the meantime, I'd slump again. After months of that, they were sure I was borderline retarded — which is exactly what I wanted them to believe.

I got to know a woman named Mrs. Folmer, who was a widow. She had only one daughter, and that girl was eighteen years old. Mrs. Folmer must have been about forty, a beautiful woman with very fine features. But her face expressed suffering so deep that I will never forget it; her eyes radiated a deep sadness. She went quietly about her own business and talked very little. Because her daughter had helped Allied pilots, the Gestapo arrested the mother when they arrested the daughter. She knew that her only child was in deep trouble, and she had no idea where this young girl could be. Mrs. Folmer was oppressed by that special sadness, perhaps the most horrible torture, of those who had no idea what happened to their loved ones.

I had put my own parents' safety in danger in the same way that Mrs. Folmer's daughter had brought suffering to her mother, not only because I was active in the Resistance, but also because one night Hein and I had hidden weapons at my parents' house. At one point we had many revolvers and rifles in our possession, weapons we didn't know what to do with. Father and Mother had gone to a family birthday.

"What do we do?" we asked ourselves.

"Let's bury them in your parents' garden," Hein said.

And so, in the dark, while Father and Mother were away, we dug a huge hole in the garden, wrapped those weapons in rubber sheeting, and buried them. Of course, we had to disguise the broken ground to make it look as though no one had been digging there.

My father and mother never knew that we had hidden all those arms there. Every day they sat in a house with a garden full of buried guns. In addition to all the other worry and suffering at Vught, I worried myself sick about it, because I knew any search of that yard would turn up those weapons. And I knew what would happen if that occurred. Just as Mrs. Folmer was arrested and imprisoned because of her daughter's crime, I knew my father and mother would be put up against the wall and shot if the Gestapo ever discovered those arms. They would be killed for something they knew nothing about, something their daughter did.

The sadness I saw in Mrs. Folmer's eyes, and the way I identified her plight with what could happen to my own parents was the reason I eventually spoke to her and told her something of the truth about myself. But there's more to the story.

According to my ID, Willie Laarman was born in Para-maribo, Surinam, and that had to be my story. My being born in Surinam was fascinating to other women, most of whom were born in the Netherlands. You need things to talk about when you are in prison; and simply chatting with others was difficult for me because of that oddity. The truth was that I knew absolutely nothing about life in Surinam. From studying geography in school, I knew it was a Dutch colony, that the capital is Paramaribo, and that the black people there have their own language. That's all I knew.

Now, a very famous celebrity, Ennie Meunier, who starred in all the great theaters of the Netherlands, lived with us in Barracks No. 4. I had no idea why such a famous actress would be in Vught camp, but I listened closely to the talk going on around me, and I discovered that she was engaged to a German. That wasn't reason to be arrested, and as soon as I heard that, I became one of the only prisoners in our barracks who wanted nothing to do with Ennie Meunier. I didn't trust her.

One day Ennie Meunier walked up to me and said, "Oh, Willie, I hear you were born in Paramaribo."

I couldn't deny it.

"When I was on my tour in May, did you see my show?"

I knew that any visit by a Dutch entertainer of that rank would be the social event of the season in Surinam.

"As a matter of fact," I said, "my father had a leave just at that time, we were out of the country, and we were so sorry we missed it." I told her everyone I knew had been talking about it. "It must have been terrific," I said.

She smiled, but then she went on. "Where did you live?" She was after a street name.

I had no idea what to say, and I was scared of her anyway. But I remembered one wonderful excuse we all used at times: we would pretend we had a sudden bout of diarrhea. "Excuse me," I said, and I ran. No one ever asked questions if you suddenly flew off to the toilet. But I was afraid Ennie would get back to me one day, and she'd been to Surinam. From then on I tried even harder to avoid her, but I thought about what I could do when she asked again.

I don't remember how I learned about Mrs. Folmer's past, but I heard someone say that she had lived in Surinam, in fact, in Paramaribo. One day, when I saw Mrs. Folmer run to the bathroom all by herself, I ran after her. If anyone had observed me, they would have merely thought, "Well, Willie had diarrhea today too." I sat beside Mrs. Folmer and started talking.

"Is it true? Have you lived in Paramaribo?" I asked.

She said she had.

"Please, don't ask me any questions," I said, "but tell me everything you know about Paramaribo. Start with the name of a street where people live."

She said "Heerenstraat." Then she told me all about the layout of the city, about its downtown, its parks, everything I needed to know. She never asked why I wanted to know, but I told her that when the war was over I would explain.

One evening Ennie Meunier came back to me again, and I knew she would pick up the conversation. She did.

"I really loved Paramaribo. Tell me," she said, "where did you live?"

This time I answered her questions as well as I could. Willie the maid must have sounded as if she knew the city of Paramaribo very well.

That Mrs. Folmer was there with me at Vught was no coincidence. It was providence. She was the one I needed for information. Of all the women I came to know during the early days of my imprisonment there, she was the only one I would have trusted because I could see her life's sadness in her eyes. There was no deceit in her.

One woman was darker than the rest of us, somewhat Indian or African, from one of the islands — Aruba, I believe. Her name was Amancia, a very exotic name in the Netherlands, where there are dozens of Cornelias or Berendinas, but no Amancias. To me, it seemed so melodious: *Amancia,* the name for a beautiful song. Her last name was Roggeveen, and it made for an incongruous

combination of names. *Rogge* means rye grass, and *veen* means peat:
a real farmer's name, a peat moss name. Amancia Roggeveen —
those two names just didn't go together at all.

Amancia began to read everyone's palms, and we all were
surprised at what she would tell us. "It's true," some women
would say. "It's absolutely true. Everything she says is absolutely
true." Her popularity grew by leaps and bounds. After all, we
were sitting there in the camp with no power over our future;
what might happen to us became a matter of constant specula-
tion for all of us. The women streamed to Amancia. "Read my
hand. Please, read my hand," they would beg.

She read the lines in their hands and even talked about their
pasts. She would tell people that this happened and that happened, and the women would say, "Yes, Yes, Yes." The moment
she looked at a hand, she would begin to speak: she would see
certain things that were undoubtedly going to happen, she'd say.
And many believed what she said.

The women who were told good news were consoled by
it, of course; they were going to get out of the prison, and this
and that would happen. Amancia couldn't give exact dates, but
many of them felt much better because of Amancia's readings.
I sometimes believed that such fortune telling could be accurate;
I doubted it seriously, but I was willing to believe it wasn't
impossible. But I thought that if the predictions came true, what
Amancia was doing was of Satan's working — because of what
we had been taught about the witch of Endor.

So I didn't want her to read my palm. Besides, I thought
that if I would show her my hand, she might say something like,
"You're not who you say you are." So I stayed away from
Amancia. But eventually everybody had gone to her, and some
had gone several times. The others said, "What did Amancia
say to you, Willie?"

I told them I didn't believe in that stuff.

"Oh, but you don't have to believe, Willie," they said. "You can have it done just for the fun." Everybody barged in on me, and I was the center of attention because I was the only one who had not yet gone to Amancia. I always tried to avoid being the center of attention. And eventually I was drawing more attention to myself by not going to Amancia with my hand out than I was by staying away from her. So I went to her, but I didn't like it at all. I did it only because of the pressure of the others who thought I was crazy for not playing along.

And when Amancia held my palm, I was actually afraid. She looked at my hand and said, "Do you have a twin sister? I see someone exactly like you."

That scared the blazes out of me. I was absolutely convinced that she saw the real me, plus she saw the one that I was pretending to be; and since she didn't know what to do with what she saw in the lines of my hand, she tried the idea of a twin sister. I never doubted that what she'd seen was my lie about who I was, but I played dumb. I always played very dumb. I said, "No, I'm the only child, and —"

"Well," she said "I see loads of paper — loads of paper. And I see you crying, crying, crying."

"I never really cry," I said.

"I see you crying," she repeated, "and I see loads of paper, and then they call you, and you get . . . you get a hearing, and it will go real long. And then you will feel real good because everything went so well, and after that, later, you get a very short hearing and you'll say something else — and *then* you will go in deeper than you've ever been before."

That's what she saw in my hand.

Time passed, and I tried not to think about what she'd said because I was afraid of what she had seen. It was too upsetting.

And yet I was ambivalent. I believed Amancia's prophecy, even though it sounded ominous. And part of what she had said could make me believe that I would be released in a normal way. But that last remark about the mistake worried me.

For some reason, I started to worry that the guys from our Resistance group might try something to get me out of prison—bribe someone or something. If the Germans caught wind of such a plan, they would know I was not just a stupid maid. One day I met a brokenhearted girl named Floortje. She had just found out that her husband had died in prison. The Germans never really told wives that their husbands had been executed; they would simply let the spouses go one day. Floortje knew that her husband was gone because they were releasing her. She was from Rijswijk, just outside The Hague.

"I have to trust you," I said to her. "When you are out of here, please go to this address. Be very careful. I don't know if the Gestapo are keeping their eyes on this address anymore or not. But just pretend that you have come for a collection for whatever cause — maybe for the hungry.

"Please go there and tell my parents that I am here and doing fine." I asked her also to tell them to let my group know that they should *not* think of getting me out since it would put me in greater danger if they tried to bribe someone or do something foolish.

"This is very, very important," I said.

And she did go to my parents. That was the first moment that they knew I was in Vught, and that I was alive and doing well under the circumstances. I had told Floortje to make sure that in describing Vught she wouldn't create too much worry; otherwise they would think their daughter was in deep misery.

The guys *had* actually been making inquiries about where I was and how to get me out. They had begun talking to my uncle, who was in the local police. But even my uncle could not have found me: I was incarcerated under a false name. I didn't want them trying to find me because I believed I had a chance of getting out by the method I had devised — by acting stupid at my hearing. There had always been a little voice in me — even that day I was arrested — that insisted I would get out of prison, even if I had to go to Germany, like so many others.

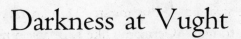

Darkness at Vught

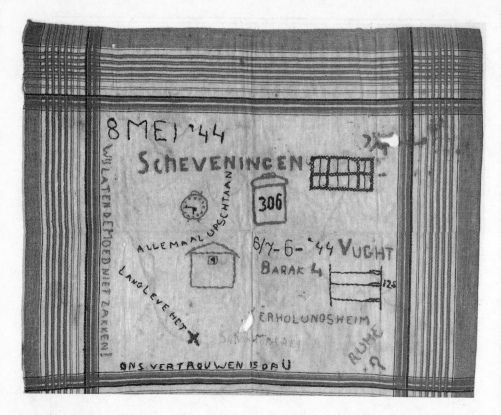

At the time of her arrest, Diet, like everyone else, carried a handkerchief, since no tissues were available. At the Vught concentration camp, the women passed around a carefully hidden needle at night so that they could embroider under the blankets. Each woman could use the needle for about seven minutes; thread was scavenged from clothing. Diet's handkerchief is embroidered with the date of her arrest; her barrack and cot numbers; various symbols, including a clock showing the time they were awakened each morning; German words that were frequently yelled at the prisoners; the title of the camp song composed by the inmates ("We don't lose our courage"); a Bible verse ("Our Trust is in You"); and "Long Live the Red Cross." Without the food supplements the inmates received from the Red Cross, many would not have survived.

At Vught Camp our barracks was the only one that specifically held female prisoners who hadn't had their hearings. Sporadically, one by one, we were called out to face our interrogators. We were always nervous and scared.

Three months passed, and through all that time God gave me the opportunity to go over my story — over and over — to learn it perfectly. From the night in Scheveningen when I'd talked to Trix about what I should say, and all through my months at Vught Camp, I worked very hard to restrain my thoughts from remembering the people I loved. Instead, I worked at creating a whole new life, a new identity for myself as this woman named Willie Laarman, a maid born in Paramaribo whose parents were now both dead.

It was very tempting to reminisce about those I loved because that was what my mind wanted to do — to relive the good times. It would have been so great to be able to think about Hein. But I wouldn't allow myself that pleasure because I still had to face my hearing armed to the teeth with a plausible story so deeply set in my brain that I wouldn't flinch for a moment when telling it. Maybe it was partially because of the rigid self-discipline I made myself live with.

When I went to my bed after a long day in camp, it would be so tempting to start thinking of Hein and my parents, my brothers and sister. I prayed for them every night, of course. I knew Hein was in the prison at Amersfoort, and Amersfoort had a horrible reputation. But other than praying, I would not allow myself even a thought of the people I loved and missed so dearly for at least the last hour or so that I stayed awake.

"You are Willie Laarman. You were born in Paramaribo. You are an orphan. Your parents have died." That's what I told myself, over and over again. I wanted no ballast when the time came for me to have my hearing; I wanted to have the whole story of my false life down to the last detail. If I were to tell my interrogators that my parents were dead, I knew I would have to explain their deaths, give dates, and be able to remember perfectly what I'd said if asked to repeat the facts again. I spent hours at night going over the whole story, trying to keep it as bare bones as I could: just me and my parents, and they were dead, and I didn't have much to say at all about life in general.

I made sure those were my last thoughts before I slept. I did not want to be caught off guard if they called me at two or three in the dark of night — which they regularly did. If they were to wake me from a deep sleep and start bombarding me with questions, I wanted to have Willie on my mind, not Hein. So I tried to put him out of my head completely, as completely as I could. I knew our whole operation was at stake.

Today, sometimes, I think that perhaps what I did to brainwash myself during those years was too much. I don't know if it was wise, but it was safest. Our minds are strange things.

During that time I always tried to keep my eye on the others, in silence, of course. I observed how one woman especially, a woman named Hanny, who was not very pretty — had horrible teeth and especially greasy hair — was called up for hearings two or three times a week. I wondered what she had done that they were calling her out so often.

You learn things when you watch as closely as I did. Most women would be shattered when they returned from their hearings; but Hanny did not come back broken like so many of them. Also, unlike many of us, who were called at any hour of the day or night — often in the middle of the night — she was called out quite often at 1:30 or 2:00 in the afternoon. And she was never nervous or scared. When she returned, she looked almost tanned, as if she'd been in the sun; and often she was even talkative, as if she'd had a beer or two.

I began to believe that she was being used to spy on us. That had to explain why she wasn't scared, even though the guards came for her so often. But she wasn't smart either. If they had been using me, I would have at least acted nervous about what had happened at my hearing. And it was stupid of the Germans to take her out and let her sit in the sunshine somewhere.

I trusted Mrs. Folmer, and I trusted a wonderful Catholic girl named Freddy, but very few others. And I asked those I trusted if they'd noticed how Hanny was never nervous when she was called out, and how she was always talkative when she returned. I told them that we should watch out for her.

One day, close to when it would be my turn to be *Stube älteste*, the one to get all the women lined up for roll call in the morning, one of my friends came up to me.

"Guess what?" she said. "Every night Hanny Janssen climbs out of that little window in the guards' room, and she disappears with one of the guards at the four corners. They go out into the woods. And the other three guards watch the corners. Then just before daylight, she comes back."

So I concocted a plan with Freddy. I told her my plan, and she said she would help. The morning I had to do roll call, we got up at five — forty-five minutes early — and checked all the windows in the whole building, then locked them all. At about twenty after five, when it began to get light, Hanny wanted to climb back in. And when she couldn't, she became desperate. She was supposedly a normal prisoner, after all, and here she was sneaking out at night.

There we all stood that morning. The keys clanked in the barracks door, it opened, and the female guards marched in. That morning I had to stand on the line, count prisoners, and report. There were always seven or eight prisoners sick, and that number varied, but the total had to be right. I told the guards that I'd counted and counted and that there should be 167, but one was missing. "I can only count 166 . . . but maybe I made a mistake," I said. "I know there are eight in bed, but it doesn't come out right."

They thought that this mistake was simply attributable to stupid Willie: she can't count, after all. But for security's sake, they started counting themselves, and what they found was that one *was* missing, just as I had said.

Then they got nervous. All the names were called out, and we had to say "Yeah," "yeah," "here," "here." It turned out that Hanny Janssen was missing. She was their spy, but we weren't supposed to know that. We were very curious to see what would happen.

There was one part of the prison at Vught that everybody was afraid of. I never found out what really happened there, but if you had done something very bad, it was said that you were sent to the "bunker." We often heard terrible screams coming from there, but we didn't know for sure whether prisoners were tortured there or what. People who had walked by and knew where the bunker was said that they had seen hands sticking out of the window or bars. It must have been a terrible place.

Once our guards discovered who was missing that morning, we got a notice that, as an example of Hanny Janssen's "trying to escape," she was now in the bunker. She would have to stay there for at least a month, they said. So for that month we lived without our spy, thank goodness. But when she came back a month later, Hanny didn't even complain. I think she was probably being entertained; she probably had a good time somewhere other than the bunker. I never knew for sure what other spies might have been among the women in Barracks No. 4, but I was sure about Hanny.

*   *   *

One night, suddenly, one of the girls started screaming with pain. She was absolutely hysterical. What could we do? The female guards had left for the night, so we went to the window and called to the outside guards:

"We don't know what to do with this woman. She's in terrible pain!"

The male guards said they would get a doctor, which pleasantly surprised us since we hadn't known that there even was a doctor. When the outside guards came back with a stretcher, they had to call the female guards because it was a very strict order that men were not allowed alone in the women's barracks. Eventually the woman in pain was carried off on the stretcher to the hospital. We hadn't known that there was a hospital either! It turned out that she had a ruptured appendix, and she was operated on right then and there.

We found out that the hospital we hadn't known about was very well supplied and that it was staffed almost entirely by Dutch surgeons, doctors, and nurses who were also prisoners. In addition, we learned, the food was good in the hospital, which was getting extra supplies from the Red Cross. And there was a dentist, also a fellow prisoner, who worked on teeth in the hospital.

Once we found out that there was a hospital, many of us wanted to go. One day in June, I suddenly had a tooth filling fall out — a large one, large enough for me to be constantly sticking my tongue in it. It didn't hurt that much, but I didn't want to be bothered by it all the time. When I heard that there was a dentist in that hospital, I thought, *Well, why not try it.* After all, prison life can get very boring. One will do anything to make something different happen.

I told the guards that I'd lost a very big filling, and they

said it was okay for me to go to the dentist. I accompanied
a group of eight or ten from another barracks who were also
going to the dentist. We had to march through the prison
camp alongside a big soldier who was yelling, "March, march,
march," toward the hospital — a hospital that I'd never known
existed. Finally we came to one end of the hospital, where
there was a small extension building, and that was the dentist's
office.

The dentist stood there in that little room with its small
window and dentist's chair; the waiting room was a tight corridor
just outside, where there was a bench and a door. All the prisoners in the camp had triangles on the sleeves of their prison
uniform. If you were a political prisoner, you got a red triangle;
if you were a murderer or some other kind of criminal, you got
a green triangle. I did not have a triangle yet; none of us in
Barracks No. 4 had received identification because none of us
had had a hearing.

I will never forget that dentist, because when I looked at
him for the first time, I saw a green triangle on his sleeve. He
was a murderer. *Maybe he murdered a German,* I thought, which
would make him a murderer in their eyes but not in mine. There
we sat on that waiting-room bench, nine of us in a row, with
the guard watching us. He would walk past with his rifle, stand
a moment, then step into the dentist's office, and walk by again.
He had to stand guard there until each of us had had a turn.
Sometimes he stayed in the dentist's office a long time, watching
whoever was in the chair. The dentist kept asking, "Does this
hurt?" And we would say, "Ah-hah."

I was sitting right next to the door that went back into
what we assumed was the hospital. At one point, that door
opened, just beyond the latch, so that it made a sound with the
wind — click, click, click — an irritating noise like a dripping

faucet. I pulled it shut to stop the bothersome noise; but a moment later it was open again, and it started into the same little clicking. I thought I had shut it, and this time I started thinking that the noise was not just irritating — it was strange. At that moment the guard walked into the dentist's room, and suddenly a hand came out of that door loaded with slices of bread and margarine!

I grabbed them right away because I was sitting next to the door; but there were so many that I quickly spread them around to the others waiting on that bench. The moment I saw the guard again, I stuck the bread inside my dress. And as soon as he went back in with the dentist, the hand came out of the door again with more bread. We couldn't really eat with the guard walking by so often; so we put the bread inside the front of our dresses and took it back and shared it with the sick people in the barracks. Every time the guard would leave the corridor, another piece of bread would appear, and we'd stow it away in our dresses. It was wonderful to get all that extra food — not only the bread, but cheese, ham, and margarine with it! We all ate very well that day.

Finally it was my turn to go into the dentist's room.

"Where does it hurt?" he asked. He was a Greek who spoke rather broken English, and just a few Dutch words.

"Well, I lost my filling," I said.

"We'll have to do some drilling and put a temporary one in," he said. So he started drilling, and the moment he did, he said, "Have you heard the latest news?"

Now at that time every business in occupied Europe was short of manpower. Jewish people were not allowed to work, of course, and many natives of occupied countries had been sent to work in Germany. In addition, many men were in hiding. Philips, the large electronics manufacturing plant in Eindhoven, which was very close to Vught, had been taken over by the Germans because it was a war industry. But Philips was always short of laborers, and the Germans were constantly rounding up people to work there.

So the Germans had allowed Philips to set up a plant inside the camp at Vught. The prisoners who got to work in the Philips plant were the lucky ones. They got extra food and were treated well by the Philips employees brought in to run the plant. We could not listen to the BBC, of course, but the prisoners in the Philips plant were able to do so indirectly. The Dutch Philips employees would surreptitiously tell the prisoners what was going on at that point in the war.

"It's good news," they would whisper. "The Allies have taken this city or that town, and they're marching up in Italy, and Patton's in Belgium — there's lots of good news."

In the evening all the Philips plant prisoners would be back in the camp, and they would spread the news they had heard. Sometimes those prisoners would get sick or have a toothache, and they would spread the news to people in that hospital. Philips became a major source of information for everyone at Vught, and it was wonderful to have.

As soon as that dentist asked me what I had heard, the German guard came back, and the dentist started again:

"Where does it hurt? Right here, you say?"

We played that game again for a while, but as soon as the German would walk back out, the dentist would start telling me all about the progress of the war. He gave me all the latest news from Philips that day. Finally my tooth was filled, so I had to leave. But he told me that the filling was only temporary and that I'd have to come back. I said that would be fine.

So a few days later, we did the whole thing again, and I

heard the latest news once more. I also wore my gabardine raincoat that time, so that I could open the pockets and let the bread fall in between the lining. That way I could bring much more back to the barracks along with all the news from the Phillips plant. I don't know how many times I have blessed that hand full of bread and cheese and meat sticking out from behind that door, and given thanks to whoever was there. And I never even saw who the person was. There may have been someone in our group who was aware that this would happen; but when it started, I was the one sitting by the door, and I had no idea. To me it was a complete surprise.

Finally the Greek dentist said to me, "It's now all repaired, and I'll have to let you go." I was so sad. And when he saw that, he said, "On the other hand, if you want to keep coming, I'll have to drill holes in some of your perfectly good teeth."

"Yes, please!" I said immediately.

And he drilled several after that. During the rest of my stay in that prison, I was in his office many times. It seemed like I always needed something done. I don't know how many holes he drilled, or how often I went, but he filled them up with some strange wartime compound. He must have done a good job, though, because those fillings lasted many years.

Years later, a dentist asked me about the strange fillings in my teeth: "I don't know what this stuff is — it's really odd."

"Oh, those are my prison fillings," I said.

I still have some of them in my mouth, I think.

*   *   *

In the summer of 1944, General Patton's army was making excellent progress against the Germans in Belgium, and soon enough we began to hear heavy artillery coming closer and closer, thumping in the distance. The Germans were beginning to get scared. Vught is in southern Holland, and since the country is very small, the distance between Vught and Belgium isn't great. We could hear Patton's artillery coming.

The guard assigned to supervise the laundry became so terribly bored after a while with watching us — sometimes I had a helper or two — that finally she just locked us up in the wash room and left us alone. She'd go and get a cup of coffee or have a beer or something, which we would smell on her later, and she'd stay away for a long time.

The moment she'd leave, we'd have a breath of freedom. You must understand how much we hated the Germans, and here in the laundry room our job was to wash out their underwear. We had to wring out all their rotten underwear with our bare hands, make sure that stuff was perfectly clean. We hated the SS worse than any of the other Germans, and there was the SS insignia, embroidered on every undershirt.

Except for one or two of them, the camp and prison guards all belonged to the SS; and in the termination camps they were always SS. The Gestapo's job was to investigate and interrogate, and they were smart; but the SS were not necessarily wily or cunning — they were simply brutal. From what I've seen in the camps, I think that the SS were specifically trained for the work they did in camp; they were trained to torture and kill. And they seemed to do it with joy. They were the worst of the Germans, and we hated them. Here I was — my fiancé somewhere a world away in some other camp, maybe alive, maybe not — and I was washing the underwear of the worst of the worst.

Once the guard would leave, my helpers and I would take those SS shirts and hold them up. Then we would gather up a nice big glob of saliva and spit right on the SS insignia. We became very good at it, really accurate. We had to do laundry every day because there were so many guards in that camp, and by the end I was really a sharpshooter. Every day my helpers and I would spit on their underwear.

It's absolutely crazy to think, now, that spitting on somebody's underwear could be that enjoyable. But we were never really sure at what moment we would be facing death at the hands of these very people. It felt wonderful to spit on that hated SS insignia that way. After the war, a psychiatrist friend of Corrie ten Boom wanted to talk with Ansje, a young friend of mine who lost her husband, and to me. Corrie said he was very interested in what we had gone through. I told him that maybe what we did in that laundry room was silly, especially when our lives were at stake. But he told us it was wise to do something like that. He said that the Germans tried hard to break our spirits, and things like spitting on underwear and other seemingly foolish things helped us to know that we hadn't let them.

We would do laundry the whole day — underwear and shirts. We would soak all our own clothing in the same gutters that we had to wash our faces in in the morning. But for the guards' laundry we had a tub. Those clothes had to be white and clean: that meant chlorine bleach and lots of scrubbing with our hands and our knuckles, the kind of scrubbing I had learned from Alie on the farm. For the SS underwear, of course, we also got soap. After a while our fingers became calloused with all that scrubbing and rinsing.

About the time we began to hear Patton's heavy artillery, one day I found my hands coming away bloody from the clothes we were washing. One shirt, light blue, was very bloody. We had to wash the bloody things in a separate trough and soak them in cold water to let all the blood run out. There was a lot of blood, and I had no idea what had happened.

One of the women guards, Frau Schenck, appeared to have

some human qualities. She had been on duty one day when I had been thinking some good thoughts and simply started singing a hymn. This was, I'm sure, quite unusual; those guards never heard any singing. I had been alone in the laundry that day, and Frau Schenck had been away from my side for a little while, so I was singing in full voice when she returned. Most guards would have snapped at me — "Keep your trap shut" — something like that. But I can still hear her say, *Du singst wie eine Heide Lerche,* "You sing like a heather lark."

Frau Schenck was on duty the day those bloody shirts came through the laundry, so I dared to speak to her.

"What happened here?" I asked.

"Oh," she said, "two guys on a motorbike had a terrible accident, and we have them in our hospital. We want this stuff clean when they come out."

So I washed it and it was taken away. But the next day there were many more — maybe eleven or twelve pieces of underwear and shirts — everything, including socks and even suits, covered with blood. This was no motorbike accident. I became very nervous because I had no idea what was going on. A few days later, when Frau Schenck was there, I spoke to her again. I asked her again about the bloody clothes.

She could have said that it was none of my business, but she didn't.

"Yeah, those are traitors, and they had to be punished," she said. In her eyes, of course, anyone who opposed the Germans was a traitor.

"But why do we have to wash their clothes then?" I asked.

"Because we have to send the clothes back to the family," she said, "and it would be very hard for the family to see those clothes filled with blood."

That was exactly what she said: this halfway decent guard

with her halfway decent lie. And that's what I believed at first; that belief enabled me to continue with this hideous task. I believed Frau Schenck, who wasn't as bad as the guards we hated. And I thought maybe she was correct — that it would be better for the families not to have to see those clothes all full of blood.

I went on washing, looking for identifying labels in that clothing; and many of the shirts and jackets had Dutch names. I was still very curious. One night I tried to introduce that mystery into a conversation we were having. I told everyone that I was wondering what had happened. I told them how the first time the bloody shirts came in, the guard had told me it was from a motorcycle accident, but how those bloody clothes had just kept on coming.

"One day," I said, "there were thirty-six shirts, and it was just terrible. I mean, it was a river of blood in that laundry room. My nerves were so wired I couldn't sleep that night."

And then Hanny, the woman we knew was a spy, said, "Oh, those shirts come from men who are being executed."

My mouth went dry. "But why do we have to wash their clothing?" I asked.

"Germany has no clothing whatsoever," she said, "so it has to be washed and sent to Germany."

I was horrified. I was just horribly shocked. I had washed those bloody clothes myself, with my own hands, the clothes of men they had killed — our guys! And now those clothes were being shipped back to Germany to be worn by our enemies! I can't describe the horror I felt. All I can say is that the feeling I had that day of my hands in our own guys' blood remains one of the most horrible of my life.

Hanny probably shouldn't have told us that either, but she was stupid. Sometimes the Germans picked the stupidest informers. She seemed proud of the fact that she knew something about what was going on on the outside, something none of the rest of us did. She said that those clothes went from our barracks to another barracks, where a whole crew had to mend the bullet holes.

I still continued to do the wash for one or two more days because I wanted to see if I could pick up any names on those clothes. Those days I spent in the laundry after I knew what was going on with all those bloody clothes were the most horrible days of my life. I started to look very closely at where the bullet holes were in those shirts, and what I found was even more horrible. Sometimes the bullet holes were not at the heart level, as ordered by the Geneva Convention, but at the stomach level, which meant that the men who died in those shirts probably suffered for hours before finally succumbing. There are no words to describe such blackness.

I examined those shirts very closely to see whether I could find names. These were Resistance people who were being executed, and I knew that I had to report the gunshots to the stomach to the Red Cross; so I wanted badly to find names, any names at all, maybe written in or sewn into the clothing. Whenever I found one, I tried to commit it to memory. These were not military uniforms but suits, some woolen suits, full of holes.

What was happening became clear to me. The men who had been executed — usually every night at sunset, we could hear the machine guns — would be lying somewhere for hours before they died. I was absolutely heartbroken. And I was heartbroken for another reason: I suspected that any one of those men being taken out and shot in the stomach and left to die could be my Hein. He could easily have been transferred from the camp at Amersfoort to the one here at Vught; I would never have seen him, even though we might have been so close to each other — in the same camp.

Hein's clothes might be among all these bloody ones, as well as Ab's clothes, Adriaan's clothes, Jantje's clothes, Aalt's clothes. The tension mounted, day by day, as I went to the laundry. I'd say to myself, "Whose clothes will I find today among the bloody ones? Will I see the clothes of the man I love today, the man I would have married?"

It was terrible. At that moment I began to be filled with hatred, absolutely filled with it. And then I lost something: I simply could not ask the Lord to help me to love my enemies anymore. I was praying, instead, for God's damnation on the Nazis, for his curse on them. I couldn't face the evil anymore; I had no strength to go on. I couldn't brace my mind anymore, couldn't hold it up with any strength, because I had none. After all those years in Underground work, and then the entire year they were constantly searching for me, terrifying my parents; after Hein's arrest, and then mine; and then waiting forever for a hearing that never came. Then the bloody clothes of men I might have known and loved — at that moment life was unbearable. The relentless fear and tension and anxiety overcame whatever meager power I could muster when I found my hands red with blood.

This was July 1944, and it started with two bloody shirts. I found out that when we heard the heavy artillery in the distance, the Germans had begun to get nervous: they wanted to empty the camp because they didn't want any prisoners to fall into the hands of Patton and be free. Hanny told me that they were executing people at sunset every day. So we listened, and we heard machine guns. I found out later that they simply picked a certain number of prisoners at random every day and sentenced them to death. No trial, no nothing — just bang, bang, bang. To have to go through that, to hear those shots and to imagine what we did, to think that every day some of our boys, possibly our loved ones, were being murdered out there, so close to us, and yet to know we were powerless — that was unbearable. At that point I couldn't go on.

I said to God, "How can you let all of this horror go on? How can you stand all this evil? This is *your* world — how can you stand it?" And I said it angrily. After all, we had done all of this work, involved ourselves for several years, suffered so much sleeplessness, so much worry, so much tension, and risked so much danger. And now, when I held those clothes in my hand, it seemed as though the death of those men was the only verifiable answer to all of my praying — all of our praying together — and everything we'd ever done.

I'm not sure what happened in me, but some impulse to continue was switched off as abruptly as if a power source had suddenly disappeared. One morning I woke up and absolutely could not move. I was lying on my side, totally paralyzed: I couldn't turn over, and I couldn't stand, not even for roll call. When it sounded that morning, I said to the others, "I can't work. I can't even move."

They turned me over, but I couldn't go to the bathroom or anything. It seemed to me that I had lost complete control of my whole body. They reported that to the guards, and the guards came in.

"You have to get up," they yelled. "You have to do the laundry! Get out of that bed!"

But I honestly could not move. I was not faking anything; I was completely paralyzed. They sent for the camp doctor — a Dutch prisoner and a very good doctor, I discovered later. He came to my bunk. I'm sure that it was probably the most difficult role he had to play: to pretend to be very tough on prisoners such as I, prisoners who absolutely couldn't go on. If he didn't appear to be tough, he would risk being removed from his job and replaced by someone much worse.

"Now get up," he screamed, and he kicked the bed. But he didn't kick me, and it didn't hurt anything. "Stop this right now." He went into a tirade, but I couldn't move. I literally could not move.

"But I can't get up," I said.

Then I heard him say something to the Germans, something about "this lousy woman," and that day they allowed me to stay in bed. In fact, I lay there for three whole days, totally paralyzed. My friends helped me to the bathroom and anywhere else I needed to move; but I have very vague impressions of those days because it was a time of complete darkness for me. Somebody told me later that what I had was a form of hysteria: my body and my mind fled into paralysis. There was nothing wrong with me organically, but somewhere inside I suffered a complete breakdown.

At some point in everyone's life, I believe, there comes a time when one feels perfectly alone, when one hits the bottom. It might be long-term illness, it might be divorce, it might be a job loss. But most often in such situations one is surrounded by friends or family, people who can help, support, and encourage. But at that moment in the camp at Vught I had nobody. I had friends, and there were some women I talked to; but all the time, even with them, I was trying to be someone I was not. I had no real communication with anyone at that time, so I was totally dependent on God. And he never failed me.

The Hearing

One of many fake identification cards Diet
used during the Occupation.

Finally, the day of my hearing came. I had gotten my story down so well, having had all that time to imagine it so deeply, that the details were burned into my mind. None of us women ever knew what was going to happen at her hearing. Whether one was interrogated horridly or not often depended simply on the case worker. I didn't even know who my case worker was; I'd never met him. I had simply been sitting in the camp for all those months. At one point I had worried that they had forgotten to register me in the system, that I would never even get a hearing, that I had been lost among the hundreds of thousands of prisoners. I was afraid that I would never get out, would just sit there until the war was over.

One day I was scrubbing the bathroom, which was part of my new job after the breakdown, and I was totally alone, my nerves very high. The others were working on rope and I was allowing myself to think about Hein, my parents, and Aalt and Alie at Watergoor. While I was scrubbing, for the first time since I had been arrested, I allowed myself to cry. I cried and cried and cried. It was crying time for me, and a dam just burst. All alone in the bathroom, so that neither the Germans nor anyone else saw or heard it, I let myself go. It was undoubtedly necessary: I had held it in for so long. So instead of scrubbing the floors, I just sat on the dirty floor and wept.

Just a few days later, a man with boots and a uniform came marching in and called for the guard in charge. When I saw him, a little voice inside me said that after all these months, this call was for me. I went on sweeping, and when this soldier found the guard, she came yelling: "Willie, go with him."

When my friend Freddie heard that, she knew I was going to my hearing. The two of us had this spiritual tie, and we had confided some things to each other. We knew and trusted each other so much that as soon as she heard that call, she pretended that she had diarrhea and flew toward me on her way to the toilet. While she was passing me, she whispered, "Willie, I'm going to storm the gates of heaven for you." And off she went to the bathroom.

I followed that officer, but what she'd said hit me very hard: "I'm going to storm the gates of heaven for you." It was such a great comfort to me that she wasn't going to be merely praying — she was storming!

Following that officer through the camp — another moment during the war where I felt I was hanging between life and death — I was considering all these things: Will they believe my story? If not, can they find out who I really am? Do they already know? I had great fear inside because we all knew that hearings were terrifying; at the same time, I was filled with hatred: ever since we had learned about the executions, I had prayed for every kind of curse and horror on the Germans, and I had hoped that God would punish them. I wanted nothing but evil done to them because of the bloody clothes and what I'd heard in the sound of guns at sunset, what I'd feared in the silence and in the darkness.

I must have walked with that officer quite a distance, but I can't remember that walk at all. I didn't even see where I was going. *What am I going to say?* I thought. *What am I going to say in this story?*

And then suddenly God's promises came to me: *Don't worry. If you appear before authorities and kings, I will give you the words.* This is what I heard in my mind: *Not a hair of your head will be harmed without the will of your heavenly Father.* God's promises came to my mind. "Okay," I thought, "I have often broken my promises to you, Lord, but you'll never break your promises. You take over now. You have promised it — now you have to do it." I said it to God as if I were confronting him: "I am going into my hearing, and you have said that you would be my God. Now I'm going to hold you to it."

Right then, while walking through the camp, my hatred disappeared. *Don't be afraid,* a little voice said. *They can't hurt a hair on your head unless it's the will of your heavenly Father.* At that moment I found comfort. I knew that whoever I would see there, no matter how cruel they might be, nothing and no one could touch me unless my God were to allow it. I went into that building in that frame of mind, with that assurance and that faith.

Now my physical appearance was something that would probably turn the stomach of those with the strongest constitutions. Just as at Scheveningen, we had received just one slice of bread early in the morning, one slice in the evening — a little bit of margarine too — and then soup, which was often practically water. That's all we ate at Vught, except for that time once every few weeks when the Red Cross gave us sandwiches and thick bean soup. Close by Vught was a German air base, which had plenty of food. In fact, all their leftover bread was thrown into dumpsters, and when full, those dumpsters were brought to our camp. The bread in them might be a day or so old, or it might be crusted with green fungus, but whatever was in that dumpster was fed to us, among other things.

There were many barracks at Vught, so our barracks, like the others, would get a turn at what the air base considered to be garbage. One day we would get what was on top, for instance, and then the next day we might get only what was left on the bottom — green bread. If you happened to be the last in line to pass the table, you had no choice in pieces of bread. The guards made sure you took what was in front of you. So at a certain point the one slice you received might be green bread, but you ate it. That's all there was.

In addition to the bad food, bad hygiene was a way of life.

We had no soap or shampoo, and certainly no deodorant. We stunk. And we could wash only with cold water. Many of us started to have itchy spots on our faces; they were always on the face, not on the arms or anywhere else. They were like hives, big hives, and they grew bigger and bigger until they were the size of strawberries, twisting one's face out of shape. Finally, the skin would burst open. They were called *phlegmones,* and when they burst open, green pus came out. Sometimes pus would be dripping down one's cheeks. It was horrible. We didn't have mirrors, but we could see each other; so all of us knew how those things looked on the others. I had at least three or four of those phlegmones.

When I was finally called out for my hearing, the officer looked at me as though I was something he would not touch at any cost. I had my prison gown on, those boils, and the hair of a woman who had not shampooed in over four months. I was ushered into the building for the hearings and brought before seven men sitting behind a table set neatly and covered with green felt. The hearing room was large, and there was a portrait of Hitler on the wall behind the table.

I had to sit on a wooden kitchen chair; my interrogators' table was quite a distance away. They started talking immediately, asking questions. Since I had vowed never to speak German, I shrugged my shoulders, playing stupid, as I had for as long as I'd been imprisoned.

"I can't understand you," I said. "I speak only Dutch."

For every word they said to me they would have to have a translator. And if they wanted to explain something to the *stomme schaap,* the "stupid sheep," they would have to go over it very slowly for me. Once a translator came, they started asking questions again. Now my stubborn patriotism gave me an advantage: they would ask the question in German first, and, of course, I understood it. Then, while the translator repeated it, I had a few extra moments to devise an answer.

That was how the hearing went, and it took much longer with the translator. I had to tell them how I had obtained my false ID. I was, of course, the maid born in Surinam, which they had no way of checking. But actually, when I was arrested, I had been delivering documents and was on my way to meet a family in Heemstede who would vouch that I was their maid. The idea was that we would see each other's faces, and I could see the layout of their house. But I'd never met them, so I had no idea of the layout of the house where I'd supposedly worked. If the Germans were to ask me a question about that, or if they would ask me to describe the man or the woman, I would have to make it up. I knew that was my weak point because that was the only thing they could check.

"Tell us what happened," they said.

I told them I was born in Surinam.

"Paramaribo? — that's where you were born?" they asked.

"Yes, I was born there," I said.

"Your parents?"

"Well, my father worked for the government — "

"What did he do?"

"He was in taxes or something. He had to do with the tax administration," I said. People pay taxes everywhere, I thought, so it would work for him to have that kind of job.

They accepted that. "Do you have brothers and sisters?"

"No."

"And where are your parents now?"

I told them that they had died. Of course, I did not want to hesitate at all, and I'd rehearsed the potential questions every night before I went to sleep. I told them my parents had both died in 1938, because in my story I'd come to the Netherlands in 1939.

The main interrogator asked if I had uncles and aunts.

Some were in Surinam and some in other countries, I told him. They couldn't check that, of course. Then I said, "We are a very small family. My father had only one brother."

"When did your father die?" he asked.

"December 5," I said, which was very easy to remember — Dutch Sinterklaas. I figured they might ask me that, and I knew they'd ask it more than once, perhaps with long intervals in between, and I'd have to say it again. So I couldn't choose just any day.

"What did he die of?" the man asked. My father must have died rather young, because I was in my early twenties.

"Well, he died of a snake bite." I figured that wasn't something a lot of people died of, but in Surinam they have very many poisonous snakes. I also wanted something a bit exotic, not something everyday like a heart attack.

Then he said, "Your mother?"

"She died right after him," I told them.

"What of?" he asked.

"My mom had a very weak heart, and when Father died so suddenly," I told them, "she had heart failure and died ten days later, on December 15."

It was difficult to act that out, because Willie Laarman's parents were only imaginary; but I had to convince them that these people — my parents, after all — were real. They had almost become my mother and father in my mind; it was a strange feeling to kill them that way, like sentencing my own parents to death. The lie gave me a strange feeling, perhaps because I felt as though I were committing a sin by telling them my parents had died.

Then I was told to explain how I got the false papers.

"When my parents died," I said, "there was no point for

272

me to stay in Surinam. I had nothing there, so I felt I should go back to the Netherlands. But I didn't know anybody to stay with, so I just became a maid. Then the war broke out."

"But how did you get to have this paper — this ID?" they asked.

So I told them that as the maid I had to do all the shopping for the family in Heemstede. All that time the Allies were going overhead on air raids, and sirens would go and you had to be off the street. I was out shopping, and just when I was on my way to the grocery store there was an air raid and I had to rush to the nearest shelter. There were shelters everywhere: some held hundreds of people, some only a few. Wherever you were, signs pointed toward them, and you had to take cover. You sat there amid lots of conversation, sometimes for five minutes and sometimes as long as an hour. You never knew how long it would last until the signal was given that it was safe outside.

I told them that I bumped into a young guy, and we started talking; it was a long raid, so we had a long conversation, sitting on the floor beside each other. When it was over, he asked me if we could meet each other again. He was a really nice-looking guy, so I said it would be okay. We agreed to meet in Amsterdam, near where he lived, somewhere in a park.

"What is this guy's name?" they asked.

"Jan Schilder," I said. *Jan* is, of course, a very common name; and *Schilder*, well, in our church we had just had a contentious split over theology, and the breakaway group was led by a man named Schilder. So I used "Jan Schilder."

And they said, "What did he look like?"

"Tall, blond, with blue eyes" — it was Hein. Of course, three-quarters of the men in Friesland are tall, blond, and have blue eyes.

"Where did he live?"

"I don't know," I said. I met him only a few times, and he was a very nice guy, and I liked him. But he didn't ask where I lived, and I didn't ask where he lived. We only met each other, let's say, often enough to go for a stroll in the park, maybe get a cup of coffee, but not much more. Because I didn't have a bike, we walked and we talked."

"Well, how did you get this ID?"

I said it was because of the curfew. "The last time I was visiting with him," I said, "he had a little newspaper. He told me it was one of those thrown out of the Allied planes that came over every night. He said it was named something like 'Flying Dutchman,' and when I left he gave it to me."

I told them that Jan Schilder had asked me to read it and bring it back to him. So I took that newspaper in my purse, where I also had my ID. But it was late, and I was terribly nervous because I was on the last train; I'd never taken the last train.

"And it was so close to curfew," I said, "that when the train stopped in Heemstede, I had to run to the home where I was maid to be there before curfew."

All during the interrogation I was playing the scared, stupid maid because I thought it was my only hope. In real life I couldn't have cared less whether I got in by curfew time or not. I also acted as if I had no idea what that paper was. I told them that Jan had said: "Be careful because you really are not allowed to read this." Those notices were dropped from planes, and I knew very well that the Germans had announced in all the papers that if you read them, you would go to prison.

"But when the train stopped at the station," I said, "and I knew the stops were very short — just a moment and you had to jump out — I was out so fast that I had run all the way home before I realized I had left my purse in the train."

"Normally," I said, "you would just go to the police station

274

the next day and say, 'I lost my purse with my ID.' But I didn't dare to do that because the newspaper Jan had told me was dangerous was still in my purse. And I hadn't even read it yet. I don't even know what it said.

"I didn't know what to do then," I went on. "I had another date with him, so I went. I told him what happened: that now I had no ID, and that I didn't dare to go to the police because of the newspaper he had given me. 'What did it say?' I asked him. He said, 'Well —'"

I told them that Jan didn't seem too worried about it because he said, "'Do you have passport photos?'"

"'I have some,'" I said.

"And he told me to bring them the very next night when we had another date."

"I must have been *so* lucky," I said to those Germans. "Jan must have been working in one of those offices where they make those papers, because he took my fingerprints, and the next time I saw him he gave me my new ID, and I didn't have to go to the police!"

I said it all as if I had never heard of stolen documents and blank IDs, or falsifications. "I was just so lucky," I told them. "But now you say that there must be something wrong with it? I didn't know that."

They sat around and started discussing my story, and I sat wondering if they would believe it. Their discussion was in German, of course, and I could understand every word; and I thought, *Thank you, Lord.*

They looked at me, and I heard one of them say, "But she doesn't really look like a maid. She seems more the type of a secretary or a teacher or something."

There must have been something about my appearance that seemed different from how I was trying to look. They stared at me for a while, and finally one of them said, "Well, we can give her a test."

And I thought, *Oh, no.*

Here they came with a magazine, a block, a pad of paper, and a pencil, and they said, "Copy this."

Once again I can say that God was taking care of me. Right away, ideas flipped through my mind. Most maids in the Netherlands at that time came from big families and could often complete only the sixth grade before starting to work in a home for another family. In sixth grade your handwriting hasn't yet been formed: schools required us to sit and write for a couple hours a week in order to acquire those beautiful curves. Early in school we would practice penmanship for a long time, and we'd be graded on it. So I thought that anyone who had only a sixth-grade education would probably think of handwriting in that way. She would write very gracefully, picture perfect.

As a maid, I thought, what would you ever write? Maybe a shopping list? If your boyfriend is in the same town, or your parents, for instance, you don't need to write them at all. Now Willie from Surinam didn't have parents; she might have an uncle in another country, but then she'd write at most maybe once a month. Such infrequent writing does not change one's handwriting such as it does, for instance, in someone who is constantly taking dictation.

Your mind works fast and you make quick decisions when your life is at stake. So when they gave me that pencil and the notebook, I sat there and I wrote as if it were a real job for me. I stuck out my tongue to make them think that I had to really concentrate in order to write beautifully. I wrote the most beautiful school penmanship, with all the graceful capital Gs and Es, and I handed it to them as if I'd done my very best. But it looked, I hoped, like the work of a sixth-grade kid from Surinam.

It must have satisfied them because I passed their examination with that beautiful writing. If I had walked into this trap without knowing any German, and they had simply given me the paper and the pencil and said, "Copy that," I might have just scribbled it out the way I scribble out most things.

During those months my whole life depended, apart from God, on so many little, insignificant things. I had to try to see through their plans, and they were trained people. They had examined many others, and they were not stupid; on the other hand, I had to convince them I was stupid, uneducated, and very scared. If they had been really smart and looked back at my papers from the arrest, they could have put me through torture, which could have broken our whole operation. They could have had my parents arrested too, since their garden was full of buried arms, and I did not know whether they had been found.

In those first hours after I had been arrested, when I acted so cocky with that arrogant Gestapo officer, I had appeared in a completely different character from the one I decided to assume early on in my imprisonment. That sassy young woman was totally out of character with the stupid maid I decided to become. It was a blessing that these men at my hearing had no inkling of the way I'd pushed the bell myself outside of the prison at Scheveningen, how I'd told that officer I'd race him through the station. If there had been some note of that wildness, the officers at my hearing would have had substantial grounds to doubt every word I'd told them. But no one had ever noted my behavior right after I was arrested; or perhaps it had been noted, but in the rush of our transfer out of Scheveningen those papers were lost. I can only say that God took care of all that stuff.

When I gave them my handwriting, they discussed it and put it aside. It was, I suppose, exactly the hand they expected from a maid. When I had entered that room my hatred had left me, and I was at peace; and I wasn't overanxious about what I would say. There they sat, well fed and well shaven, with loads of decorations on their uniforms; and here I sat with those horrible pus things and my prison gown and greasy hair. And I thought to myself, *You big shots think you can decide on my life, but I have news for you: you can't touch a hair on my head without the will of God my Father, because he is on my side.*

The greatest miracle was that in the end I could actually feel pity for those men because they were so deluded: they *thought* they had power and really they had nothing. I will never forget it. And from that moment on, I've never really hated anymore. It all turned around when I sat there thinking what poor empty souls they were. I've always felt very strongly that when we do evil, we will have to give a final accounting for everything. And then I thought, *I would absolutely hate to be in your shoes, boys.*

It is very difficult to explain, but I felt a sudden peace come over me in the middle of that hearing, a hearing I had dreaded for months because it was so dangerous, not only for me but for Hein and our group and my parents. I was eventually so much at peace sitting there that I can only attribute it to a miracle, and that's what I wrote to Hein later. I knew very clearly that both sides in every war say that God is on their side. In many wars, God isn't on any sides — he's crying. But in this war it was absolutely clear to me that the Nazis did such evil things that they were evil personified. We had God on our side. I would not have dared to say that on my own, but in this war it was clear right from the beginning. Who asked the Germans to attack us? Who begged them to come marching into the streets of The Hague? No one. And who did all those horrible things to the Jews?

At length, one of the interrogators looked at me and said,

with all his decorations and stuff glittering: "I have done nothing else my whole life but hearings and interrogations. That is my area of expertise. I've done many of them — hundreds of thousands — and I have developed a sixth sense. I can *feel* what is true and what isn't true." He looked me straight in the eye. "I can't put a needle in your story. It fits — all the way through. But my sixth sense tells me that it's all made up."

That was frightening to me because, of course, he was absolutely right. That man spoke only once during the entire hearing, but he sensed that it was all baloney. When he said what he did, however, it also gave me the feeling that I was going to be all right. When this officer said he couldn't find a gap anywhere in my story, it gave me another sense of the great security of being held in the hands of God.

Release from Vught

DE VLIEGENDE HOLLANDER

DAGBLAD VERSPREID DOOR DE GEALLIEERDE LUCHTMACHT

No. 64. VRIJDAG 27 OCT. 1944

Groote overwinning op Japansche vloot

- Russen diep in Oost-Pruisen
- Britten naderen Tilburg en Breda
- Canadeezen op Zuid-Beveland

Londen, 27 Oct.—De Japansche slagvloot heeft in de wateren om de Philippijnen een zwaren nederlaag geleden. In een zee- en luchtslag die drie dagen duurde, zijn, volgens de jongste officieele gegevens van Admiraal Nimitz, tot zinken gebracht een groot en een klein vliegkampschip en vier kruisers. Twee Japansche slagschepen en een groot vliegkampschip werden waarschijnlijk tot zinken gebracht. Deze cijfers zijn nog niet volledig. De Japanners hebben reeds het verlies van een slagschip erkend. Hun smaldeelen trokken zich, na den zwaren nederlaag, in verschillende richtingen terug en werden daarbij door Amerikaansche zee- en luchtstrijdkrachten achtervolgd. De Amerikanen verloren een vliegkampschip. Tot de beschadigde eenheden behoorde de Australische kruiser "Australia," vlagschip van het Australisch eskader.

Tweemaal hebben in dezen oorlog zware Japansche vlooteenheden slag geleverd met deelen van de Amerikaansche vloot: in Mei 1942 in de Koraalzee, in Juni 1942 bij Midway. Bij beide gelegenheden leden de Japanners ernstige verliezen, vooral aan vliegkampschepen. Sinds den zomer van 1942 heeft de Japansche slagvloot den strijd vermeden. Japan aanvaardde het risico dat de Amerikaansche superioriteit steeds grooter werd—Japan aanvaardde het risico dat de Amerikanen steeds verder doordrongen in de richting van het Aziatische vasteland—omdat Japan het nog veel grootere risico van vernietiging van zijn slagvloot, grondslag van zijn op voet gebouwde Imperium, niet durst aanvaarden. Toen Amerikanen echter landden op de Philippijnen, waardoor Japan afgesneden dreigde te worden van zijn aanvoerwegen van grondstoffen in het Zuiden, werd het critieke punt bereikt. Uit Tokio kwam het sein dat de Pacific-vloten van Amerika moesten worden vernietigd, en de landingslegers in zee gedreven.

Drie Japansche smaldeelen stoomden naar de Philippijnen. Twee, waarbij zich uit van slagschepen bevonden, kwamen uit de Zuid-Chineesche Zee en ongeving en een derde, dat tevens vliegkampschepen bij zich had, kwam uit Noordoostelijke richting, van Formosa vandaan. Bij dezen strijd die zich ontwikkelde, hadden de Japanners het voordeel te beschikken over vliegvelden op de Philippijnen. Alle Amerikaansche toestellen moesten opstijgen van de vliegkampschepen, waarvan echter een formidabel aantal voorhanden was.

De Amerikanen hebben officieel bekendgemaakt dat zij in den Pacific beschikken over minstens 16 slagschepen. De Japanners wisten dat een Britsche slagvloot naar het Oosten onderweg was, die zij al sterk genoeg was, den strijd met de Japanners aan te binden. Vandaar dat de Japanners hebben gepoogd, bij de Philippijnen den Amerikaan zoodanige schade toe te brengen dat zij daarna konden afrekenen met de Britten. Deze berekening is feilaar mislukt. De Japanners hebben zulk een zwaren nederlaag geleden dat de bewegingsvrijheid van de Geallieerden in den Pacific nog grooter is geworden dan zij reeds was. Pearl Harbour en de Slag in de Javazee zijn gewroken.

Russisch offensief

De Russen hebben in de afgeloopen dagen hun stellingen in Oost-Pruisen verdedigd. Over een breedte van meer dan 100 km. zijn zij nu ruim 30 km. diep op Duitsch gebied door-

gedrongen. Het bericht van dit offensief heeft in Moskou groot enthousiasme verwekt. Onder bevel van den jeugdigen generaal Tsjerniakowski doorbraken troepen van het Derde Wit-Russische front twee sterke Duitsche linies. De Duitschers hadden daar bunkers gebouwd met betonnen wanden van 3 m. dik. In vele van deze bunkers was geschut geinstalleerd dat aan een vollen cirkel in het rond kon draaien. Dichte Duitsche mijnenvelden waren plaatselijk meer dan een kilometer breed. Prikkeldraad stond onder een sterken electrischen stroom. De Duitsche officieren en soldaten hadden opdracht, geen meter te wijken. Zoo machtig was echter het Russisch offensief dat de Duitsche verdedigingswerken in enkele dagen onder den voet werden geloopen. Duitsche doorbraken werden van den aardbodem weggevaagd. Koningsbergen wordt door de Duitschers ontruimd.

In het hooge Noorden is de eerste Noorsche stad, de haven Kirkenes, door de Russen bevrijd. Stalin maakte op Woensdagavond 25 Oct. bekend, dat geheel Transsylvanië van Duitschers was gezuiverd.

In Nederland

Op Dinsdagavond 24 October bereikten Engelsche troepen Den Bosch, langs den grooten weg van Grave. Zij reden den weg en spoorweg naar Hedel af en drongen Woensdag diep in de stad door. Woensdagavond was de Noordoostelijke helft van Den Bosch in Engelsche handen, terwijl de Duitschers zich nog verdedigden in de Zuidoostelijke wijken. De Kathedraal van St. Jan werd door de Duitsche cultuurbeschermers als militaire observatiepost gebruikt.

Tusschen Den Bosch en Eindhoven trokken enkele Britsche colonnes in de richting van Tilburg. Berg Boxtel, Oirschot en Moergestel werden bevrijd. Donderdagmorgen bereikte de Britsche voorhoede den rand van Tilburg.

Felle strijd is in de afgeloopen dagen geleverd bij Bergen op Zoom. Ten Oosten van Bergen op Zoom. Ten Zuidwesten van Bergen op Zoom zijn de Canadeezen den rest in Brabant zijn het Kerekerak Zuid-Beveland binnengedrongen.

In Zeeuwsch-Vlaanderen veroverden de Canadeezen op Woensdag 25 October het fort Frederik Hendrik.

Het Vijftiende Duitsche Leger dat in Brabant en Zeeland vecht, wordt ingekluist hulptroepen, geschat op 70.000 man. Daarvan zijn ruim 15.000 afgesneden in Zeeuwsch-Vlaanderen, en op Walcheren en Beveland. De positie van de rest in Brabant is vooral bedreigd door het verlies van de spoorwegverbinding via Den Bosch naar het Noorden.

DE PRINSESJES BEATRIX, MARGRIET EN IRENE met hun Moeder in Amerika gefotografeerd, kort voor het vertrek van Prinses Juliana naar Engeland.

Verdiend loon

Fransch verradersjournalist ter dood veroordeeld

Parijs 23 Oct.—Het Parijsche Gerechtshof, ingesteld ter berechting van de collaborateurs, is een reeks van processen tegen 1500 beklaagden begonnen met de behandeling van de zaak van den verradersjournalist Georges Suarez, hoofdredacteur van het weekblad "Aujourd'hui." Honderden Fransche en Geallieerde journalisten waren in de rechtzaal aanwezig. De voordracht voor de samenstelling van de jury—waarvoor men kan kiezen uit de verzetsbewegingen. Suarez werd beschuldigd van verraad; heulen met den vijand, het afschilderen van De Gaulle als verrader, het rechtvaardigen van het dooden van gijzelaars en het aischen van massa-arrestaties onder de verzetsbeweging.

Er waren geen getuigen à charge. Tegen den beklaagde zouden slechts zijn artikelen getuigen. Uittreksels uit 103 daarvan waren bij het Hof gedeponeerd. Vele daarvan werden tijdens de zitting voorgelezen.

De verdediger van Suarez had een aantal getuigen à décharge gedagvaard. Een daarvan deelde mede dat hij, toen zijn zoon als gijzelaar geëxecuteerd dreigde te worden, op Suarez een beroep had gedaan voor interventie bij generaal von Stülpnagel. Meer dan een kort uitstel van het doodvonnis had Suarez niet verkregen.

De openbare aanklager somde op hetgeen tegen Suarez in het geding was gebracht. Hij betreurde het dat hij schrijven van talent zijn pen aan Hitler en de vijanden van Frankrijk had verkocht. Hij besloot: "Bewust van mijn verantwoordelijkheid en n plicht, eisch ik den doodstraf. Werkzaamheden als de Uwe mogen slechts eindigen aan den galg."

De verdediger van den beklaagde merkte op, dat Suarez oprecht in de politiek van samenwerking, met de Duitschers had geloofd en geen Franschen had verraden. Hij vroeg om clementie.

De jury verklaarde Georges Suarez schuldig aan landverraad. Het Gerechtshof veroordeelde hem daarom ter dood—een vonnis dat met luid applaus werd begroet.

BOMMEN REGENEN NEER OP DUITSCHLAND

Dit Britsche toestel laat ze bij honderden tegelijk valln op het hart van de Duitsche oorlogsindustrie : Essen in het Ruhrgebied.

The Flying Dutchman, a newspaper printed and distributed by the Allies, was an important source of information for the people of Holland.

Oₙe evening in August, after my hearing, a number of us were sitting and fantasizing about liberty. We talked about what it would feel like and what we would eat and where we would go. One of the girls, José Smeets, who was from a very wealthy family, said she wanted to eat white asparagus: "I would give anything for white asparagus!" At my home, we had never had white asparagus; all we ever ate was the everyday Dutch food like kale and *zuurkool*, green beans and sprouts.

Then somebody said, "Willie, if you could choose what day you would get out and be free, what day of the week would you choose?" I felt so filthy with all the pus on my face and greasy hair and filthy clothing that I immediately thought of the way we used to feel on Sunday morning, when the whole family was squeaky clean. When I was young I had not always wanted to go to church twice on Sunday; but right then I would have given anything in the world to go to church any number of times.

So I said, "If I had the opportunity to choose, I would want it to be a radiant sunshiny day! And I would love it to be a Saturday morning. I'd go home and take a bath and soak and shampoo and put on clean underwear and clean clothes! And then Sunday morning I want to go to church and thank God for freedom — with capital letters."

I had always taken freedom so much for granted, but now I knew it was a gift. And then I told them, "Of course, if it's Monday morning, I'll go too — even if it's pouring." I didn't even know then whether I would ever get out to freedom at all, but that inner voice I was learning to trust kept telling me that I would get out.

The Germans wanted to empty Vught, so they were executing many men; we could hear the machine guns almost every sunset. The wives who had been arrested with their men were

now widows, and the Nazis felt that they were no longer dangerous to the Reich. So they released them. And then there was
stupid Willie Laarman, too stupid to be any kind of a problem
for them. It seemed that I now belonged to a group that could
be released. They had to empty the camp. It happened to be on
a gorgeous Saturday morning, August 19, a radiant sunshiny day.
The women who had tuberculosis and other illnesses were lying
on their cots, sick with fever or whatever. The camp doctor had
to come by to check that it was really a sickness they were
suffering from, that they were not putting on an act. Then a
special detail came with food for the sick prisoners. I was mopping floors, and the girls were lying there, and I said, "Well,
girls, remember what I said: this is my gorgeous Saturday morning. This is it. I'm going home today."

And then I said, "Now let's repeat the addresses. Freddy,
you live at Noordermarkt 32, Amsterdam. Ina, you live in The
Hague . . ." And I repeated all the addresses of the people who
wanted me to visit relatives or family and relay messages. Once
I had them all named, I said, "Well, that's it. Now I'm going.
Bye-bye."

But I grabbed my rag again, of course, and went on mopping
floors. In a moment, however, the head of the guards marched
in, a woman with icy eyes. Whenever she came in, we had to
jump to attention. When she addressed us, we had to say,
"Jawohl, Frau Hauptwachtmeisterin" or "Nein, Frau Hauptmachtmeisterin." I could easily say that, but I had to make it
appear difficult, because I wasn't supposed to know any German.

"Jawohl, Frau Hauptmachtmeisterin," I stuttered.

"Willie, get your stuff — get ready," she announced.
"You're going to Germany."

That was my worst fear. Everyone knew that Germany
meant those infamous camps where we knew they were killing

people. But my little inner voice immediately said, *You are* not *going to Germany — you are getting out.*

At Vught we could keep a few things that we might need, and I had a navy blue sweater, a raincoat, and a navy blue flannel plaid skirt with red and yellow, the one I was arrested in. I had used that, rolled up, as a pillow because we received no pillows.

I picked up that stuff, but I was so convinced I was going to leave the prison that I ran to the bed of a girl who was just my size and had nothing at all, and I gave her the skirt and my woolen sweater, thinking she might have to go to another prison in Germany eventually. I was in my underwear, because I had to give the prison dress back to the Nazis, but I had my navy blue gabardine raincoat over my underwear, and I was ready. That's how convinced I was that I was going to be free; if I were going to Germany, I would have needed the clothes I had given to the other girl. But when Frau Hauptwachtmeisterin came back, she scared me to death. "Before you go," she said, "you get another hearing."

I immediately remembered what Amancia the palm reader had read in my hand: "You have tears, loads of paper, and I see police" — that was the Gestapo, the secret police — "and when you think you have licked it" — and I had thought that my hearing had gone well, because they couldn't prick a pin in my story — "then you have a small hearing, and you make a mistake, and you'll be in as deep as you have ever been in before." That's what Amancia Roggeveen had told me. I thought of that as soon as that guard said that I would have another hearing.

When I had walked out of my first hearing, I had felt confident about my possibilities because I felt it had gone well. But success was always relative and tenuous. Two Jewish girls who were originally in our barracks, sisters or cousins, had had their interrogations, and one apparently could no longer hear when she returned. The Nazis had taken the legs of a chair and beaten that girl on the ears until she was deaf. They put the other girl in a very hot bath, then in a very cold bath, then hot, then cold again — to try to get something out of her that they thought she had been keeping from them. It was horribly cruel.

The worst fear in the hearings was that you would get some evil interrogator: you could never know what might happen then. No one who lives in a free country will ever understand that kind of fear. What is most horrifying is the realization that you have no idea what *can* happen, that your life is totally in the hands of someone in the chair in front of you, someone who might well be a demon. They had not tortured me, of course; and when the sharpest of them had said he couldn't put a needle in my story, I had felt great relief. But my life was still at stake in what might happen the next moment.

In spite of the fact that I had some inner peace, I knew one little slip-up was all I would need to get back into deep trouble. That's why I trusted that God would not let me say something stupid and would make my thinking very clear.

Frau Hauptwachtmeisterin had told me I was going to Germany only because she wanted to be cruel. It was a lie, and somehow I knew it even when she said it. It was the same kind of trick the guards at Scheveningen had used when they called me out for a shower. To them, it was amusing: they got their kicks out of doing things to get your hopes up, and then destroying them. In this case, even though she knew I was leaving, she said I was going to Germany just to scare me. It was normal, everyday intimidation.

I did have to go back to questioning all right, but not to that same group of seven officers. Instead, I went to my case worker, the man who had taken me to the original hearing and had looked at me with revulsion when he'd taken me from the barracks and marched me down the street of the camp. He was sitting there in the office, and he said, "We are going to let you out."

"Oh, that's wonderful," I said.

"What are you going to do?" he asked. "Are you going to see that guy again?"

"I don't want *anything* to do with him anymore," I said, throwing up my hands in anger. "I spent months and months of my life in this misery because of him; I don't want anything to do with him."

"Tell you what," he said, "why don't you go back and try to find him, and then go on seeing him. When you know who he is, come to our offices and tell us where he lives, okay?"

I nodded. *You bet*, I thought, *I'll be sure to do that.*

Then he said, "He has hurt you so much, he deserves his just reward, don't you think?"

"Of course," I told him, "he made me suffer a great deal."

He stood up behind that desk and said, "Alles Gute! Alles Gute!" and let me out of the office.

He called a regular soldier over. In the meantime Ansje den Dool, another prisoner, had finished with her case worker just then, and the two of us got our papers and our belongings back. Accompanied by that soldier, we were marched to the gate.

Ansje and I walked to the front gates of Vught prison, they opened, and we walked out — free at last. There we were in the beautiful sunshine, but we had no idea where to go. There was no road or path, just a track made by wagon wheels and some horse manure. We didn't even know which way to turn. We had been herded there in the middle of the night by soldiers and Dobermans, and we had no idea how we got there. The only thing we could see was that a cart drawn by a horse must come along once in a while. That was it.

We were undernourished, and Ansje was pregnant. In addition, she didn't know whether her husband was alive or dead. Nor did we simply shake away our deep fear of the Germans. You don't quickly forget the cruelty, such as the way the guard with the icy eyes had said, "You're going to Germany." Even though we were outside the electric fences, we still felt as though we were subject to their reign; and we were afraid that at any minute the gate would reopen and they would grab us and drag us back in, that our getting out was all a joke.

We wanted to get away quickly. But where? We started walking to the left, and as we did we saw a little dot that grew bigger the closer we walked toward it. A horse-drawn cart full of manure was on its way out to the fields. There was so little of anything left in the Netherlands by that time that all kinds of manure was valuable.

Clock, clock, clock . . . the horse came plodding along. When the farmer driving the wagon saw us, he said, "Girls, you just came from the camp?"

We told him that we had. He looked back at his cart, not seeming to know whether he should offer us a ride in all that luxury or not. He turned toward us and stammered, "Would you? — would you? — "

"Yes, please!" we said, and we sat on the little bench of that cart, behind the horse, and we simply loved the smell! We really did. It stank pretty bad, of course: manure was caked all over the wagon. But we were free. Right then I was elated with a sense of how faithful God is to his promises; I was free, and I was smiling joyfully on a manure wagon. As we ambled along, I laughed to myself when I thought of God's sense of humor in delivering us that way. Even today, the smell of manure reminds me of freedom.

The farmer drove us into the town of Vught. I had never

been there before, but he knew the way to the station, where there was a Red Cross post (the Red Cross kept a post staffed day and night just a short distance from every concentration camp). The woman on duty in that office that morning was very friendly.

"Oh, I am so happy you're out," she said. "Now, shall I get you a train ticket to where you want to go? And are you hungry?"

We were hungry, of course, and we were amazed to meet a human being who was interested in our needs — even our desires.

But the train was just about to leave when we got there; the steam from the coal fire was already making the ch-ch-chugging noise. By that time there weren't many daily trains running anymore, and the Red Cross woman wanted to get us to our homes on the first train possible. So she ran to the station master to get us our tickets.

The station master was holding what they called a "fried egg," the red signal with a handle that they raise to allow the train to move forward. He was just ready to put it up when the Red Cross lady pulled his arm down.

"Can you wait a moment?" she asked.

She quickly gave us bread and then hopped onto the train along with us because she couldn't keep it waiting any longer. So while we ate a little lunch, she told us that the Red Cross always sent telegrams to prisoners' families to announce that they were coming home.

"Where do you want me to send your telegram?" she asked.

The train was full, and I saw people wearing NSB badges, so I gave her my most recent false address in Heemstede, the home of those people where I was supposedly employed as a maid when I had been arrested. I was still scared: I saw spies everywhere, and I wanted to be sure no one would catch me on anything. So the Red Cross sent that cable to those people in Heemstede.

Poor Ansje! She had not yet heard that her husband had been executed; she would have to go through that later. We parted at Utrecht because she had to go home to Deventer. I wanted to see my parents very much, but I was still suspicious about Nazi spies keeping an eye on their home for signs of Diet Eman. So even though my ticket was for Heemstede, I got off the train with Ansje in Utrecht and went to another ticket office; I still had this fear that the whole thing was a set-up, that I was being followed, and sooner or later they would arrest me and take me back to Vught. Before I got on the next train, I walked around and around, watching to see if anyone was following me. Once I was convinced I was not being followed, I took the next train to The Hague.

But I still didn't dare to go home right away because of the Eichorns, our neighbors up the block. The woman of the house was a native German, a bossy woman who had married a very meek Dutch man (she may have even been a maid for years in Holland: that was how a lot of simple guys met women and got married). I was suspicious of their only son because I thought he had some connection with the Nazis. He was half German himself, and if you were German you really had to take a stand. He was maybe fourteen or fifteen years old and in the Hitler *Jugend.*

They might very well turn me in, and I certainly did not want to take that chance. But I simply had to see my parents — to make sure they were all right. The only safe way I could think of was to go to my father's business associate, Mr. Gerritsen, an upholsterer. As far as I knew, the Gerritsen family was not at all active in the Underground, but they *were* friends of my parents. I didn't know, of course, what my parents might have told them had they ever asked about me. When I had first gone into hiding but still saw my parents a few times, I found out that Father and Mother had simply made up excuses for my being gone. You couldn't tell people anything. The simple souls were often the most dangerous, because in their innocence they would say things that would be revealing. Mother told me that she'd told people I was off to live with Hein's folks for a while, where I was going to learn everything about cooking and laundry and kids. People had accepted that because they knew I was engaged to Hein.

I rang the bell at the Gerritsens, honestly expecting them to say, "Oh, it's Diet — how wonderful to see you! How terrific that you're okay, and how are you?" I thought they would react like that because of what I had gone through in the year or more since I'd been able to visit at home.

"Oh hi, Diet," they said in a very nonchalant and matter-of-fact way. "Why don't you step in?"

Father and Mother had told their own little lies very well, and I realized immediately that the Gerritsens didn't know a thing. And yet, my realization that they didn't know what I'd been through was like a cold shower for just a moment. Here I was looking at the first really familiar faces I'd seen in over a year, and they acted as though I'd merely been on vacation.

"Have you seen Father and Mother recently?" I asked.

I was so afraid that they had been killed.

"Ja, we saw them around last week or so," they said.

"How are they?"

They kind of looked at me as if they thought I had gone a bit batty on my vacation. "Fine," they said.

Then I told them everything: how I'd just been in prison and a concentration camp, and how I wanted so badly to go and see my parents but was still afraid of going home because of the Eichhorns.

"We can ask your parents to come here," the Gerritsens said.

"But there is so much to tell them," I said. "I would prefer to be home with just them. Will you please go to their house? I don't know how much of a shock it would be for them to see me again if I just walk in unannounced," I explained. "Would you tell them I'm here, and if they will leave the front door unlocked, I'll go to the corner and look to be sure the Eichhorns aren't there. If the coast is clear, tell them I'll just shoot in quickly."

When he came back, Mr. Gerritsen acted like he was very important: he knew something nobody else knew. Even so, he was a very nice man.

So I walked down that side street, and once I saw no movement at the Eichhorns', I flew into the house. Father wasn't home, but Mother had the door open. It was wonderful to see my mother again, so wonderful! How can I describe it? We hugged and hugged, and talked and talked.

Suddenly the doorbell rang, and I fled through the kitchen and into the bedroom. But it was only the baker or the milkman at the door. What food we had at that time was still delivered to the home: the little ration of milk from the milkman and bread from the baker. One rarely went to the shops in those days. While Mother was at the door telling this man what she needed, and I was hiding in the bedroom, Father stepped inside. Mother could not warn him that his daughter was home — not in front of this delivery man; you couldn't trust anyone, so you always kept your mouth shut. When Father walked into the kitchen unexpectedly, I came forward. I knew that whoever was at the door couldn't see me from there anyway. Father caught sight of me, and I expected him to come up right away and hug me. Instead he wheeled around immediately and ran into his bedroom.

I was astonished. I couldn't understand what was going on.

I thought perhaps he was angry about all the suffering I'd caused both of them. He never touched me, never said a thing; he just shot into the bedroom. It made me think that he didn't want to see me at all. But when Mother closed the front door, I ran after him. And then I saw the tears streaming down his cheeks. I had never seen my father cry before — never. He had turned away because he didn't want me to see him that way, so emotional.

I will never forget my father's reaction when I came home from Vught so unexpectedly. If Mother had been able to warn him that I was on my way or that I was already there, he would have been prepared for it. But when, suddenly, there I was, it took his breath away emotionally. He couldn't really handle seeing me in the flesh — for a minute or so. It was too much for him.

I loved my parents . . . always.

But it was too dangerous for me to stay in The Hague. After I visited my parents for just a night, I immediately went to Ab van Meerveld's place in The Veluwe, and he told me that Hein had been transferred from the prison in Leeuwarden to the concentration camp at Amersfoort — and that they had an open connection.

"You write him a letter," Ab said, "and I can see that we get it smuggled in."

It was very dangerous smuggling in mail because Hein was there under a false name, and I had to write very vaguely, not mentioning his name. "Dearest" — that's the way I started it, and I signed it *Famke*, an endearing Frisian name that he always had for me: *"Mijn famke,"* he'd say always — "my little woman."

Any letter to Hein, smuggled in or out, was stamped "A-W-S," indicating Hein's section of the prison camp. A man carried the messages in and out of the camp under loads of potato peelings. Thousands of prisoners were kept incarcerated at Amersfoort, and each of them had to get his turn. This man couldn't smuggle thousands out of that camp at a time; so each section got its turn, and Hein's section was A-W-S.

"Dearest H.," I wrote, "How *dolblij* — how "ecstatic" (meaning "more than happy") I am that at long last I can write you, because you must have been thinking, 'Why does that child never write me?'"

▲   ▲

Dearest H.,

How ecstatic I am to be able to write you at long last, for you must have been thinking, "Why doesn't that child write?" I didn't write because on May 8 I was caught during a train search. It so happened that my ID was not in good order. The guy insisted that it was printed in 1943 and issued in 1941 — how on earth is that possible?

Of course, how the official who issued it could have been able to perform such a miracle was a total mystery to me. But I was requested to go along to the Oranje Hotel [Scheveningen prison]. When the invasion took place, we were transported to Vught with approximately 1600 other prisoners. That was a scary moment for me because I thought we would all be taken to D [Germany].

Well, my hearing was not as bad as I expected. Of course, I played a stupid sheep, very scared. Thank God the case went well. Later, you will hear the whole story in detail, but I am so happy that I experienced this too, my darling. When I first heard what happened to you, it was nearly too much for me to bear. But from the moment that the door of my little cell closed behind me, I did not shed a tear any more. Still, what was difficult was not knowing anything else about you and the others from our group. I was not allowed to write anyone or receive parcels, and I'm sure the others found it equally difficult not knowing anything of how or why I had disappeared.

But all that belongs to the past. Last Saturday, all of a sudden they set me free. What a terrific experience! In a little while you will find that out for yourself. Every morning when I wake up, I still think that I am dreaming.

At home everything is fine — fortunately, for I was afraid of that situation. And now I have to split myself into many pieces because everybody wants me to come and visit them.

Darling, I have deep faith in the future. My story is one great miracle, and now that God spared me so miraculously, I know for sure that everything will turn out well. What was really true for me was that "my help comes only from the Lord," for I didn't know a thing about you any more, and there seemed no possibility of my ever getting any more information. Everything at the camp was very strict.

Still, all the time I had such an inner peace like I have never had before, and I met such great women and girls. You will meet them too, for these friendships undoubtedly will remain.

How wonderful it will be when you get out, and how much we have to tell each other. It's great that you were able to meet some friends there [other arrested Underground workers] and that we can be in contact. Now I can take the sadness more easily. Don't worry about me. I know what you're going through, and now that I can read your letters I'll be just fine.

Maybe you won't believe this, but since I got out I gained some weight, thanks to the Red Cross! Everyone here is so wonderful to me that it makes me a little self-conscious. Little

Teun [son of Ab and Riek van Meerveld] has grown so much. He is crawling, laughs and jumps! I was so surprised! Yesterday I arrived here at Teun's and I will make the rounds to all the people again. Some of the others [in the Resistance group] want to put me in a glass showcase!

How is your case coming? I understand they have not yet made your protocol? Are there lots of guys in your barracks? In the end, we had 175 women in ours. In spite of everything, we had lots of fun.

My brother Albert said goodbye to his bachelor life. I am still full of blue spots from his embrace when he came home all of a sudden after I was freed!!

Hey, are we still going to get married in September? Didn't we agree upon that? I have taken care to be home on time, so now it's your turn! You can't be a spoilsport now. Actually, we will probably be the last married [of all our friends], but the best married! Couple number two is now married, and soon it will be our turn. What a party that will be!

What a terrific future we are going to have with you free and peace on earth. It will surely be over soon. There is so much to tell you still, but I will do that in a few weeks when we can speak together "when He, who is almighty, with his wonderful guidance, has completed the work which now gives us so much hurt . . ." [paraphrase of Psalm Hymn 411 in the *Zangbundel*].

Darling, I hope to hear something from you soon.

A whole regiment of kisses . . .

Famke

letter from Diet Eman to Hein Sietsma

▼ ▼

Ab smuggled that letter into the camp, and Hein received it and answered quite quickly. The potato man smuggled his reply back out on August 29, 1944. He wrote his letter right on my letter, in the open white spaces.

▲   ▲

August 29, 1944

My darling Diet,

What a surprise it was for me to receive this letter. All the time I thought it very strange to hear nothing but "W[illie] is okay." When I heard that you had withdrawn from the work and didn't do anything anymore, I really wondered whether it was possible for you to become such a meek lamb so quickly.

First, I was a little irritated that I had not known the truth about what had happened to you. But that you are free again seems almost too good to be true. Driek [a fellow Resistance worker also held at Amersfoort] told me that it was at your explicit request that the guys kept me in the dark concerning your arrest, but I can't believe that. Did you receive the table from G & L [furniture for our apartment when we were to be married]? Please remember the instructions and stay out of Friesland for some time to come. Will you please visit John Wassenaar [false name for Louis Chaillet from the aviation laboratory in Amsterdam] for me and give him my best regards? Will you also please arrange everything related to the insurance of our household stuff and the life insurance? I hope that we will see each other soon again, for now that you're free I'd prefer not to have to stay in this place a whole lot longer. Last Sunday

297

we had to do knee bends for ten minutes — our whole block. Now we are all limping along with stiff thighs. It's quite silly to see all these young guys hobbling along like old men.

Darling, how brave you have been. All that time and no news from home or our friends. I feel as if what's happened to me isn't much at all when compared to your suffering. I enclose here your own letter because I don't want to keep it here, but I want to have this later as a memento of what happened.

Last night I went to a movie. I hardly ever go, but it has really lifted my spirits to see some nice girls on the screen, and there were some dances. All of a sudden you feel for a moment as if you are someone else, lifted somewhere out of this world of walls and men only.

If your brother gave you black and blue spots around your neck, just be ready for the time when I'll see you again. You'll be completely black and blue the moment I get out of here. This letter jumps around a great deal, I know, but that's because I'm trying to write in such a hurry. Next time it will be better, I assure you.

a kiss from your *jongen*

letter from Hein Sietsma to Diet Eman

▼   ▼

The words of that letter were the very first words I heard from him after I was released from the camp at Vught. It was very important to me then, and it still is.

The Hunger Winter

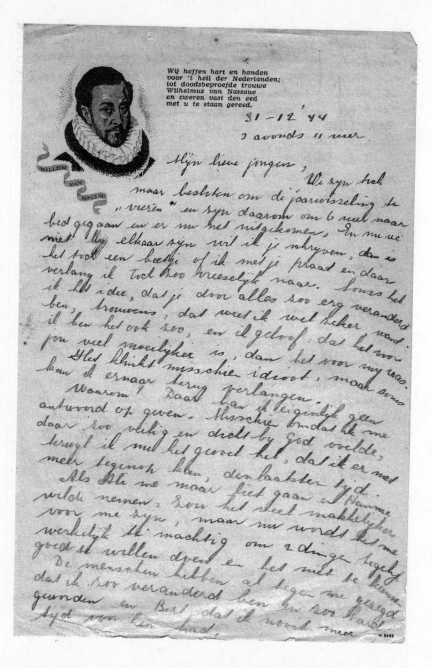

References to the Dutch royal family were forbidden during the Occupation. Diet's letter to Hein was written on paper decorated with a portrait of William of Nassau (1533-1584).

▲   ▲

September 17, 1944

Came back yesterday to Alie's. I don't understand how
restless I am. There is not much to be done here. I'd better
go first to Haarlem and then south. If it is quiet in our
work, then I have to sit at Alie's and do knitting, and I just
cannot do that now. Yesterday I bicycled through "Laan
1914," only five hundred meters away from Hein in his camp
at Amersfoort.

Many Tommies in the sky. They shoot at everything
that is moving on the main roads. The Huns are scared
stiff.

O *jongen*, now that I am back and miss you everywhere,
I am so hurting inside from longing for you. I'll take refuge
in writing.

Did you feel these days how close I was to you in my
thoughts and prayers? My darling, a year ago we were
together in Friesland, and we were walking outside to buy
flowers for Gerk and Lena. We looked at each other and
had to laugh for we had our crazy little secret, and when
we looked at each other we felt so overflowing with happiness that words would have spoiled it, and therefore we
only laughed.

Darling, today I read in our diaries. How much you
did love me and idealized me!

from the diary of Diet Eman

▼   ▼

After my release from Vught, I returned to Aalt and Alie's because I was needed by our group even more than before my arrest. Driek had been arrested, and he and Hein were already in Amersfoort. We were strapped. I went back into Underground work very quickly, almost instinctively. In those first months after Scheveningen and Vught, I was often tired and emotionally exhausted, but I don't remember ever feeling the slightest fear about rejoining the Resistance effort. By that time, I had seen firsthand what the Nazis were doing, and I hated them and their whole system.

All during that time I kept the name Willie Laarman because it was now safe to move around with it: Willie's sentencing was over and she'd served her time. Furthermore, I had been Willie before at Aalt and Alie's. Alie's own family never knew a thing about what I was doing; to them I was simply the maid, and they knew nothing about my capture or imprisonment. After the war, when they found out that I wasn't simply someone who had come from the city searching for food, they couldn't believe it.

Aalt and Alie also needed my help after I was released from Vught: they constantly had a houseful of people. I told them that after I'd seen my sister and the men of our group who weren't in prison, I would make their farm my base again and help out as before.

What affected us more than anything just then was the Allied air attack on Arnhem. The British General Montgomery had a plan that was called "Market Garden." The plan was to land a force of paratroopers north of the Rijn, Waal, and Maas rivers in the Netherlands while marching a major force up from the south at the same time. When the two forces would join, the German army's hold on the Netherlands would be severed and the Allies would have an opportunity to move toward Germany itself much faster than they had otherwise anticipated. By September 1944, Hitler was already reeling because of the devastating war in Russia and, of course, the toll that the invasion on the beaches at Normandy had taken.

The idea was to land at Arnhem with storm troops parachuting from airplanes and gliders full of supplies and munitions. Those gliders would be released from the planes tugging them and would come down at a certain spot with tanks, guns and whatever other supplies the paratroopers needed. Meanwhile, the army in Belgium would drive across the rivers and join this large paratroop detail dropped near Arnhem. But the paratroopers would have to hold out until the Allies were able to move up to meet them.

This huge strike would free the Netherlands, and the Allies could then move more easily into Germany. If it had worked, it would have ended the war much more quickly.

But it was a big defeat. The German army was stronger in Holland than the Allies had realized, and those troops dropped at Arnhem could not hold out long enough for the Allied troops to meet them. There were horrible battles, and many were wounded and killed.

▲ ▲

October 5, 1944

The whole day the heavy artillery is booming. We are close to the battle front.

O Lord, make haste to help us;
O Lord, make speed to save us.

O *liefste*, I am longing so very, very much for you, and sometimes I don't know where to turn anymore. Sometimes

I have the feeling that the future we hope for is just a castle in the air. I cannot believe or imagine that what we hope for will come true. But deep, deep inside, I know that everything with us will turn out completely okay.

Psalm 130: "O Israel, put your hope in the Lord, for he himself will redeem Israel and his goodness never fails."

I thank you that we both may know this and can cling to this.

from the diary of Diet Eman

▼   ▼

The city of Arnhem was bombarded and completely evacuated. It was a strict order: everyone had to leave. Hundreds of thousands of people living in that area were sent out. Even when babies had just been born in the hospitals, the Germans said, "Out! Out!"

So thousands of people were walking the country roads of The Veluwe. Many of those refugees were sent to Ede and Barneveld and other small towns in the region, where they were taken into schools and housed there. Kids from Nijkerk or any other little town couldn't go to school anymore. The Red Cross jumped in to help, giving out blankets for those who slept on the floors and food for all the hungry people.

What affected all of us in that region was that suddenly every farmer and every household was visited by Germans, who would take a look around and confiscate rooms. They would evaluate the size of your house and then tell you — not ask you — that you would be taking a certain number of those Arnhem refugees. They didn't offer choices; they simply said, "You *will* take so many people." The Germans determined the number of refugees you had to take; local Dutch authorities were responsible for making assignments of specific people to specific households.

Each of the refugees had his or her own ration cards; but their presence still meant much more work for the family. The new hosts were simply commanded to open their homes to total strangers, who could be criminals or Nazis or NSBers. Nobody knew what kind of people they would get. And yet, beyond those newly housed, thousands of people simply roamed the area with nothing — and nowhere to go. Many were taken to empty old schools and movie houses, wherever there were large spaces.

In addition, there was so much hunger at that time that women and children from other cities were wandering all over the countryside searching for food. Cat owners in the cities wouldn't let their pets go out of the house for fear that hungry people would cut off the heads and tails, skin them, and sell them as rabbits — *dakhaas,* "roof rabbits," is what they were called. People bought them, not knowing that they were going to be eating cats.

In the Netherlands, sets of little silver spoons are often given as wedding presents (here in America no one uses them, but in Holland they are part of a serving set). They are often decorated with silver or gold flowers, and are very precious. Many of those hungry mothers would take their own precious silver or fine linens and trudge out to farmers to try to barter for food for their families. The longer the Occupation went on and the weaker the Germans got, the scarcer the food became. At first, those women went just outside The Hague or any other large city; but during that Hunger Winter of 1944 those women went farther and farther away from home. Sometimes they'd be gone for weeks, looking for food, pushing their carts everywhere they could, trying to trade their linen and silver and crystal and china for a bag of grain or barley, some potatoes and beets, maybe dried food — whatever they and their children could eat. It was very sad.

Just as was true everywhere else in The Veluwe, the Germans demanded that Aalt and Alie put up some of those Arnhem refugees. All of the rooms in the house at Watergoor, plus the loft over the *deel*, were already occupied. In addition, there were often wanderers at that farmhouse looking for food (*passanten* they were called, because they were "passing by"). Everywhere you looked, people were walking — the homeless, the hungry, the refugees. At curfew, of course, those people had to be off the streets. So each of the villages — Barneveld and Nijkerk and Putten — had their school gymnasiums full of hay or straw, and at night all the *passanten* came in. They had to keep their carts and things outside, but they tried to keep an eye on what they had. A lot of thievery took place, because no one had anything. In those places you slept when you could with your stuff under you head. There were fights too, and the police had to keep an eye on those places because people would steal from each other in the darkness. At times it was chaos.

Some were very good people, and some were not very good at all. But Aalt and Alie took them in. Even when they had said, "Oh, we can't take anymore, and it's already so late," they would still put somebody up somewhere. They would make places up in the *hilt*, the loft over the *deel*, where the animals were, with hay and grass, and the *passanten* could climb up a ladder and sleep there. They took people in almost every night, in addition to the Jews they were already hiding, and each one would get a mug of milk, very much treasured, and a slice of bread. It might be twenty or thirty people! But everyone there got milk and bread. God really had to bless them, for Aalt and Alie were so good to all of those people they took in off the road, who otherwise would have had nothing.

What they gave to *passanten* was not the bread Alie baked, however; it was the bread we received from coupons. It tasted a bit like brown cardboard to us, it even had the smell of cardboard, and it was *klef,* "soggy." But it was bread all the same, and in those days of hunger it was precious. For Aalt and Alie to give all those *passanten* a piece was no small thing at all. Because they were farmers, they could also get flour from their relatives to make their own bread. And though Aalt was a dairy farmer, he also had a little piece of land where he grew rye; he would grind that rye, and Alie always baked rye bread.

One night there was a terrible screaming up there in the loft. Aalt's brother Frits hopped up there because he was more or less in charge of those people who came and needed a place to sleep. Alie was pregnant, and Aalt was busy with all the responsiblity of the Jewish people and so on; so Frits was in charge of the *passanten.* If a *passanten* couple was married, they were allowed to sleep together, of course. But that night a couple who had just met in the street but pretended to be married were staying upstairs. Those two got into a terrible fight, and the young woman was yelling and screaming. When Frits went to look, she yelled, "Oh, come here please — I'm not married to this man." She wanted protection from him.

Aalt and Alie were responsible people, and they felt that this event taught them a lesson. After that night, they told people who stayed overnight that they had to show their IDs so they could be sure they were married. Aalt and Alie kept those IDs overnight and in the morning gave them back. Some of the *passanten* didn't like that, and if they didn't, they simply had to move on. Aalt and Alie were a bit strict with them, but with all kinds of people streaming through, they had to be.

Those were days of suffering, but they were interesting days too. Every night there was some kind of surprise with so many people wandering all over the country. In addition to all those *passanten*, though, Aalt and Alie were then required to take in Arnhem refugees on a permanent basis. In this they were helped by Ab van Meerveld. Ab went to Barneveld, where there were hundreds and hundreds of refugees housed in a school. Some Dutch people were involved in arranging the relocations; they worked at the town hall or in other ways tried to alleviate problems.

Our biggest worry was that, because Aalt and Alie had this farm with two extra rooms, plus the *heerd* (a big, beautiful room), the Germans would say that three rooms were not being used. One of those little rooms had Uncle Ben and Tante Marie in it, and the other was mine. Uncle Ben was still doing all the fake IDs for downed pilots and everybody; in fact, Watergoor had become a headquarters for fake IDs in that whole part of the country.

I could have moved somewhere else, but I would have hated to leave Aalt and Alie because they were almost like a sister and brother to me. We couldn't move Uncle Ben around very easily at all; he needed a quiet place with no disturbance, and no one could know he was there either.

The Germans determined that Aalt and Alie were to take in six Arnhem people. We worried a great deal about what kind of refugees we would get. Ab was worried too. His small family lived in a little apartment over a shop in town, and they had no room to take anyone in. They had very little more than one bedroom where their new baby stayed with them, plus a closet. I sometimes slept there myself if I couldn't make it back to the farm before curfew. The woman they rented from lived downstairs.

Several other farmers where we had Jews hidden also had to take in some Arnhem refugees; but we were most worried about our Uncle Ben because he was so important to our work. When Ab went to Barneveld, he found most of the people from Arnhem in a daze after all the things that had happened to them. They had lived so quietly for a long time, and then suddenly they were in the middle of air raids, bombing and shooting, and the bridges blowing up. Allies dropped out of the sky, the gliders flew past silently, and awful shooting surrounded them for days on end. Many died in that horrific fighting; blood was all over the city. On top of everything else, they had had to leave their homes. There were no cars, of course, so everyone walked or traveled on bikes. Some of them did crazy things to try to take important possessions along, even pulling them along the road behind them in children's wagons.

In the school at Barneveld, Ab heard a large family talking: it was a father and mother with four children, and the daughter had a little baby who was a year old. They were worried to death that they would be split up. Ab thought they would be the right ones for Aalt and Alie's farm. This happened to be the very day that this family was supposed to go out and be relocated.

"Under these circumstances I know it won't be easy," the father said to Ab, "but we are seven people and we want more than anything to stay together in all this danger."

Ab discovered that they were a devout Catholic family, and then he made a couple of political remarks to see where they stood with respect to the Germans. And the man responded, not knowing that what he was saying was very important to Ab. At a certain point Ab realized that they were okay, that is, they hated the Nazis and felt horrible about what was happening to the Jews. "Oh," the man said, "we feel terribly sorry about what the Nazis are doing to them."

"I can get you a farm where all of you can stay together," Ab told the man. "But there are Jews in hiding at that place, and if you're scared, I won't put you there. But if you feel that you can stay there, I'll put your entire family at that farm."

The man went over and talked with his wife about it, because it was a big risk to go where there were Jews. This was late in the war, and Ab told him that these Jewish people had been in that home for years already. By this time everyone felt that it wouldn't be long before the war would be over.

When he came back, the man said, "We want to stay together, and we are proud that people like that are willing to help the Jews. We will happily take that risk. Will you take us there?"

So suddenly Aalt and Alie received another seven people! My room went to the father and the mother; a big double bed was placed in the *heerd*, and that's where Annie slept, the daughter with the baby (Aalt and Alie put a little cot in that room for the baby); and the other two sons slept where the *knecht* (Aalt's brother, the hired hand) had slept. One sister left; she had a boyfriend somewhere, and a job. We had fulfilled the Germans' requirement. Annie, whose husband had left her, was a year or two older than I; she was a nice girl, and I liked her a great deal. Whenever I was at Aalt and Alie's, I usually crawled in that double bed with her.

For me, the new family did not make much difference because during that winter I was gone so much of the time carrying cards and rations; there was a great deal of work to do supporting all those Jews in hiding. I walked most of the time because my bicycles were often stolen by the Germans. One day at lunch time, I arrived at a little farm whose owner was a widow with a son; they had also taken in a young Jewish man. "Willie," the woman said, "do you want to eat here?"

"Yes, please," I said, because I was always on the run and scrounged a meal wherever I could.

Farmers didn't throw anything out then, and that woman was serving sauerkraut that day. Sauerkraut is a popular dish in the Netherlands, usually cooked in a certain way: the potatoes are placed in a big pan, the sauerkraut laid on the top, and on top of that a piece of ham or smoked sausage — something with a smoked flavor. Everything is boiled together, and then the meat is removed before the rest of the meal is mashed together. It's a winter dish, and I always liked it.

So the woman placed on the table the big pan, blackened by smoke because it was cooked over a wood fire, and began to ladle out the meal to each one at the table. I wondered what kind of meat they would have that day, since any kind of meat was in very short supply. When she lifted the lid off the pan, I couldn't believe my eyes. There were two strips from the belly of the sow, and there on that meat stood two whole lines of nipples staring me in the face. Now I was a city girl from The Hague, and I had already learned a lot about farm life at Watergoor, but this was too much. I didn't think I would ever get those nipples down.

Nothing was asked, of course, and I was given my portion of the sauerkraut and then my portion of the strip of belly. Several nipples stared at me. I started discussing the whole thing with myself: *Between nipple and nipple is just meat and skin*, I thought, so I started eating. All the others were simply eating it too. But I just couldn't get those nipples down. So I put one in my mouth but hid it behind my cheek, then another behind the other cheek. I got all the meat down, except for the nipples I was saving in my cheek — several of them.

At that time we didn't have paper napkins, but everyone carried handkerchiefs. I generated a coughing spell in order to take out my handkerchief; and when I faked that cough, all the nipples went into the handkerchief. After the meal I had to go to another village, so I hooked my rucksack on and started walking down one of those little roads in the woods. I met a very skinny dog, so skinny you could count that creature's ribs. If there wasn't enough food for people during all that time, I thought, there certainly wasn't enough food for cats and dogs.

"Dog, do you want to have a party here?" I said. And I shook all those nipples out of my handkerchief, and he had a feast during that hungry winter, a feast all to himself.

Because I was staying at Aalt and Alie's most of that winter, I didn't feel the pain of hunger as did so many others in the Netherlands during the last winter of the war. But I worried about my parents in The Hague, though years had passed since that first time the Gestapo had come to my house. Their surprise visits continued for months and months, but eventually they came with less frequency.

I wanted to visit my folks, but there was no safe means of transportation anymore, and bikes that were in good condition were routinely confiscated by the Germans. Of course, with our Jews all over, we had to keep traveling throughout the Netherlands because those families had to be kept supplied. During that time I literally walked all over Gelderland almost every day of every week. That winter I was traveling so much that I decided I would risk going home to see my parents in The Hague. The work was exhausting and always trying, and I needed to be with them, to refresh myself. The guys gave me some work to do in The Hague, and I decided to take that opportunity to visit my parents — even if it was only for a little while.

Toward the end of the war, the British controlled the major highways in the Netherlands completely; their air power was largely unchecked by the Germans, who were obviously beginning to lose the war. Even though there were no Allied troops in the area, British Spitfires roamed the skies and regularly patrolled the highways. I would often see overturned trucks and train wrecks along the roads, victims of Spitfire attacks. Dutch people had been warned by our queen that the Spitfires would attack anything that moved: we were told not to attempt to travel on certain highways, because if we stayed off those roads, the Brits would know that whoever was on them would be Germans or German sympathizers.

The Germans built deep manholes along those roads so that troops could take immediate cover when they heard that piercing noise Spitfires made when they started to dive at whatever moved. Once they swooped down, they would rake the ground with their machine guns — "rick-a-tick-a-tick." It was very dangerous.

When I was set to go see my parents in The Hague, I had somehow gotten hold of a bike, and the guys gave me something very precious: what must have been one of the last bike inner tubes in Holland. It had been stolen from the Germans, I remember, because inner tubes simply were not to be found anywhere anymore. I put this inner tube on the back wheel of my bike, and on the front I had wound a rubber garden hose, just as many people did at that time.

When I came to De Bilt, near Utrecht, people I met going the opposite direction told me that a little further up the road the Germans had set up a trap where they were confiscating bicycles with any good parts. So I went to the nearest farm and asked for a tire lifter to take the tire off my bike. I removed the precious inner tube, tied it around my waist under my winter coat, and walked my bike the rest of the way to The Hague, since what was left on my old bike was a garden hose and a steel rim.

Now I faced a difficult question. Walking my bike made traveling much more difficult. There were two roads: the straight highway one that led directly to The Hague and was controlled by Spitfires, and the other, lined by trees, full of cover, and not regularly patrolled. But the safer road was much longer, and I knew that I had little time for this visit. So I prayed. I asked God for protection, and I took the straight highway, thinking that if our Allied friends were so adept at shooting anything that moved, they must have great sights in those Spitfires, sights that were sharp enough to recognize a young girl walking on the highway.

I made it past the German "trap" because my bike was so old and rusty they didn't give it a second look. They didn't spot my precious inner tube either. The highway I had decided to travel was competely deserted that day. I met absolutely no one, and I knew very well why.

Three Spitfires suddenly appeared in the sky above the road. I was struck with fear, even though I knew they were our friends. I had the choice of diving into the manholes, which were every-where. But I was confident that if the British flyers were to spot a young woman, they would leave me alone for the rest of the day. If I were to dive into one of the manholes, I guessed I would spend most of the day in and out of those things.

So when they began to dive, I prayed again. I stood in the middle of the road like a willing target and waved my white handkerchief as high and hard as I could. They dove. I heard their horrible shrieking, but I kept waving and praying for dear life. They swooped directly at me, so close I could plainly see their faces and they could see me. Then, suddenly, they pulled themselves up and soared over my head.

Many, many times that day I saw them patrolling that highway that led to Germany. It was as if they had become my only friends on that lonely road. And they *were* my friends, of course; eventually they would become our liberators.

Walking my bike that way, I made it only to Zoetermeer by nightfall. Curfew was at eight o'clock, so I had to leave the highway and go into the village, where literally hundreds of people like me were being housed in a school. That night, I slept on straw like the others, and I never took off my shoes. Because my feet hurt so badly, I was afraid I would never get them on again. The next day was Sunday, and I still had another twelve kilometers to go to get home, so I left early and entered The Hague just about the time when most people were going to church.

The Gestapo had not been to my parents' home for quite some time, but I was still afraid of going directly to their address. That moment was another one of those times during the war when I was depressed, tired, and emotionally drained. But I wanted to see my parents, and I was determined to pay any price. When I was almost home, I met a man named Mr. Semeyn, whose daughter Coby had a beautiful singing voice and had often been a visitor at our house when we made music, before the war. He was on his way to church, but when he saw me, without saying a word, he took the bike from my hands and walked it himself, right beside me, directly to my parents' front door. He never asked me any questions, though I must have looked like a tramp. That may seem like such a small thing, but what he did thrilled my soul.

Mr. Semeyn rang the bell and the door opened. Mother started to cry the moment she saw me. She helped me take off my shoes, because the soles of my feet were like beefsteak, raw and bloody with no skin left. I can't describe how much I ached. But at least I was home — if only for a little while. I'd brought some things from the farm along with me, hidden of course:

flour and bacon and milk that Aalt and Alie had given me for my parents, who had very little. It was a great blessing that I could bring them food from the country. It was also wonderful for them that I could be home again. Even though the war was all around us and this house was not at all safe for me, it was home for all of us. I still couldn't breathe easily when I was there, but it seemed enough of a relief that at least some of my anxiety would disappear, even if my stays there were only for a few hours.

On December 8, 1944, the Nazis raided the home of Dries Klooster, a highly respected man from Barneveld, because they had received a tip that Allied pilots were being hidden there. Dries, like many others, had created a hiding place in his home, just in case such a raid were ever to occur. He had hidden me there, as well as downed pilots; but we had gotten out before the raid. Dries himself climbed into that hiding space and was able to escape.

But Ab van Meerveld was not able to escape. Ab was at the Kloosters' almost coincidentally on the 8th, and when the Gestapo suddenly came in, they captured him. They were very happy to snatch Ab, because he had become known to them as "the man in the leather jacket"; he was on their most-wanted list. Ab was Hein's best friend and the co-leader of Group HEIN. He and his wife, Riek, were our dear friends. The last meal I had with Hein before he was arrested was at the van Meervelds'. It came as no great surprise to me when Ab was arrested. Getting caught by the Nazis was always a possibility, even a reality one lived with daily. But the sudden loss of someone so important in the day-to-day functioning of our Resistance work was difficult to calculate; and the personal cost, the pain to Riek, was immense.

At the beginning of the war we had had the sense that the Occupation could not last long. We had been wrong: it had seemed to go on forever. But by the end of 1944, signs appeared everywhere that the German military presence, so powerful a few years earlier, was rapidly losing its hold. Ab's arrest was very painful; but what helped buttress our hopes, even in our suffering, was the growing sense that the Occupation would soon be over. The proximity of liberation offered hope that Ab — and Hein too, though he'd been arrested much earlier — would soon return home. But it was sad to live without them.

I was able to return to The Hague late in December, and I celebrated New Year's 1945 at home, sitting in my room as the clock proclaimed the end of the old year and the beginning of the new. We had gone to bed early and set our clocks to awaken just before midnight. It was a time for reflection for me, not celebration. I took out of a piece of my favorite stationery. It was contraband stationery, since a portrait of William of Nassau appeared at the top, along with a little poem:

"We lift our heart and hands
for the blessing of the Netherlands,
for faithfulness till death,
Wilhelmus van Nassaue;
and we take the oath
to stand ready to die with you."

I sat there in my room that New Year's Eve and wrote Hein a letter, even though I had no idea where he was and no means by which to send him what I'd written.

▲   ▲

December 31, 1944

My dearest jongen,

We have decided after all to "celebrate" the change of years, and that's why we all went to sleep at 6 P.M. and just got up now. Now that the two of us cannot be together, I want to write you, for if I write, it almost seems as if we can talk together. Sometimes I have the feeling that through this all you will have changed a great deal. Judging by myself, I am sure you have changed, and I have the feeling that prison is much more difficult for you than it was for me. Maybe this sounds ridiculous, but sometimes I find myself longing for the time when I was in prison. Why? I cannot really answer that. Maybe because there I felt safer and closer to God in spite of everything. Now I have the feeling that I can't handle things anymore.

People have told me that I have changed and become hard! Bert said that I don't seem to have any time for them anymore. Yet I know the work could be enlarged and much more could be done. Other jobs need to be done. I *know* that you would do those things, and that you expect the same from me. But how can I do this all when I don't have enough time?

And here in The Hague. You always attached such great importance to Klassen. If Bob [Resistance worker] goes away, then can Tilly [another worker] do his work? And if I stay here [in The Hague], then how will things go back there [in The Veluwe]? It's impossible for me to stay here.

To be honest, I would love to do completely different

318

work. I would love to help at Jantje and Piet's. Darling, how hard it must be for you not to be able to do anything now! How you would have enjoyed what we are doing now, all this added work. Where are you now? Are you sleeping or are you awake? Are your thoughts with me? Are you still healthy? Are your shoes still in one piece? Are you walking around in wet feet? Are you coughing a lot? I suppose you can still hang in there, darling!

From your last letter and the one time I spoke with Adriaan [who had spoken with Hein in the Amersfoort camp], I got the impression that you have changed. Because your character is always full of ambition, the news of my being locked up must have been much harder on you than it was on me. When I was arrested, it was almost a relief to know that I could now experience what you were experiencing yourself. I am so afraid that they are breaking your spirit. And you did not get a chance to escape on The Veluwe, an area you know so well. Oh, there are such huge mountains of problems now for you and for me. There are so many dangers which threaten you physically and maybe also spiritually.

Often I have the feeling that I cannot go on one step farther. And then I think: "You [God] don't give more than we can bear and than my strength can take," but now I can't take any more, Lord! Sometimes I honestly have the feeling that I just can't go on, that I'm really cracking up, going crazy. But thank God, it has not happened. He has saved me from that, and I don't believe it will happen. But what has happened has left scars.

Darling, it is like I am relentlessly being pushed on.

Inside, everything in me hurts and I yearn to talk to somebody who will be able to understand me. That's why, with all the work I have to do already, I still run from one person to another. But I still feel alienated everywhere. Everybody is so full of their own difficulties. These times don't leave space and time for anybody. With all of my old friends, I don't seem to be able to converse in depth anymore. But I don't blame them. I tried so many times, but maybe, when I look back at it, it was good that I never got to have a good conversation with them, because I don't think they would have been able to understand what I'm feeling. Besides, I know where I have to go for my medicine. Why should I go to people if I can go to him who said, "Come unto me all who are heavy laden, and I will give you rest." *Heavy laden* — that's what I am. Laden with pride, often thinking myself better than others while we have to think the other one better than ourselves.

Laden with my own egotism.

Laden with all my sins.

And when I went to bed last night and thought about everything and wanted to bring all those difficulties to God, I couldn't even find the words! I thought, I'm going to tell him everything just as if he were standing next to my bed and listening, for that's where he is. But I didn't even know where to start. But I also knew that he knew it all already. Yes, darling, thank God, both of us know where to go with our troubles. But I'm human, and it would be such a relief, I think, if I could talk to someone about it all.

What makes me happy is to hear our friends talk about you. Oh sweetheart, I was so deadly unhappy, and it was such a chaos inside me that I took the luxury for once to have a good cry. And now, when Mother called to wake me up for the New Year, I first wanted to pray, but it turned into thanks, darling, for all that God had given us this year. For his wonderful ways with us, even if we don't understand it all now. For his love, that in all our disappointments and sorrow he himself helps us to bear it all, so that all this turns into a blessing because we feel his nearness and can take up our cross joyfully. And so we may know, and we do experience, that his power is made perfect in our weakness.

12 Midnight — change of 1944 into 1945! Sitting with the light of a candle. Mother also said a prayer of thanks with us.

May the Lord keep you and may you abide in the shadow of the Almighty.

May the Lord make his face to shine upon you and be gracious to you and may he lift up his countenance upon you and give you peace.

He will guard you so that you will not strike your foot against a stone, and he will also keep your soul.

Hein, darling, can it really be better: I give you as an offering into his hands, body and soul.

What can hunger or cold or anything else in creation do to you?

Nothing will be able to separate you from the love of God that is in Christ Jesus.

He will lead you and me by his counsel and afterward he will take us into his glory. I cling to all his promises. You are in the shelter of the Most High and you are under his wings. You will only observe it with your eyes, but no harm will befall you.

"Because he loves me," says the Lord, "I will rescue him and show him my salvation. With long life will I satisfy him."

His name is Wonderful Counselor, Mighty God, Everlasting Father, Prince of Peace. For this God is our God!

Darling, how will it be next year at this time?

Will we be together again?

Dearest, some time in the future you can read everything I've written. And then you can tell me about all your thoughts and together we will thank him. This pouring my thoughts out on paper has relieved me. I feel better and full of confidence and resolution that with God's help we enter this new year. I pray that in this coming year he will bring us together again.

Dearest, how great is your love for me, and how egotistical is my love for you.

from the journal of Diet Eman

▼   ▼

Over the River

Photograph by Emmy Andriesse in *Amsterdam Tijdens de Hongerwinter* (Amsterdam: Contact and De Bezige Bij, n.d.).

In February 1945, I had to walk from Nijkerk to Ermelo, where we had an elderly Jewish couple. I hadn't been there in a while, so I brought them ration cards. They were hidden in one little room, kept there on the second floor in the back of the house, and almost the moment I got there the old man started to cry.

"Juffrouw, juffrouw," he said, "we are going crazy! The two of us here, locked up in this room! Is there nowhere we can be where we can walk around outside?"

I told him it would be very difficult to move them at all, but I did know a couple in Hulshorst who wanted badly to get out of the house where they were. The man was a rabbi from Amsterdam, Rabbi Tal, a well-known leader. They were horrified by what was going on there: the woman who owned the house was carrying on an affair with a Jewish man, a man considerably younger than she. Rabbi Tal and his wife were very religious people, very strict and orthodox, and this situation appalled them — as it did us when we heard about it. The rabbi had complained strenuously; he said they couldn't in good conscience go on living there when they knew that this great sin was happening right there in that house.

But we couldn't find another place for them to live just that quickly. So when this older Jewish man hiding at Ermelo began his lament, I remembered Rabbi Tal saying that he didn't care if he was locked in some tiny room, he couldn't stay at his address any longer. I thought it might be possible to have those two couples trade places.

I told the man in Ermelo I couldn't promise definitely, but I said that it might be possible to move them to a spot where they could escape the limiting confines of their single room. So I walked all the way to Hulshorst, where I spoke to the rabbi and his wife and told them I could arrange for them to get that little room in Ermelo. Yes, of course, they said; they wanted out of that place of sin.

Now the problem was how to get those people moved. In the first place, there were no more cars or trucks. Many of the trains were no longer running, and it was far too dangerous to take Jews on the trains anyway, since the British regularly bombed the trains. Besides, these people were in their sixties. At Hulshorst, the lady of the house where the rabbi was in hiding told me that the baker in town was someone who could be trusted. She thought maybe he could arrange something for us because he still had a horse and carriage. So I went to that baker. I had to tell him who had sent me to let him know that I was okay. But even after I had talked with him for some time, I was sure that he wasn't completely convinced I was safe. It was very difficult to trust anyone during the war.

"May we please use your horse and carriage?" I asked. "We'll pay you — we'll make it even with you. . . ." I tried very hard.

But it was scary to go anywhere by horse and carriage. By that time in the war, everything that moved on the road was being shot at. I didn't blame him for being reluctant. But I begged and I begged until finally he gave in, and in the end I got him to promise that he would move those people between Hulshorst and Ermelo on Monday afternoon.

I walked all the way back to Ermelo. It was February: very cold and snowy, dark weather, not a good day at all for walking. But inside I was happy because I thought those two couples would at least be happy. Everyone knew that the war wasn't going to last too much longer. I knew the old couple would be happy at Hulshorst, where they could walk outside; and the rabbi and his wife would be thrilled to be out of the house of sin. I figured that the old man at Ermelo would be very happy to hear it was all arranged.

"It's all taken care of," I told him when I got back there. "Monday afternoon, five o'clock, there will be a little horse and carriage and you and your wife just have to get into —"

He looked at me angrily. "Who do you think you are? You're so young and you think you can decide about *our* lives! You think we don't have any say about how we live? Just who do you think you are?"

I was too young to understand that this was probably a kind of emotional breakdown for him. I was worn out by that time myself, after doing all that walking and figuring, scheming and negotiating. I wasn't thinking of his plight at that moment, how he and his wife had had to sit for those years in that one little room. What did come to my mind was the book of Exodus, how the children of Israel had grumbled and grumbled, always murmuring, as Moses said. And suddenly I had had enough of that kind of whining. I'd walked all those miles that day in terrible weather, exhausting myself trying to help them, only to have him tell me that he was angry at me for arranging something that had been very difficult.

"Dammit!" I said, "You *are* going!" I shouldn't have said that word, I know, but I couldn't help it. It just exploded out of me.

"You can't make me," he said. "I'm *not* going. You see if you can get me in that carriage."

I slammed my fist on the table and said, "You *are* going."

"Oh yeah?" he said.

And then I said something else I'm not proud of. I asked him if he had read the paper: just a few days earlier, there had been an article reporting how the authorities had found a couple of Jewish people in the woods nearby, without papers and shot to death.

"Do you remember that article? If you don't get in that carriage," I said, "there will soon be another article just like it."

Then I left. I had come to their address full of happiness, but I was leaving angry. What I had said was nasty, but I was at my wit's end.

Back at Aalt and Alie's that night, I met a man named Wim who was a member of the *knokploeg*. He had a gun.

"Wim," I said to him, "are you busy on Monday?"

"No," he said, "what can I do for you?"

It was a good plot, I think; in fact, I'm surprised at how good it was, even if it wasn't nice.

"Will you go to this address in Ermelo on Monday, and when you get there, lay your revolver on the table — just play with it. You don't even have to say a thing, just play with your revolver. You'll see a couple run into a carriage." And that's exactly what happened.

▲   ▲

"When you come back you will not recognize me anymore, my love. There is not a bit of softness in me. I am stone, stone-hard, and I'm tired of the whole mess. I'm embarrassed to write you this, and I'm asking for you to understand it or that you will be angry with me. Maybe if you would still be here, I could handle it better. But now I have to struggle along here alone, and it is just too heavy for me.

Do I disappoint you? Oh God, I am just aching for the end of it. And what will be then? Now I still have hope. From the moment that there is peace until the time that I finally hear something from you — that will probably be the most difficult time of my life.

Over the River

I don't know how I'll ever get through it.

a letter, never sent, from Diet Eman to Hein Sietsma

▼   ▼

The Germans made it known at that time that all the bridges over the IJssel, a large river running north and south, were going to be closed. What that meant, of course, was that the river itself would become something like the wall in East Germany, a boundary that stopped any kind of movement whatsoever. We had so many people hiding Jews on the other side of the IJssel in Friesland that its closing became a terrible problem for us. The guys said we had to have one last contact across the river. "Diet," they said, "you have to go once more — with loads of ration cards and information."

A bike ride from Aalt and Alie's across the river to Friesland was normally a day's travel. But during the war it took longer, because I was walking most of the time. For this last, sudden trip, I had one day to get there, one day to do all the necessary things in Friesland, and one day to get back — before the Germans were going to shut down the bridges. And it didn't matter where I was when they closed them; the whole river was going to be closed off.

I had two options: one way, along back roads, was safer but would take longer; the other way, along the dike, was faster but much more dangerous. Because of the time limitations, I decided I would take the dike. I came to the river at Zwartsluis, at a very wide point, and stopped to look at what was happening on the other side. It was a forbidden zone, *Sperrgebiet*, and you needed a special permit from the Germans to travel there. I saw a ferry boat with fifty or sixty people on it crossing the river in the rain. The land was at a high point and the river was deep down, so people had to go downward to a wooden platform, on the river's edge, where they would stand with their bikes and wait for the ferry to return.

I watched them cross the river, get off the ferry, then go up the bank on the other side. The road was straight there. Up the road a bit stood the guard house occupied by a single soldier with a rifle, and he was inside, out of the rain. As the ferryboat arrived, I noticed that the single guard waited until the people came up from the river toward him. Then he would come out and search their papers and permits. The guardhouse itself stood at a place where the road up from the river split into two directions, north and south.

Almost all of the area around the Beulaker and Belterwijde, a couple of lakes near Meppel, was completely forbidden territory. Only the people who lived there could get in, and they had to have a special permit. I asked a woman how to get a permit, and she said that I would have to ask the Germans. I knew that would require a full investigation, and I needed to get over the river now. I had to get into that forbidden zone, but I had no legal way of gaining entry. I felt, once more, that my life was really at stake. I assumed that if I was going to get through this one, as I'd been through the arrest and the hearing and so many difficult situations, it was going to be only because the Lord wanted me to do his work over there.

"You know, Lord," I prayed, "I have to get across. You know that in two days the IJssel is going to be closed, and I must get to the other side. I don't have the time to go back to Zwolle or anything — I have to go now." I asked the Lord again to take care of me. I told him I needed his hand, demanded it, if I was going to make it. It was one of those prayers that I think of as being somewhat disrespectful, like Tevye's in *Fiddler on the Roof* — nearly commanding God what to do. But I'd once heard a sermon in which the pastor said that God loves it when we hold him to his promises.

When the ferry came back, I got on it with my old bike. By that time another fifty or sixty people had gathered, many of them with bikes. I deliberately went to the very front of the ferry. I saw that the German soldier was once again inside the little guardhouse on the other side, trying to stay out of the rain. I knew that when I got off, he wouldn't see any of us right away, since he was waiting until the whole bunch would come up the long hill to pass his guard house.

So I was the first one off that ferry. The others weren't in the kind of rush I was. I tore off quickly and shot up the hill, leaving the rest of the passengers at the bottom behind me. The guard in the shack had more or less timed his coming out into the unpleasant weather, since he knew about when he could begin to expect the crowd coming up the hill. He might have seen one figure coming up the road to his guard house, but he was still inside and probably was not interested in coming out of his dry room for just one person when there were another fifty still coming up the hill behind me.

He was alone, thank God! I pedaled as fast as I could and was almost past the guardhouse before he came out and yelled, "Halt, halt, halt!" as I went past him. I took an immediate left, to the north, toward those lakes. Rushing past that guardhouse was my only chance. I always said a prayer before I did those things, and I told the dear Lord exactly what I needed, left it up to him to take care of me in his way.

I'm not really sure what happened. Maybe the guard could have shot me. But sixty others were coming up from the ferry in a swarm, so suddenly he was confronted with a tough decision: do I chase down this one young woman and risk losing more in the larger group, or do I deal with the sixty people who are right here at my door? He was probably young and not very experienced; but had I been a man, I believe that he would have simply shot me. I pedaled as fast as I could, wondering if I would get a bullet in my back. All I could do was pedal and hope that I wouldn't be instantly dead. I zigzagged, just in case he would shoot.

And again God delivered me. After all, I had to get over there because I had the last bunch of ration cards and necessary information. It would be the last contact with the people we worked with in Friesland before Liberation, and I made it. My delivery of those ration cards was a sad time, and yet somewhat hopeful. When I talked with those people on the other side, we knew we wouldn't see each other again until after the Liberation. We hoped and trusted it would be soon: the Germans themselves would not have closed the IJssel, we figured, if they did not know that the end of the war was very near. But what price would be paid before the end? Who else would suffer? Who would die?

Once I got into that area, I wasn't stopped anymore. The next day, when I got back to the river after making all the deliveries on the other side, it was not hard to get back across. This time I took the open roads through territory that wasn't forbidden. The work was done.

That afternoon, when I crossed over the IJssel bridge, near Zwolle, the line was endless: swarms of people didn't want to be on the German side once the IJssel was closed. Hundreds were taking this last opportunity to go west, back to their homes with food they had found. It seemed as if I would stand in that line forever. The Germans checked your papers at the bridge and asked you what you were going to do. I had my papers in order, so I wasn't worried. In the meantime, I was at the very end of my stamina once again. I had returned to Resistance work very quickly and had been working hard ever since I'd been released from the camp at Vught. But the effects of my stay in prison had been more severe than I thought they were at the time — both physically and mentally.

Right there, standing in that endless line of people on the bridge, I prayed to God again, asking for something more than just safety this time, asking instead for him to get me out of the Underground work. I'd had enough of it. What never stopped in the Resistance was the tension of knowing that at any time you could be caught and maybe killed, along with others you loved. That fear never diminished; it was relentless. You lived with it at all times.

For years after the war, I would have a dream that I was being chased by the Nazis down a street of The Hague or some place I couldn't identify. I would see them behind me so vividly that I would shake. And then suddenly a miracle would happen. I would shake my arms and wave them all around until I lifted myself up like a bird, very slowly, all the time my flapping arms getting more and more tired, until finally I would let myself down to rest on a balcony somewhere. Then the glass doors of that balcony would open, and it would *always* be someone with a Nazi insignia coming out, and I had to start flying again! I would wake up after that dream, completely worn out, my shoulders aching.

To live with that constant fear of getting caught was one of the worst things about Resistance work. You were never safe — and never free of the tension. That's why I told God on the bridge that I wanted to drop the whole thing. I wanted to go somewhere where there was peace and quiet and safety. I could weep just thinking of such a place. I wanted to go somewhere and just read a book. *I don't want it any longer, God!* I told him. *I've had it!*

That afternoon on my bike I had terrible cramps, and I felt as though I had diarrhea. There were no public bathrooms anywhere, so if you had to go, you had to find your own place. And I couldn't really find a place to go because the roads were clogged with people, mostly women wandering and looking for food, or begging from farmers. It was March — no shrubs, only bare trees. I was miserable. I had waited in line at that bridge forever, and I had such horrible cramps that afterward, when I finally crossed the river and was back on my bike, I didn't dare to get off. I knew I would have an accident for sure if I did not get home soon.

All I was longing for was to get home to Aalt and Alie's place, where I'd be okay at least for that night. I was riding a very old, rusty bike Aalt had given me; I don't know where he got all those old bikes, but he was always finding something for me after the Germans had taken mine. This one was a very rusty man's bike, with that bar you had to swing your leg over. I made it back to Nijkerk, to that little *kinderhoofdjes* street, the Brink, the cobblestone street where I was close enough to see Watergoor in the distance. I felt miserable all over, physically and emotionally. I had to go to the bathroom so bad, but I didn't dare get off that bike.

Right there, on that plaza, within viewing distance of Aalt and Alie's, an old man stepped off the curb and walked right in front me. I wasn't going fast, and my first reaction was to veer to the right to miss him; but he saw me, realized that he had stepped in front of an oncoming bike, and stepped back instead of continuing forward. When he stepped back, I had to veer the opposite direction. Then he stepped in front again, moving the same way I did, back and forth, almost like a circus routine. I lost what little speed I had, and I had to get off my bike to avoid hitting the man.

As soon as I got off the bike, I had a terrific accident in my pants, right then and there, on the cobblestone streets of Nijkerk, so close to Aalt and Alie's that I could see the house from there. Terrible diarrhea — it was the most humiliating thing that could have happened! I had been sitting and squeezing all afternoon, holding it back in with those awful cramps, and then when I was just about home, I lost it. I had to swing my whole leg over the bike's bar in order to get off, and I stood there in the street, utterly miserable. I had to crawl back on that bike and continue to the farm in that condition. Here I was, twenty-four years old, and so thoroughly exhausted that I said, "Lord, now why did you have to let this happen?" I was angry with God. I thought that this was not necessary. If he could do everything, I thought, then why on earth couldn't he at least keep that man out of my way.

I didn't want to get back on the seat again, but I did because it was still too far to walk. I was angry, depressed, and I had no strength. I was going very slowly when, just like that, something cracked, and I was left holding the whole steering mechanism in my hand. That old rusty bike cracked in half, and I was looking down at a sharp piece of old iron sticking straight up at me. If I had had any speed built up, I could have been severely hurt or even killed. I would have fallen forward, and I would have caught that rusty metal shaft right in my chest.

I do not think that it was just coincidence.

The bike was broken, so I put it on the curb in two parts and walked to the farm with my dirty pants. It was very dark by then. When Alie saw me, she didn't know what she was seeing, she told me later. I must have looked like I was at the very limit of everything — physically, emotionally, and spiritually.

"Willie," she said, "you look terrible."

You don't want to know how I feel, I thought.

"Sit down, sit down," she said.

But I couldn't sit. So I told her what had happened, and I just broke down and cried . . . and I cried. I couldn't hold it in anymore. It was like that morning in the Vught concentration camp: everything broke in me and I couldn't stop weeping. I told both Aalt and Alie that I had had enough of the whole business. I was cold and I was dirty, and I couldn't do it anymore, and I wanted the war to be over. Alie hushed me and consoled me, and that was good.

My friend Alie knew how broken I was, so she heated a whole bucket of water for me, and we did not split that one! That bath was all mine, and it was wonderful. Then I put on clean clothing, and I felt much better.

That night I read my little book, the biblical diary book I'd received from my parents when I'd left home. It was always like something of my Mother and Father to me, wherever I was. When I opened the book that night at the end of February 1945, it said, "Being exhausted, yet keeping up the pursuit" (Judges 8:4).

Even after what I had said of wanting out, even after that humiliation, the physical exhaustion, the deep despair I felt, those words were my new marching orders. The next morning, I swung my rucksack over my shoulders and was off again.

▲　　　▲

April 3, 1945: In the night, two o'clock.

Dear Hein, where are you? Is there not a chance that you can smuggle out a note so that I know what is happening? Today I was longing so much to be arrested again because I really thought it was better to be there than here. I am so absolutely fed up with the whole thing. Riek told me that two days after Ab had been arrested she found it easier to bear her cross, and she could not understand that it would be more difficult after a long time. But today she also said that she found it was getting more and more difficult. If we only knew that you both are coming back — both of you — it would be easier.

And the worst is that I feel so far away from God. There seems to be no contact — I can't even pray anymore, and that's what I need more than anything right now. If I only knew something about you. But I'm so afraid that you won't make it because of the hunger. There are so many dangers all around you, but even if I feel far from God I know one thing — and that is that God is more mighty than all those dangers and that he will protect you like the apple of his eye. If I couldn't cling to that, I would go stark crazy.

And what would life be without you? I am now racing from one side of the Netherlands to the other, and I do things that I can't understand where I get the strength to do. This restlessness in me, I think it's only because in my subconscious I'm searching for you, trying to find you, and I don't find you anywhere.

Sometimes I feel so hopeless and lonely, and then I think that maybe it's longing to go home, and I try to go to The Hague and see my parents for a night, but then when I'm there it's almost worse.

Please come back to me soon, I miss you so terribly. And I don't know where to look for you anymore.

Oh, what am I — an egotist! How are things with you? And how strong your longing to get out must be.

O God, bring us together again.

from the diary of Diet Eman

▼   ▼

The End of the Occupation

In Mei leggen alle vogels een ei!

After Liberation, the Allies dropped food to the starving people of Holland.
Translation: "In May every bird drops an egg."

P. de Zeeuw J. G.zn., *Vrij* (de Bilt: Uitg. Comp. De Branding, 1945).

The Lozeman family and the resident Arnhem refugees at Watergoor farm,
taken shortly after Liberation in 1945.

The End of the Occupation

One Sunday afternoon at Aalt and Alie's, I had my military charts and maps in front of me because I was supposed to make reports for the GDN (Geheime Dienst Nederland), the Dutch spying network. In order to do that, I had to spread those large maps out over the whole floor. It was difficult because even Aalt and Alie didn't know that I was doing that kind of work; I didn't want them to know that I was also spying.

I had collected a lot of detailed information for my friend Klein Jantje, the spy. I had to measure it all out on those detailed maps, which showed railroads, bridges, and farms — even objects like trees. I had to mark everything I'd seen and measure it in degrees: where I'd seen troop movements and where I'd seen fortifications being erected. But I had this problem of when and where to do it because I had to be alone. Mother and Father Engels, the refugee family from Arnhem, always took a nap on Sunday afternoon, and Uncle Ben and his wife were in their own little room. Annie Engels, the young single mother, was resting or reading, her little baby sleeping in the *heerd*. And Aalt, who was always very tired from working so hard, could not go to church twice; he would often fall asleep by five o'clock. So Alie would go to evening worship, and he would often stay home. I would take care of the little kids.

But this Sunday Aalt had awakened from a nap and told me he was going to have a chat with the neighbors. There was no one around, so it was a great opportunity for me to get my work done. I got all of my maps out of their hiding place and spread them all over the table.

For some reason, right in the middle of all of that map reading and marking, I happened to look up — and I thought that my heart would stop! There, at the end of Aalt and Alie's very long driveway, I saw two *Landwachters*, Dutch Nazi volunteers in green uniforms — in my mind, the lowest of scum. They were

341

collaborators who checked to see if you had an illegal pig or a bike you hadn't reported. Everything was regulated, and if they found anything at all, they would confiscate it for the Germans. Every farmer had a pig hidden somewhere, or something else stuck away. If you had new bikes by that time in the war, you hid them; you would never use them.

There, on Sunday afternoon at about five o'clock, those Dutch Nazis had turned into our driveway on their bikes. Bikes go slower than cars, so I had a bit of time before they would actually get to the house. I picked everything up in a panic and flew around the house. I started in the *heerd*, where a mirror hung, hiding the forbidden radio; I slipped that mirror to the side and put all the spy maps I was working on behind the mirror.

"Annie," I yelled, "get the Jews underground right away! Tell them that they may not call up. Tell them that this time it's for real."

Aalt and Alie had butter and other things that were contraband, so I tried to clean up as much as I could of the things they were not supposed to have in the house. Then I scurried outside, because I wanted to catch those collaborators and stall them while Annie was getting Uncle Ben and his wife into that hole under the table in their room.

Annie was not in the Resistance work, and I didn't know how she would react to danger. I was very nervous.

I stopped those men outside and said, "Hi, can I help you?"

"Whose farm is this?" they asked.

"Aalt Lozeman's," I said.

"Where is he?"

I told them that he had gone to see the neighbors.

"We want to take a look around."

"I'm only the maid here," I said. "Would you mind if I get him from the neighbors?"

"No, we want to see it *now*."

"But he's not home —"

"We don't care," they said.

Thank God, they did not go into the house first! They went into the barn, and that gave Annie more time. But I wanted to keep my eyes on them, so I couldn't run into the house and be sure that every trace of the Jews was gone. All the work that Uncle Ben was doing on IDs for us had to be completely out of the way.

I delayed and misguided them as much as I could, but they found two bikes and a hog that Aalt should not have had. That made them furious.

"We want to see this house," they said, storming in.

"I hate it that Aalt isn't here," I told them. "I'm only the maid and I never go into their bedroom or anything. It's their house."

They came in anyway, and they found the churn with butter, another item you weren't allowed to have. They went into the *heerd*, where Annie was with her baby, and then they went into the Jews' room. There was a spinning wheel there, but Annie had been able to hide Uncle Ben and Tante Marie under the floor. Those *Landwachters* both had heavy boots on, so I hoped that Uncle Ben and his wife would hear the pounding and understand that this was no drill we were doing. I was hoping that Marie would not call up, as she usually did, "Please may I come out now?" I hoped Annie had made it very clear that this was no exercise.

I told the men that this room and the next were the rooms in which the seven people from Arnhem were living. And they fell for it. And they never looked behind the mirror, so they never found the radio or the maps I was working on. They went back into the kitchen, into Aalt and Alie's bedroom, and into the *kelder*, the basement, where we kept cheese and cool things.

When they had looked all over, they came back to the kitchen and sat down to make a report. That was when Aalt returned. When he stepped in, he turned three shades whiter. He had no idea what had happened, nor did he know what they had found; he did not know whether the Jews had been hidden. He didn't know anything. So I stood behind those *Landwacht* guys and signaled to Aalt that everything was okay, so he would know that the Jewish people were out of sight and safe.

"We found *new* bikes!" one of those guys said.

"Ja, ja, everybody keeps their bikes out of the way these days," Aalt said.

"We found a pig!" the other one said.

Well, every farmer did that as well. For hoarding bikes, a pig, and a little butter, Aalt got a fine. But that was all they found. I'm sure that when they left they congratulated themselves on the fine job they had done: a pig, new bikes, butter. But they'd missed a whole world of important things in that house, everything that would have been really dangerous for us.

When they were gone, I told Aalt what had happened. By that time Alie had come home from church. That was one other time when my whole body reacted to the fear and went out of my own control. My nerves came apart completely, and I started vomiting and vomiting. I couldn't stop. It had been such a narrow escape. I kept telling myself that I could take all of the pressure; but there were those times that my body seemed almost to shut itself down, to scream that what was happening was just too much.

If I hadn't paused for a moment to look up — and why I looked up is still a mystery to me — and spotted the collaborators in the driveway, they would have been at the door just like that. Who knows what would have happened with Uncle Ben and his wife and the spy maps? We may all have been arrested

—and some of us executed. Nobody in that house knew the extent of the danger we had been in.

That was in April 1945. At about the same time, the Gestapo returned to the home of Dries Klooster in Barneveld, trying to find him again, just as they had in December when they had arrested Ab van Meerveld, who happened to be there that time. They knew that Dries was aiding downed pilots. I had lived in his house for several weeks myself, just after returning from Vught and just prior to taking up my base at Aalt and Alie's farm. I'd been there several times after that as well. Dries was the father of seven children, and those kids knew everything that went on in the Klooster house. I always considered that dangerous. Those kids were having fun learning English by joking around with Allied pilots. Of course, the fact that they spoke some English words would have proved to anyone that they'd been in contact with Allies.

Once the raids began at the Klooster house, I couldn't go there anymore; no pilots could hide there anymore either. In fact, Dries himself couldn't stay at home after the raids began; so he went into hiding. We knew that the end of the war was just a matter of weeks away. But that time the Gestapo again came to search for Dries and found him absent, they took his wife, Jo. The Gestapo often did this, because most men would have the impulse to return and save their spouses. There was no prison in Barneveld where they could put her, so they took Jo Klooster to Apeldoorn, the Willem III Armory, which had been turned into a Gestapo prison. What that meant, of course, was that all those kids were alone, their father in hiding and their mother arrested. Under those circumstances, I felt that I should go to Barneveld to be with those children, because I had lived with them for a few months before.

We had to send Dries the message that his wife had been

taken prisoner. The Gestapo thought Dries would turn himself in, but we warned him, "Don't do it, don't do it — not with liberation so close at hand." But it was very hard on Dries to know that Jo was in the Gestapo's hands. He hid in a place called Drie, very close to Nijkerk. By that time the Canadians were already advancing, and we were constantly being shelled; they were shooting long-distance artillery into the area, that's how close the liberation was. One of those shells made a direct hit on the farm where Dries was hiding. The farm was damaged, of course, and Dries was killed — the only one on that farm who was.

I don't think it's possible for me to describe how horrible that death was to me. Many people were killed during the Occupation — hundreds of thousands. But this one, after all our suffering, with the end so close, seemed more horrible, more of a waste, more absolutely unnecessary than so many others that were just as awful and just as costly. Dries Klooster was much beloved in Barneveld, where he worked in the post office, and his death hit all of us terribly hard.

Why, Lord? I asked then, as did everybody. This was a father of seven kids, and he'd done so much good during the war. Why does this good man have to die so shortly before the end? And by our own friends' shell?

When the children heard the news from their pastor that their father had been killed, it was just shattering. The Underground sent a message to Apeldoorn on April 17, via the Red Cross, to the commandant of that Gestapo prison, asking them to free Mother Klooster because her husband had been killed. Even if the Germans wanted him, he had already been killed by Allied shelling, and there were seven children. They did let her go. The Germans themselves realized that it was simply a matter of days for them.

After staying with those children for a couple days, I went back to Aalt and Alie's. The whole area was very tense because the Allied shelling was advancing closer and closer. The closer they came, the farther the range of their artillery extended. At one point we were directly in their range, and for three days and three nights we sat in that house, all of us, listening as those shells fell all around — SSSHHHEEEEEEE-boom! We could hear them whistling, every one of them, and we never knew exactly where they would hit; but we knew, after it fell, that at least it hadn't hit us. Three days and three nights, from April 17 to 20.

▲   ▲

April 19, 1945

Today everything is quiet again. All the barbed wire blockades are put in place, and Jilt had to pass Watergoor to go home because the Allies are two km. away from Nijkerk. On the Holkerweg every fifty meters there is artillery. There is not much flying going on, and only a little shelling. Only this afternoon quite close, some machine gunning and even some regular rifleshots.

I think they will be here tomorrow! Wageningen and Ede are also liberated. How long still before Holland is free? Father and Mother must be thinking of us.

And Hein, have you already been liberated — are you free? They are twenty-five kilometers from Hamburg, and Bremen has been surrounded. Many prisoners are free already. But *where are you?* When I heard about Buchenwald I turned ice cold, but Psalm 91 is for us: "Because he loves me, says the Lord, I will rescue him. I will protect him for he acknowledges my name. A thousand may fall at your side, ten thousand at your right hand, but it will not come near you."

O darling, how happy we will be.

from the diary of Diet Eman

▼   ▼

It was still occupied territory, even though the end was obviously near. We were being liberated by battle, and we happened to be in the battle zone. There were still Germans all around us; but the Allies' plan was to soften up what was left of the German resistance, to shell and shell until all the lines were broken and all the men were fleeing. Then the Allies would roll in with the tanks, take that area, and move on.

All of the people staying at Aalt and Alie's sat in the tiny space of the *kelder* for three days and nights. Much smaller than a basement, it was a narrow space under the kitchen stairs. We had enough food down there for a little while at least, and nobody left. The men didn't even go out to milk. You simply didn't know what would happen.

Then, after three days, all the bombardment stopped on April 20. Suddenly there was nothing — just silence, deadly silence. We were still scared: we didn't know what was happening because we hadn't been outside for several days. Finally I told them I was going out; I would be the dove out of the ark. I wanted to see what was going on.

"Willie, be careful, be careful," they all said.

But someone had to go: Aalt and Alie were the parents of those three kids, and Uncle Ben and Tante Marie certainly couldn't go out either. So I figured it was best if I did. Everywhere I looked, there were dead cows, with swollen bellies, lying on the ground with their hooves in the air. They'd been hit by shells or shrapnel. It was another picture I'll never forget. I walked tentatively toward the road, and all of a sudden I couldn't believe my eyes: as far as I could see there were tanks and tanks. The Canadians were coming from the east.

I wanted to run back to the farm and tell Uncle Ben and Tante Marie that they could come out because it was over, that their long captivity had finally come to an end. I wanted to scream out, "It's over, it's all over."

But when I turned around, there, across a *sloot* and along a row of weeping willows, were three heavily armed German snipers who were covered with branches and leaves for camouflage. They were crawling in the brook, under those long weeping willow branches. They were aware that I had seen them. For me to run to the farm, of course, would put my life in danger, as well as the lives of the rest of those hiding in the house. I knew they would want to get me because I'd seen them.

So I wheeled around the other way and ran as fast as I could in the direction of those tanks coming up the road. I zigzagged in case the snipers would shoot.

I could speak English, so when I got to the front line of the tanks, I stopped them and told the man up on top that there were snipers ahead under the weeping willows.

"Where?" the soldier said.

"Under those trees," I said, pointing, "and they are heavily camouflaged."

This Canadian guy immediately said, "Okay, hop on," and he pointed to the top of the tank. So I actually hopped on that tank. The rest of the column kept going straight, but three tanks veered out, and I was riding on top of one of them. They moved terribly slowly, like elephants, as they turned off the road and up into the meadow, rolling along until they were right up to the *sloot*.

"There they are," I screamed. "There they are — do you see them?"

The tanks stopped, and their big turrets aimed directly at those Germans, who had seen it all happen. Just like that, the Germans threw up their hands. There I sat on the top of one of those tanks. It was my own private triumph: I felt at that moment as if I'd actually won the war. I was so happy when they took those Germans and put one on the front of each of those tanks, like a mascot, and swung back up to the road.

"You speak English very well," the Canadian said to me. He was happy to find a native who could talk to him. "What else can you tell us?" So I told him everything I could.

That was liberation day for me. Everybody in Holland has a different memory of liberation, of the moment that spelled the end of the Occupation. For me, sitting on the top of that tank and rolling through that field to capture those three Germans in hiding — that was the day I won the war.

"There will be a big thanksgiving service on the plaza in Nijkerk," the Canadian soldiers told me. "We will have our chaplains there, so spread the news. The chimes in the church will ring, and there will be a celebration of the liberation."

I flew back to the farmhouse and told everybody what had happened — about the three Germans and the tanks and the liberation — and all the people finally came out. The Jews could walk around outside, and everybody in hiding could come out. The kids didn't have to stay inside anymore. There was great, great joy.

That evening we went to the plaza, and we sang the *Wil-helmus*, our Dutch national hymn, and the tears streamed down our cheeks. We hadn't been allowed to sing that hymn for many

years. The Allies sang their national songs too, but the farmers
didn't know them. By nighttime many Allied soldiers had arrived.
The Dutch girls kissed everybody, and the liberation troops were
all invited into our homes. There was so much fun.

The next day, with all of those dead cows, we had lots to eat
for the first time in a long while. None of the cows had been killed
by disease; so the farmers checked to see which had been killed
most recently, and then they simply started to butcher. It was a big
loss — whole herds had been killed — but nobody was complain-
ing. We were finally free! We had a big celebration, with loads of
meatballs, from whatever could be saved.

We also found dead Germans who had been killed in the
shelling. We could see just how devastating that shelling had
been, and how we might have been killed if we'd have been out
there. I got on a bike and went here and there to see how all
"my" Jews were. It was just wonderful that they all could come
out, that I could speak with them openly. Some, of course, hadn't
seen each other for years. How can I describe it? It was a feeling
that a great cloud had been lifted, and we were finally free.

Uncle Ben and Tante Marie had been there with Aalt and
Alie for years. And the next day their son came back from the
place where he'd been hidden. All of that happened on April
20. What was especially poignant to me was that that day was
Hitler's birthday. Every year on April 20 — even now — I think
of Hitler's birthday and the joy of liberation.

▲   ▲

April 20, 1945

When it was quiet again, we all finished the work that
had to be done and then I went with Alie to the home of

her parents. On our walk, every time we saw Canadians there was spontaneous greeting. They were all driving the tanks.

At her parents' house there was so much to talk about. I told them that April 20, today, also happened to be Hitler's birthday!

On the way back a Canadian gave me a cigarette on the Brink. He hooked his arm in mine and walked with us to the farm. He told us he was a Catholic and had already been in the war for five years!

Alie and Annie also arrived with a Canadian in tow, also with cigarettes in their mouths! It was quite a sight! They came along to Watergoor, where they washed up a bit and there was a lot of talking and laughing. . . .

In the afternoon I went to see Tante Geertje and Hannie [two Jewish ladies in hiding] to see if everything was okay there. There, also, a lot of talking, and we got cigarettes and chewing gum from the Canadians!

I went to see all the nearest Jews, that evening to 't Veen, where everything is fine with Bert and Ben and Lotje. Zwartebroek is still in the hands of the Germans. Near Hoevelaken was heavy fighting and in the evening I went to Holk [Hein's family].

That evening I slept alone in my bed. There was some shooting and gunfire again.

from the diary of Diet Eman

▼   ▼

On May 5, 1945, the whole country was liberated, and the queen, who had already moved to Breda in the liberated south of Holland, spoke over the radio. There wasn't a dry cheek anywhere in the Netherlands. What I didn't know was that branches of the Resistance movement had already prepared very well for a whole interim government to take over ruling the country until the regular government could be reestablished.

It was also a very difficult time, because the collaborators, such as the NSBers, the *Landwacht,* and the other trash, tried desperately to escape to Germany or anywhere they could. And it was an ugly time, because those women who had gone out with Germans were grabbed and treated very badly, often shaved totally bald so that everyone could see who they were. Some were taken prisoners. There had been so much suffering during the war because of the betrayal of those collaborators, so many killed and hurt because of what they had done to families, that the mood for revenge against the traitors was very high. It was not right, but it was understandable. That time right after our liberation had difficult aspects as well as joyous aspects; but everything was influenced by the fact that it was over. The Occupation had finally ended.

▲   ▲

Sunday, April 22, 1945

What am I supposed to do now?

To Barneveld now that Joop has to go back to the office and Mother Klooster is so tired?

Stay with Alie, who counts on my not leaving her right away?

To my parents, for whom I am longing so much and who maybe will need me if things are getting difficult there?

Oh, my darling, I cannot enjoy liberation to the fullest

now since you are not here to celebrate it with me. I feel just as restless as when I had just gotten out of the concentration camp. Nowhere do I feel at rest. May I now leave our work here?

Please show me what I am supposed to do.

from the diary of Diet Eman

▼   ▼

Picking Up the Pieces

Above: The last letter Diet received from Hein, dated December 10, 1944.

Right: Notice placed by Diet in a newspaper, June 1945: "After years of struggle against the NSB, my deeply loved fiancé, Hein Sietsma, died in the concentration camp at Dachau sometime in January, 1945. . . ."

Na jarenlange, onver-moeide strijd tegen de nat.-soc. beginselen, liet medio Januari in het concentratiekamp **Dachau** zijn leven mijn innig geliefde Verloofde

HEIN SIETSMA,

in den ouderdom van 25 j. God leidt ons naar Zijn raad en heeft Hem reeds in Zijn Heerlijkheid opgenomen.

DIET EMAN.

Den Haag, 19 Juni 1945. van Brakelstraat 98.

Liever geen bezoek.

▲   ▲

April 26, 1945

It is a year ago that you were arrested, dearest. How much has happened! And now, within a little while, I should be hearing something from you?

Spoke to Riek, went to Barneveld. Everything okay also at Hymen and Wim's.

April 28, 1945

Rumors about complete surrender by Himmler!

Everybody is pulling me to come and work for them: The NBS [Netherlands Interior Forces] in Barneveld, the family Klooster, Alie, the NBS in Nijkerk.

But I don't want to bind myself to anything, because when you come back I want to be free!

April 29, 1945

In the morning to church. Rev. Brinkman. Isaiah 26. We sang Psalm 66 and in the end the *Wilhelmus*.

April 30, 1945

In the morning to the office of the *Landelijke Organisatie*. In the afternoon spoke with Capt. Roos, when all the Jewish people came together. At the synagogue in Nijkerk the NSB had to clean the building and all the people were shouting for joy. The Jewish people were screaming, *"Schnell, schnell, schnell"* and drove them faster. It was being filmed.

357

Still something inside of me did not feel good about it. Covenant people of the Lord were standing there with such satisfaction and *Schadenfreude*, such unholy glee. However, it is understandable. . . .

May 1, 1945

In the morning to Riek and went for my residence permit and an application for a ration card under my real name.

Today I feel so much like having a good, good cry. I must be crazy, for now I have every reason to be happy!

Darling, please come soon.

May 4, 1945

I have not written for a few days. At 8:45 P.M. the radio told us that the Germans had capitulated to the Twenty-First Army of Montgomery. That meant that the Netherlands, Denmark, and northwest Germany are free.

We rushed to Nijkerk and there the Canadians and the people were celebrating, crazy happy, jigging and dancing along. All the church bells were ringing and flags everywhere!

When we came home the radio played all national songs and we all joined in singing them. After this, Aalt read Psalm 103 and we sang "Now Thank We All Our God."

from the diary of Diet Eman

▼   ▼

After the liberation, trucks and bikes came out of hiding again, but the trains didn't run right away. The government that sprang out of the ground was made up of prominent people who had arranged, with the government in London, for some kind of structure when the end of the Occupation would come, so the country would not descend into chaos.

At first, no one was allowed to travel very far from where they were staying. The idea was to try to prevent traitors from escaping. So I could go around in the area of The Veluwe within a certain limit, but I was not allowed to travel back to The Hague, which, of course, is where I wanted to go. I wanted to be with my parents.

I had no idea where Hein was, but I thought that everything would be okay. That belief did not agree with that little voice in me that had told me earlier that we would never get married. But there was such a flush of victory at the time, such a happy mood and so much joy, that all that seemed left to make it complete would be for our Resistance comrades to return.

Riek van Meerveld was missing her husband, Ab, just as I was missing Hein; she and I often went to the church in Zwartebroek together, along with her little boy, Teun. We had long conversations, and we would read to each other, especially from Psalm 37: "They will fall to your right and to your left, but it will *not* come to you. Because you have trusted in God, you will live to see many, many days in the land of the *living*." We told each other that we had to cling to that promise of the Bible. Riek was hoping so hard, with so much emotion, that it sometimes scared me. She wanted badly to convince me that we'd both get our guys back. I'd sometimes tell her that it might be God's will that they would not return. We had to consider the possibility. But it was difficult to say those things, because saying them seemed to indicate a lack of faith. We had long and deep conversations about all of that, while we waited for some news — any news — about Hein and Ab.

When Aalt saw how much going home really meant to me during those first few days after the war, he arranged for me to get a pass from someone in the new government. There were control points everywhere set up to try to catch those Nazis and collaborators who were trying to escape. And even with a permit there was no way to get to The Hague: there was no transportation. The roads were still clogged with army tanks and bombed out military vehicles. But one day somebody called me from the town hall and told me that if I wanted to, I could hop on a truck, sit in the back, and get a ride all the way back home. Someone had been killed there in The Veluwe, and the family wanted his body back home near The Hague.

I climbed on board the truck with my pass, and I sat next to the coffin. The family was sitting there, in the back as well; it was very depressing, but I didn't ask any questions at all because I didn't want to seem curious. If the woman wanted to talk, I thought she would open up the conversation herself.

I knew that the most difficult point to pass would be on a small river east of Amersfoort. Most of the bridges were out by that time, so if this river still had a bridge, it could not have been a very big one. When we came to the check point near that small river, sure enough, I was not allowed to go on. I wanted very badly to get back to my family, so I went over to the office; they told me that they couldn't let me go. They were nice, but they would not let me pass.

So I waited and waited, just sat there for a time, and then when no one was looking I simply walked away. I went down to the river and walked along the bank until I found a place where it was very narrow and the bed was full of stones. There was nothing but trees there, and no one could see me. I had loved jumping ditches since I was a girl; so I jumped from stone to stone to stone until I was on the other side. Then I walked awhile in the woods until I got back to the road. At least I had passed the checkpoint.

Another truck came along, and when I showed the driver that I had a pass, he told me to hop on. And that ride got me back to The Hague.

My anticipation of Hein's coming back — and the fear that maybe he wouldn't — dominated my mind during those first few weeks at home, and as a result my homecoming is not very clear in my mind. I remember only that my brother Albert came back from Zwijndrecht soon after I had returned home. Everything else is a kind of haze.

Soon the papers started showing the horror of what had been found in the concentration camps. The Americans who opened the doors to those camps were shocked at what they had stumbled upon. I loved the story of one of those American officers: after finding all those dead and suffering, he went into the nearest village and got every person from town — even the mayor — and he made them all, every last one of them, including children, walk through that camp at Dachau with their eyes open. He forced them to look at the horror, so they would all see what they had done and would never, ever forget.

Many of those who were sick in those camps died even after the liberation. Some were rushed off to Allied hospitals, but transportation was no good. Everything in Europe, it seemed, was in ruins.

At the same time that news of what had happened in those camps was coming out, we started to get notices from the Red Cross that this one and this one and that one — men and women we knew or worked with — wouldn't come back at all, that they had died somewhere in Germany or elsewhere. They were twenty-one years old, twenty-two years old, twenty-three years old, and all of them had given their lives for their country. It was overwhelming — hundreds and hundreds and hundreds. In the following weeks the notices kept on coming; the papers were full of obituaries of young men. Pages were full!

Then I received a card from Riek, Ab's wife, that read: "Dear Willie, This morning I received a note that Ab died on March 14 in Germany. How terrible this is. How different God's ways are from ours. This I want so deeply in my heart — that you will get better news from Hein and the other guys."

I was paralyzed.

The whole of the Netherlands seemed paralyzed, not knowing what to do, where to turn. Until I would know something about Hein, I was really unable to do anything at all. What I knew was that I couldn't simply sit in an office from nine to five every day, typing and translating. I couldn't just sit there, after years of being on the road and arranging my own day. I had nothing to look forward to either. All that time Hein and I had been thinking that we would be getting married — that's what I had seen as my future life. But it seemed, as the days passed, that it was not to be.

But I didn't want to realize that the end of the Occupation was also the end of all my dreams. I didn't want to realize that. I'd tell myself that Hein wasn't dead. We'd heard that the Russians had taken prisoners who would have to be freed, and I'd tell myself that he would be one of them for sure, that soon he would be back with all the others.

On June 5, in the evening, the doorbell rang and a gentleman by the name of Mr. Dekker stood there. In our Underground work, Hein had often mentioned a Wim Dekker, from another Underground group in the Eindhoven area, with whom he had become friends. I'd met Wim as well. This Mr. Dekker was our friend Wim's father. He didn't know my parents at all.

"Well," he said, "I've just come from Nijkerk, and I thought I'd stop by here."

"Isn't it great that the guys are coming back now?" I said. I was just bubbling over with happiness.

"Yes, yes," he said, "but of course you have to realize that some of them will not be coming back."

I didn't want to think about that, so I changed the subject. "Yes, but isn't it wonderful that the Germans have been defeated and the war is over?"

"I have just come from Nijkerk," he said, "and I have a letter from Hein's father for you, and the news is not good."

I think I must have made that evening very difficult for Mr. Dekker. I was standing there bubbling at the door — "Ja, isn't it great the boys are coming home?" — and then he had to give me the worst possible news. He tried very hard to break it to me softly by saying exactly what I used to say to Ab's wife: "Not everyone will come back."

The letter from Hein's father said that he had received notice from the Red Cross that Hein had died in Dachau, and that Jan, his middle son, had died in another camp; and that Henk was sick with tuberculosis in Eindhoven. Father Sietsma wrote that Dominee de Ruyg from Hilversum had come back from the camp at Dachau, where he had known Hein, and that Hein had died on the night of January 20, 1945.

After Mr. Dekker left, I went to my room and didn't want to see anyone. Father and Mother came in to stay with me, but I had to be alone. A couple of very bad days passed. They were days in which I couldn't really think, days that are gone now, and it's well that they should be.

▲   ▲

June 7, 1945

Why?

Why did I have to come through it all. Why couldn't I also have died?

Hein, why did you leave me alone? I cannot live without you. What am I going to do without you?

I am happy at least that I can go to Rev. de Ruyg and hear about you.

I think to be a survivor is the most difficult. But when I think that way, then I think I am happy that I am the one. For it also would have been so difficult for you if the situation were the opposite now. May I be so egotistical as to wish you back here? — for now you are in heaven.

You were ready.

Jongen, why did you read John 14 the last time we saw each other? Why was there always a voice in me that said clearly, *"Kijk nog maar goed naar hem"* when you brought me back to Aalt and Alie's farm? You noticed it yourself and started to laugh, and said, "Why are you staring at me all the time?"

Now I will have to put into practice what I once told you: "Even if something should happen to us, we still have to be very grateful for these beautiful years we had. These few years will be worth all the rest of my life — and the sorrow."

God, give me strength to go on from day to day, from hour to hour. Show me the way you want me to go.

from the diary of Diet Eman

▼   ▼

At Aalt and Alie's I had often slept in the double bed with Annie, the young single mother from the Engels family of Arnhem. We slept in the *mooie* room, the *heerd*, where it was always very cold since there was no heat anywhere in the house except the kitchen. We had heavy wool blankets on us, and that little baby was in his crib, well covered.

I remembered I had come back from a trip somewhere, and I should have gone to bed, where Annie was. But there was such an unrest in me on one specific night, January 20, because I was thinking of Hein, that I didn't go to bed; instead, I started to do what the Dutch call *ijsberen*, pacing up and down in that room, the biggest room in the house.

"Willie, come to bed," Annie Engels finally said to me. "You'll get so cold just walking back and forth." It was bitter cold.

I told her that I couldn't. "There is something wrong with Hein — I can just *feel* it. He's terribly sick, I just know he is." And then I said, "What is today's date?"

"January twentieth," she said.

"I'll have to ask him, when he returns, whether he was sick on January twentieth — or whether something happened."

That night, of course, he died.

▲   ▲

June 14, 1945

Darling, if I think of all I miss now, I will go crazy.

I should not think of that.

I only want to think of all that I still have, and then I am rich.

Your spirit is always around me, in your diary, our

letters, all the things you got for our household. How proud we were of that! And the nearly six years! O God, I thank you for those years. If I never had met you, I would now not have all the sorrow; but I would have missed these riches — and do these years not abundantly balance the lonely years I face without you?

Fortunately, you don't have to suffer this horrible pain, unbearable, which I am going through now.

All of these thoughts have come into my mind:

"Couldn't you fight a little longer for your life, *mijn jongen?*

If Henk had been able to come to you, would he have been able to help and give you courage to go on?

Was it very difficult for you to get detached from this world and from me? You were still so young and we expected so much of life.

Did you have a chance to give Rev. de Ruyg a special message for me, with which I will have to go on living, and will I be able to?

I always hoped so much that we would have sons and bring them up so that they would be like you. And I always thought how wonderful it would be that when they would have grown up to tell them about this time of our struggle and of God's help and wonderful, miraculous deliverance, time and time again.

Sometimes I am sorry that I did not want to get married during the war. You wanted it very much, and I did too, but I thought all the time that we should not take the risk at a time we were hiding and already a danger to those who were hiding us.

Oh, all these thoughts. It is understandable. There is only one answer, and that gives me rest. Psalm 73:23-24:

"You have guided him with your eternal counsel and have now taken him into glory."

Sometimes I am longing so much for you that I wish my time will also come soon; it would only be sad for my folks.

Sometimes I think that if you had died at home, from an illness, that I could take it better. Then I could have nursed you and taken care of you and we still could have talked so much, and we could have said goodbye to each other.

But could such a farewell have been more perfect than what we had . . . ?

And there in that strange country, far away from all who loved you, did you not feel God's nearness even stronger?

from the diary of Diet Eman

▼   ▼

I'm sorry to say it, but it was hard on me to see life continue all around. A few days passed and I hopped on my bike to go see Uncle Frits, who had helped us so much. He and his wife, Tante Lenie, had survived. Herman, my friend from the bank — and the first Jew we hid — came back to The Hague; his sister Rosa came back, along with Herman's girlfriend, Ada, and her mother. For the most part, they had stayed in the same place we had found for them right at the beginning of the hiding. These were the people who, in those first few weeks, had launched the whole project. They had all made it, thank God. Some of the Jews who had been in Mies's apartment had been arrested, but we had not originally placed people there ourselves.

All of the Jews we had hidden with Christian farm families made it — every single one. One of them, Albert, whom we had placed with Ab's brother, a simple, good Dutch farmer who read from the Bible every day, accepted Jesus as the promised messiah. Albert became engaged to the daughter of a pastor and later married her.

None of the people we hid really knew what to say to me when it was over. They had come through it, but I had lost my true love. The war was very difficult for them — and for me — and it was likewise difficult for them to deal with what had happened. I wasn't bitter, but it was a great irony that we all felt. We had known from the beginning that death could be the price we would have to pay. What could they say?

In those first few weeks after I heard that Hein had died, I wasn't bitter but I was angry — even angry with God. Hein had been moved from the camp at Amersfoort to Neuen-gamme, a horrible camp near Hamburg during the "hunger winter" of 1945. That's where all the men from the town of Putten in The Veluwe had been incarcerated after their mass arrest because a German oficer was killed by the Resistance just outside their village. Nearly every one of them died. Hein was with them, on the same transport, but he survived that camp.

After Neuengamme, they took him to yet another camp, Ladelund. Those two camps were the worst camps in the north: very few people survived them because the Germans gave them very little food and forced them to dig trenches on the borders of Denmark in the winter, standing in water with no heat, nothing. Many died there of tuberculosis, typhus, pneumonia, and malnutrition. Every time they were transported anywhere, they were herded like cattle on railroad cars, so many of them in a car that they couldn't sit or lie down. They were crammed in so closely that they couldn't even fall down if they died. If a military transport had to pass them, that cattle train would stand on a sidetrack somewhere in Germany without water, food, or anything for its inhabitants for long periods of time.

Hein survived Ladelund too, and was then transported all the way across Germany to Dachau and placed in a barracks with many clergymen who had been imprisoned. When he was arrested, his false papers claimed that he was a dominee. He died there, in Dachau, in the company of preachers.

When I had heard of all the suffering that Hein had to go through, I wondered why. *Lord, was that necessary? Why didn't he just get an honest bullet and have it over with? Why was all that suffering necessary?* That's the way I talked to God. I was in so much rebellion because it seemed to me that it just wasn't fair. We had gone into the work because we thought it was the will of God himself directing us to take up the cause of the poor Jewish people who were suffering so badly. I told God that I wasn't even grateful that I was alive. I told him that I wished I were also dead, like Hein. I asked him, over and over, why it was necessary for Hein to suffer so much.

Then I began to receive letters from people I'd never known — farmers, pastors, other men from the Underground: they said that they had met my fiancé in this camp or that camp, and that in the deepest misery they faced, Hein had spoken of his faith in God's promises. He was a light in their darkness, they said.

▲   ▲

Langenzwaag, July 9, 1945

Dear Miss Eman:

One morning, when the sun was shining, the birds were singing, and everything around breathed new and strong life, I received your notice, the notice of Death. The contrast was unspeakably cruel — for me, who had lost his best friend from the camp, but so infinitely more for you. Maybe it will console you a little bit — it is such a trifling bit of consolation — if I tell you a little about Hein.

He was a comrade of mine. He had very strong feelings about society; he was witty, full of pep, spontaneous, and generous. He was a splendid fellow, the most beautiful camp prisoner I ever met.

I knew Hein (we called him Hendrik, Hendrik de Jong) for ten weeks. When I received your card, for the first time I realized fully what I missed and what grew during those ten weeks. Life is like a film screen: pictures come, make an impression, go, and then make a place for new pictures with new impressions which obscure the previous ones. Some of those old pictures fade, but the impressions they leave will never pass away. Such an impression is the image of Hein Sietsma — a joyful Christian who loved life so much but was still willing to give it to the great, good, and holy cause.

I hope that God will give you the consolation to go on in life, not lonely and cold and heartbroken, but able to think of that which never disappears, always spreads its warmth, and can even make life rich without Hein.

With highest regards
R. van Tuinen

letter from R. van Tuinen to Diet Eman

▼ ▼

I received many letters like that, and then I knew that Hein had been a missionary in all those camps where he had suffered, a very special missionary. I could then accept his death, because I knew from others — not all of them Christians either — that Hein, even in his greatest misery, had been a light in their darkness.

Herman and his girlfriend Ada got married very quietly. I think it was wise of me not to attend because it would have been very hard for me to be there; I don't think I could have taken it. I visited them later, when they had their first baby, and by then some of the old pain had slowly slipped away. It was a painful thing for me to see all those young couples Hein and I had known getting married — very painful. My wedding dress was still hanging at home, and we had wanted so badly to get married. And though I was not envious, I felt sad that I couldn't share in their happiness. When I knew I had to express my happiness to them for their joy, I could not — and I knew I could not. How can one describe that emptiness?

▲   ▲

November 24, 1945

Everything is so empty. I cannot write and have nothing to write anymore.

The work is nice and busy, but if I think that this has to fill my life for the future, I could just scream!

O God, could it really not have been different? Could you only fulfill your purposes for our lives in this one way? At some moments it penetrates to me, like recently the shock I got when I said for the first time "when Hein was still alive"! At that moment it really penetrated to me that this part of me is now the *past*.

Be thou our help when troubles last
and our eternal home.

from the diary of Diet Eman

▼   ▼

While he was on one of those horrible prisoner transport trains, Hein wrote me the last letter I ever received from him. The train was nearing Rijssen, close to the German border, and he was conscious of the fact that his chances of ever returning to the Netherlands were very poor. It was dated "10/12 '44," and he wrote it on a single piece of thin toilet paper he had been given by the Red Cross. He folded that little letter very small and wrapped it in a strip of brown paper. Then he addressed it to me at my parents' address in The Hague and threw it from the railroad car. It must have fallen along the tracks. Someone, somehow, picked up that fragile, tiny piece of correspondence, and later — I don't remember exactly when — I received it. Whoever picked it up sent it off just as Hein would have requested, just as he'd hoped. I received it long after he had left the prison at Amersfoort.

▲   ▲

October 12, 1944

Dear Diet,

Our move still happened quite unexpectedly. Really, I have to say that we didn't think it would happen anymore. But I am happy that we have said farewell to Amersfoort. Yesterday about nine in the evening we left, and now it's seven in the morning. We passed Rijssen. I think that the trip will be quite long.

372

Darling, don't count on our seeing each other again soon. I have the feeling that it will take at least a year. But we are with friends altogether, and you will soon be in a free country. So we have many reasons to be optimistic.

And here we see again that we do not decide our own lives. *Dieneke*, even if we won't see each other again on earth, we will never be sorry for what we did, that we took this stand. And know, Diet, that of every last human being in this world, I loved you most. And it is still my great desire that we will become a happy family someday.

▼　　　▼

That is the last letter Hein sent, the letter he dropped from a railroad car headed for Germany with the great hope it would somehow reach me. When I think of how wet the Netherlands is, how rainy and foggy, and how little chance there was for that frail piece of toilet paper to hold its message and not become soggy and lose the words Hein wrote; when I think of how unlikely it was that someone would even find it there along the tracks, and then realize how noble that person must have been to take that letter and send it on; when I think of all of that, and then realize that I still have this letter — Hein's last — in my hands today, fifty years later, then I know that even though I don't have him, I have truly been blessed.

Sometimes people ask me whether I wish I could skip that whole part of my life, if I could live my life over. I tell them that I do not. That part of my life was very, very difficult; I cannot think about it today without crying, even though I never cried much at all for most of that time. But I tell people that those years of my life were very special, the time when I was very close to God — so close, in fact, that I not only *knew* that he kept his promises, I actually *experienced* his faithfulness. The God of creation did not renege on what he'd promised me as his child.

One thing I know is sure, and that's what I had remembered in my cell and scratched into the bricks of the Scheveningen prison wall: Jesus' last words before he returned to heaven were a promise. We all break our promises, but our Lord never does.

He told us, "Lo, I am with you always."

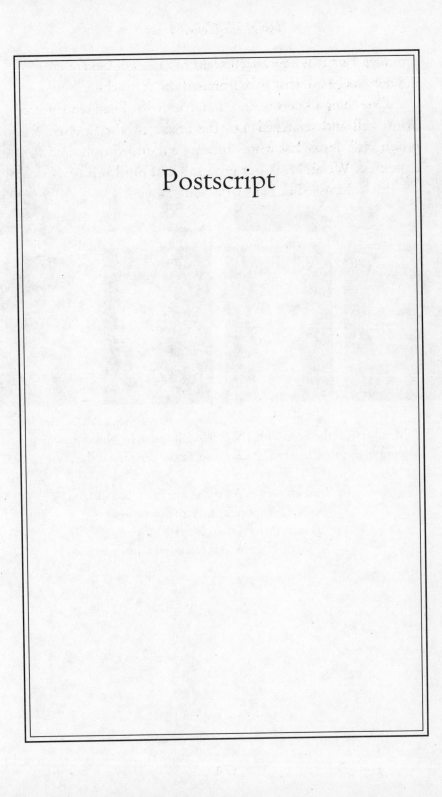

Postscript

Members of the group HEIN (Help Elkander In Nood, meaning "helping each other in need"), who died in the service of the Resistance.

Top, from left to right: Aart Oskam, Hein Sietsma,
Bouwe Nieuwenhuis, Aarjen Brouwer
Bottom: Piet Hartog, Dries Klooster,
Gerk Numan, Ab van Meerveld

To write a book about these difficult years was the last thing I wanted to do. I wanted to forget, and I even left the Netherlands after the war to do that. To start a new life in a country where there were no memories and never talk about that time again. I succeeded quite well till Corrie ten Boom came to our town in 1978 and spoke about her experiences and God's faithfulness.

After that my conscience started to graw and it seemed that every time I opened the Bible something like "Tell the great things I have done" stared me in the face. Then a pastor who knew that I had been in the same prison as Corrie asked me to speak to his church. I wanted to scream, "No, I want to forget," but I didn't dare. So I went, but it was very difficult.

More requests came. A psychologist-friend said, "Go, it is good therapy for you."

Approximately eight years ago my son Mark insisted that I write a book about all my experiences. My immediate reply was, "No way!" In the nearly fifty years after the war I had tried three times to read those letters and diary scraps, but every time I started to cry and put them quickly back. Mark kept telling me that it had to be done, even if it was hard. He said that I should pray to know God's will.

Three years ago many things happened that convinced me the book should be written. At that time I was asked to speak at the "Suffering and Survival" convention in Sioux Center. After I had spoken Jim Schaap came up to me and said, "I want to write your book!" At once things fell in place.

At that time, too, the neo-Nazis started to show up again. When the war ended we all said, "This can *never* happen again." But now polls show that 22 percent of the U.S. population does not believe there was a Holocaust. The story *has* to be retold so that history does not repeat itself.

People sometimes ask, "Would you like to skip that part of your life?" My answer is "No," for I would never have met all the wonderful friends, especially those in prison and the camp, surrounded by evil and cruelty. There no human being could help me. I was totally dependent on God. And God was right there and kept all his promises. I could say with David: "The Lord is my light and my salvation, Whom shall I fear?" and "For he will hide me in his shelter in the day of trouble" (Psalm 27:1, 5). That is just what he did. My response is, again with David, "Praise the Lord, O my soul, and forget not all his benefits" (Psalm 103:2).

Father and Mother Eman went through a lot during the war, but they survived and lived to the ripe old ages of 91 and 93 respectively. Since their daughter Fanny was their only child to remain in the Netherlands, after retirement they moved to Apeldoorn, where Fanny and her family lived. There they made many friends again, and they were interested in everything that happened in the world around them.

Arjan Eman, my older brother, had left the Netherlands before the events in this narrative began. In 1938 he reported for active duty as a member of the Dutch Royal Air Force in the Dutch East Indies. When Japan attacked, he was shot down with his plane, seriously wounded, and hospitalized with a piece of shrapnel in his thigh. Because he could not walk, he was not guarded. But he practiced walking during the night, and when he was able to, he escaped. He was later arrested again by the Japanese and put in the Sukamiskin, one of the most horrible prisons, of which it was said that nobody got out alive. We later heard that he was tortured to death. In one of the last letters he wrote to his parents, he quoted

II Timothy 4:7-8: "I have fought the good fight. I have finished the course. I have kept the faith: henceforth there is laid up for me the crown of righteousness. . . ."

Fanny Eman, my older sister, married Jo Reupkes, a widower with two small children after her fiancé was killed on the first day of the Nazi invasion. It was a happy marriage, and they had an additional two sons together, Hans and Frits, who are, of course, now grown men with their own families. Fanny's husband Jo died a few years ago, but Fanny still lives in Apeldoorn.

Albert Eman, my younger brother, became even more active in the Resistance after Hein and I were arrested, especially toward the end of the war in Zwijndrecht, where Adriaan Schouten had asked him to join a military group. After the war, Albert worked with severely handicapped children, initially in Sweden. He received a degree in this work and was asked to open an institute in Denmark. He built this institute up from a small home to practically a village, with schools, farms, shops for silversmithing, painting, woodworking, and weaving. The complex has an orchestra and a theater group, which play in churches and have played on television. Albert retired two years ago, but he is still on the board, and he still directs the orchestra a few times a week. He composes music and writes plays, often based on the Danish national history and saga.

Ab van Meerveld was, with Hein Sietsma, the co-leader of our group (Group HEIN). He went to Barneveld to warn Dries Klooster; but Dries had already disappeared, and Ab was arrested at the Klooster address in December 1944. He was brought to Apeldoorn, and from there to a camp in Amersfoort. Despite being tortured for information on other Resistance workers, Ab kept silent. He was transported to a camp in Germany, where he died on March 14, 1945.

Riek van Meerveld, Ab's wife, brought up their son Teunis, who was a baby when Ab was arrested. She moved from Barneveld to Terschuur, where she is still living today. Teun later married and established a flourishing business in interior decorating. He and his wife, Ria, had two children, and he was a good father and husband. But a few years ago, at the age of forty-two, Teun suffered a heart attack while playing ball with his young son, and died. Riek has had much grief, losing her husband and only son, but she has kept the faith.

Henk Sietsma, Hein's younger brother, came back from Dachau with a large hole in his lungs. He never knew that Hein was only a few barracks away from him at Dachau. He spent several years in a sanatorium, and he married one of the nurses. They have three children. Henk worked for several firms, and he retired in 1984 from the Fokker Aircraft firm, where he had been chief of the human resources department for thirteen years. In his free time he is involved in social work, help for addicts, and so forth. He has been back to Dachau several times.

Jan Sietsma, one of Hein's younger brothers, was nineteen when he was arrested for Resistance activities with some local friends. The other friends were sentenced to death, but Jan was sentenced to a prison camp in Germany, Ziegenhain, where he died in March 1945.

Father Sietsma lost not only two sons, Hein and Jan, but his brother, Dr. Kees Sietsma, the pastor, who died in a German concentration camp. And his son Henk came back from Ger-

Behind Diet, from left to right: Corrie van Driel, Aalt and Alie Lozeman, and Jan van Driel in Diet's home in Grand Rapids in 1986.

many very sick. Hein's father was a widower when I first met him, but he was remarried during wartime, and he and his second wife had an additional three children. He retired and died of old age.

Aalt and Alie Lozeman continued their life after the war as they had lived it before. They had seven children, five daughters and two sons. Both sons are farming near the town of Putten. Watergoor and the surrounding farms were bought by the local government, and the area was made into a large sports complex. Aalt and Alie retired to a small farm, and Aalt always helped his sons. The Lozemans studied English after the war, and they remained interested in everything around them. When one of their daughters married an American and settled near Boston, they traveled to the United States several times and naturally visited me in Grand Rapids. In 1987, Klein Jantje and his wife, Corrie, came to visit me in Grand Rapids, and Aalt and Alie were also able to make a five-day visit at the same time. When we all sat around the dinner table that first evening and remembered how we all had been sitting around the table at Watergoor amid all the danger in 1944, it was very emotional. If someone had told us that we would all be sitting around a table in a place called Grand Rapids more than forty years hence, none of us would have believed it.

Some years ago, Aalt was afflicted with Parkinson's disease, became weaker and weaker, and passed away on September 22, 1992. He was a wonderful human being, loved by everybody, and missed very much by Alie and all his friends. Since I was working with the Red Cross after a typhoon in Guam at the time of his death, I did not learn of it until much later. I was very sad not to have been able to go to Aalt's funeral because I loved him like a brother.

Alie keeps busy with her family, her choir, visiting elderly people — and she still travels to the United States regularly to visit her daughter in Boston. When she does, I fly to see her again.

Herman and Ada, who were married after the war, had two daughters. Herman studied economics, and later became the administrator of a large hospital. The fearful time of the war and the persecution of the Jews was so traumatic for them that they cannot talk about it even today.

Rosa married her fiancé after the war was over, and they had one daughter. Rosa is a widow now, but she keeps very busy traveling and organizing activities at a center for senior citizens. She was actually the first of our Jewish friends to go into hiding, since Herman was still thinking it over when Hein brought Rosa to Aalt and Alie's in August 1942. Since Nettie (which was Rosa's false name during the war) lost nearly all of her family, Aalt and Alie became her family. They have always kept in close contact with each other, and in August 1992 — fifty years later — a bouquet of fifty red roses was delivered to Aalt and Alie from "Nettie."

Aart Platteel kept on working for the Twentsche Bank until his retirement. He died of complications from gall bladder surgery.

Mattijssen disappeared during the war and was never heard from again.

The **Versteeg** family was able to get through the war all right.

Adriaan Schouten, of Zwijndrecht, was arrested and imprisoned at Amersfoort at the same time Hein was there, so they were able to support each other. But Adriaan, who had done much in the Underground, was able to pretend during his hearings that he was "just" a black marketeer — for which there was little punishment under the Nazi system. Thus he was released quite soon. He survived the war, and right afterward went to the Dutch East Indies as a volunteer soldier, as did many young Dutch men, in a Dutch-governmentsponsored "political action" aimed to liberate Indonesia from Sukarno and the Japanese. Adriaan later moved to Australia and died there of a heart attack.

Johan ("Bram") Boetze worked for years in Zwolle as an editor for a newspaper. He later became the editor of the in-house magazine of AKZO, a large industry in Arnhem. He is now retired, and he and his wife, Nel, keep busy. They have two children, and Johan still loves to write and loves music, and Nel keeps a loving eye on lonely elderly people around her.

Johan van Gelder went back to work at Shell after the War, and he was sent to Curaçao. He and his wife, Fokje, had two sons. When I was working as a nurse in Venezuela and had to bring patients from there to the Curaçao hospital several times, I visited the van Gelders there. Johan is now retired from Shell, and he and Fokje live in Amersfoort today.

Uncle Ben and Tante Marie (Ben and Marie Kanis) survived the war at Watergoor, Aalt and Alie's farm, and returned to The Hague, where Ben worked and eventually retired. Both of them died of old age.

Uncle Frits and Tante Lenie also got through the war, and both died of old age.

The **Pon** family, who gave me the magnificent hiking shoes, had a bicycle business, which grew after the war. Henk Sietsma worked for them for some time. Mr. Pon gave me a brand new bicycle after the war. The Pons have now died, but their bicycle business still exists.

The **Engels** family, who came to live at Watergoor after the bombing of Arnhem, returned to Arnhem as soon as they could after the Liberation. Contact between them and Aalt and Alie was maintained for a long time — until the parents passed away.

Beatrix Terwindt was the bravest woman I ever had the honor to meet. She was brought into my cell (Corridor A, no. 306, Scheveningen prison) one evening in late May 1944, after having been in solitary confinement for eighteen months! She was the fifth person in our one-person cell. The others slept on straw sacks on the floor that night, but Trix and I talked the whole night, sitting on the concrete floor of the cell. She told me her whole story up to that moment. Although she had a fear of flying before the war, Trix was in London working for M.I. 9 (Underground Intelligence). About twenty men had been dropped by M.I. 9 over occupied Holland to obtain information; after some successful early drops, a number of men had recently simply disappeared and were not heard from again. Since they were considered spies and thus not protected by the Geneva Convention, they could be summarily shot. Up until that time, no woman had been shot on Dutch territory by the Germans —nor had any woman parachuted into the occupied zone. So Trix, despite her earlier fear of flying, *volunteered* to jump out of a plane at night into occupied territory. But the Nazis had infiltrated the airdrop system, and they were there to seize Trix when she landed.

I was the first person that she felt she could talk to after her year and a half of solitary confinement. I will never forget the look in her eyes. That night she also gave me good advice for my upcoming hearings, for which I will always bless her. She had had a lot of experience!

Trix survived the war, but she suffered immensely, and the camps ruined her health. After the war she returned to KLM, where she became head stewardess. Later she lived in Canada for a time, but she returned to the Netherlands.

Trix wrote the long poem that appears on pp. 213-19 when she did not expect to survive. After Scheveningen she was transported to Ravensbrück, and later to Mauthausen. Her piece was published in *Aantreden* ("Fall-In"), the magazine of the Ex-Political Prisoners Association, on the occasion of her death a few years ago.

Freddy Ponger also lost her fiancé because of his activities with the Resistance. After the War she studied nursing, and she later married and had two children. But she died quite young. Corrie ten Boom and I kept in contact with her for some time after the war.

Corrie ten Boom used the prison camp experience for the basis of her book (and movie) *The Hiding Place*, as well as other books, including *Prison Letters*, and she traveled the world evangelizing. She died on her ninety-first birthday in California.

Mrs. Folmer came through the war and the camps. Her daughter, who had been in concentration camps under the "night and fog" rule, which because of its psychological torture was one of the cruelest (no contact with anybody), also survived the war.

"Klein Jantje" (Jan van Driel) married his girlfriend, Corrie Kros, after the war, and they have two sons. Jan worked for several firms, the last being Van Leeuwen, a large tubing firm, from which he retired after many years.

The last six months of the war, Jan worked for the GDN, the Geheime Dienst Nederland — "Front Spionnage" (Netherlands Secret Service — Espionage on the Front), during which I accompanied him on a few trips to draw attention away from him because I was a woman. On his often lonely and dangerous trips he had become accustomed to the idea that each one would probably cost him his life. So when Liberation came, and he biked from Rotterdam to Zwijndrecht, where he lived, it was a shock to him that he had survived and was still alive. This influenced the future of his life: he knew that there was a task for him. He became deeply involved in social, community, and church work, and is still doing that today.

Jan always says that he was no hero — simply a very scared young man who was doing his duty. He never wanted any recognition, and he never did accept the medals and citations the Dutch government offered him. The lonely years on his bike made him very philosophical. He said: "Fear drives you into the arms of God."

On the occasion of their fortieth wedding anniversary, Jan and Corrie van Driel visited me in the U.S.; the trip was a gift from their two sons.

Piet Hoogerwerff worked in Zwijndrecht in a different Resistance group, the *Binnenlandse Strijd Krachten*, but our group worked with his. Before the war was over, he became commander of that group in his area. This organization, which was government sponsored, began to maintain order in the country once the war was over. Piet also worked until his retirement for the Van Leeuwen factory in Zwijndrecht, and he still lives there with his wife, Mijntje. They have three children.

Jean Louis Chaillet had a high position with Shell Oil Company. When the Germans invaded Holland, they placed a colonel of the German Air Force in Shell's National Luchtvaart Laboratorium in Amsterdam as "protection." Shell, in turn, assigned Chaillet, who was a very strong character and personality, as a counterweight to the German colonel in that lab. It was a chess move. Chaillet counteracted much of what the Germans wanted. He took Hein into the company on false papers, and since there was a good deal of gasoline there (meant for the Germans, of course), he allowed Hein and Gosse and Corrie vanden Berg steal the gasoline for use in Resistance work. He was in a position to smooth over any discrepancies or other trouble that might become dangerous.

Chaillet was also, we found out later, high up in the Raad van Verzet (Resistance) structure in the Netherlands, directed from London. He was later arrested, suffered very much in Germany, but survived. After the war he was in charge of the NAM (Nederlandse Aardolie Maatschappij — the Dutch Petroleum Company) project in the Netherlands. He retired and passed away years ago; his wife died just recently.

Gosse and Corrie vanden Berg were married during the war (1944) by Hein's uncle, Dr. Kees Sietsma. They have three children, two daughters and a son; the son is named Hein, after Hein Sietsma. They immigrated to Canada in 1957, and they now live in Burlington, Ontario, where Gosse (George) is now retired.

Aarjen Brouwer, my Oom Arie, my mother's only brother, was arrested at his home in January 1945, along with Bob Visser, with whom he often worked. Both were imprisoned at Scheveningen and tortured, then sent to Germany. Uncle Arie died during a death march from one camp to another in snow and ice. He is buried in the *Heldenkerkhof* (hero cemetery) in Loenen.

Bob Visser (false name of Bouwe Nieuwenhuis) was imprisoned and tortured at Scheveningen, then sent to Germany. He ended up in a concentration camp on the Baltic Sea. During the Liberation, when it was clear that the Nazis had lost the war, some fanatical SSers manned some German warships, filled them with prisoners from the camp, and went out to sea. What they hoped would happen, happened. The British thought that the warships were full of escaping Germans and bombarded them. Few reached the shore. Bob was one who did make it to shore; but despite the care he was given, he died there — a few days after the liberation of the Netherlands.

Diet Eman. Although I had training in business and languages, I studied nursing after the war and left the Netherlands in 1949, bound for Venezuela as a nurse for Shell Oil Company. For emotional survival, I felt I had to get away from all the memories. In the following years I had little contact with people I had known during the war, except for Aalt and Alie Lozeman, the Boetzes, and Jan and Corrie van Driel. I married an American, Egon Erlich, in 1959, and have two children, Mark and Joy. After a divorce, I moved to Grand Rapids, Michigan, in 1969, where I became export manager for an export firm. I retired in 1986 and now do volunteer work as a translator with Christian doctors (the Luke Society), the Red Cross, and the Christian Reformed World Relief Committee in Central and South America.

Those of Group HEIN who gave their lives:

Albert van Meerveld

Hein Sietsma

Gerk Numan,
Hein's cousin who worked in Friesland

Piet Hartog,
who worked in Gelderland and Amsterdam

Bouwe Nieuwenhuis, "Bob,"
our contact with the LO in The Hague

Called to Die

Aart Oskam "Driek," Heemstede

Aarjen Brouwer ("Oom Arie"), The Hague

Dries Klooster, Barneveld

*They did not love their lives so much
as to shrink from death.*

Rev. 12:11